GOD'S ACTIVITY IN THE WORLD

American Academy of Religion
Studies in Religion

Charley Hardwick, Editor

Number 31

GOD'S ACTIVITY IN THE WORLD

The Contemporary Problem

Owen C. Thomas, Editor

GOD'S ACTIVITY IN THE WORLD
The Contemporary Problem

Owen C. Thomas, Editor

Scholars Press
Chico, California

GOD'S ACTIVITY IN THE WORLD

The Contemporary Problem

Owen C. Thomas, Editor

Library of Congress Cataloging in Publication Data

Thomas, Owen C., 1922–
  God's activity in the world.

  (Studies in religion / American Academy of Religion ;
no. 31)
  1. Providence and government of God—Addresses,
essays, lectures. I. Title. II. Series: Studies in religion
(American Academy of Religion ; no. 31)
BT96.2.T5 1983   231.7   82-19148
ISBN 0-89130-602-1

Printed in the United States of America

PREFACE

I became interested in the problem of the activity of God in the world through Langdon Gilkey's 1961 essay, and I explored it in a chapter on providence in an introductory text in which I discussed five of the essays in this volume.[1] Then in response to the invitation of Professor Charley Hardwick of American University, editor of the "Aids to the Study of Religion" series of the American Academy of Religion, I suggested that a volume of essays on this issue would be a useful teaching tool in the study of religious thought.

The significance for religious studies of the question of divine activity in the world lies in the diversity of issues involved. It has been a central problem in western theology since the medieval period, and it has received a good deal of attention in the latter half of this century as a result of the work of Bultmann and Gilkey. It involves complex exegetical and historical issues. It raises fundamental cosmological or metaphysical questions, especially in relation to the nature of causality, the theory of action, and the mind-body problem, all of which seem to be to the fore in contemporary philosophy. All in all the problem of God's activity in the world encompasses a number of important issues in religious studies.

This volume would have been enriched by the addition of essays from other religious traditions. This, however, is beyond my competence and would have required the omission of several important essays which are now included.

I am indebted to several people for important suggestions in regard to this volume: Professor Frank Dilley of the University of Delaware, Professor John Cobb of the Claremont Graduate School, Professor Avery Dulles, S.J., of Catholic University, Professor Hardwick, and the members of a seminar on this question at the Episcopal Divinity School in the spring term of 1982.

O.C.T.
Cambridge, Mass.
August, 1982.

---

1. *Introduction to Theology* (Cambridge: Greeno, Hadden & Co., 1973), ch. 7. Revised Edition (Wilton, Conn.: Morehouse-Barlow Co., 1983).

CONTENTS

1. INTRODUCTION

At the heart of Christian faith is the affirmation that God
is present and active in the creation to carry out the divine purposes and to achieve the divine goal of the fulfillment of all
creatures. Much of the impetus in Western societies for individual
action and social programs aimed at the alleviation of human misery
and injustice has derived from the conviction that God loves all
people and is active in the world to fulfill their lives.

Throughout the Bible and the Christian tradition it is affirmed that God acts, that God does things, that God creates,
judges, saves, guides, inspires, destroys and raises up. The question of the character of the divine activity in the world has a
broad context and a narrower focus. The widest context of the
divine activity in the world is the doctrine of creation which
states the fundamental relation between God and the world. Then
the focus narrows as we move from the doctrines of preservation,
providence, and history to the doctrines of salvation, incarnation,
resurrection, and miracle. The wider context raises the following
kinds of questions about the divine activity in the world: Does
God control and guide all events in the cosmos? How does God carry
out the divine will and purpose in human history? What does it
mean to say that God is the Lord of history? The narrower focus
of this question involves more specific issues: What is the relation of divine activity and creaturely activity? How is God's
action related to the finite causal nexus in nature and history?
Is God active in all creaturely activity or does God intervene in
this activity?

These questions were not especially pressing in the early
period of Christian thought. Augustine, however, developed a
rather complex theory of the relation of divine activity to creaturely activity. On the one hand the divine sovereignty, decree,
and providence reign absolutely over all of history, and God con-
trols all creaturely action. On the other hand, God does not act
as a finite cause but in and through finite causes, both natural
and human. God acts intrinsically or from within finite causes
and also extrinsically or from without through the mediation of
other finite things, especially the angels.[1]

1

Thomas Aquinas clarified these issues and established the
form of later tradition in his doctrine of primary and secondary
causes, and Roman Catholic theology has generally followed this
pattern down to the present.[2] In the treatise on the divine government at the end of the first part of the *Summa Theologiae* Thomas
draws on the categories of Aristotle and the medieval schools to
explain how God acts in the world. God can act immediately in the
world and also mediately through finite causes. Using Aristotle's
distinction of four causes, material, final, efficient, and formal,
Thomas explains how God is the source of all material causes, the
goal of all action, the first cause of all agents, and the source
of all forms. If it is objected that one action cannot issue simultaneously from two agents, Thomas responds, "The one action
does not issue from two agents on the same level; there is, however, nothing against one and the same action issuing from a primary and secondary agent." (Ia, 105, 5 ad 2) Furthermore, such
an action is not done partly by God and partly by the finite
agent, but it is done wholly by both, although in a different manner. Thomas offers the analogy of artisans and their instruments.
(*Summa Contra Gentiles*, III, 70) God can also act apart from the
normal order of the world and produce the results of secondary
causes without them or surpassing them. (*S.T.* Ia, 105, 6)

According to Calvin God is in absolute control of the world,
and the divine will is the cause of all things, although Calvin
denied the nominalists' attribution of absolute power to God.
Thus every drop of rain and the flight of the birds is governed
and determined by God's will and plan. (*Institutes*, I, xvi, 5)
God sometimes works through intermediate or secondary causes,
sometimes without them, and sometimes in contradiction to them.
(I, xvii, 1) In spite of this Calvin affirms human responsibility
and the reality of secondary causes and denies God's responsibility
for evil actions. In a chapter on "How God Works in Men's Hearts"
Calvin explains how God, the Chaldeans, and Satan are all active
in the one event of the Chaldeans attack on Job's shepherds and
flock. They are distinguished by the end or goal and manner of
their acting. (II, iv, 2)

These ideas were elaborated thoroughly in the Protestant
orthodox theology of the seventeenth century under the doctrine
of providence in its three parts, preservation, concurrence, and
government. The second of these refers to the cooperation of divine and creaturely action in which divine providence participates
with secondary causes in their action and effects. J. A. Quenstedt

(1617-1688) states:

> God not only gives second causes the power to act,
> and preserves this, but immediately influences the
> action and effect of the creature, so that the same
> effect is produced not by God alone, nor by the
> creature alone, nor partly by God and partly by the
> creature, but *at the same time by God and the crea-
> ture*, as one and the same total efficiency, viz.,
> by God as by the universal and first cause, and by
> the creature as the particular and second cause.[3]

God however, was also understood to act occasionally beyond or
without secondary causes in miracles. This traditional view of
God's activity in the world raised difficult problems in regard to
human freedom and evil. If God is the first cause of all events,
then human freedom and responsibility are put in question, and God
seems to be made responsible for evil events both natural and
human.

The development of modern science in the seventeenth and
eighteenth centuries with its sole concern with natural causes and
its ever-expanding interpretation of natural events led to fundamental doubts about the reality of divine activity in the world.
The deist theologians of the eighteenth century held that God like
a good watchmaker had created the world at the beginning and determined its laws but does not act in the world thereafter.

In reaction to what it saw as the barrenness of orthodoxy and
deism the liberal theology of the nineteenth and early twentieth
centuries held as one of its central themes a strong emphasis on
the divine immanence, the universal presence of God in the world.
Now the action of God was understood as the continual, creative,
and purposive activity which works in and through all the processes
of nature and history. The liberal theologians affirmed human
freedom and the reign of causal law and saw the activity of God
in, if not identical with, these processes. The divine providence
was understood as the purposive power manifest in the progressive
development of life and society in evolution and history toward
ever higher forms. As a result the interpretation of divine
activity in the form of miracle tended to disappear. All processes
were seen as miraculous in the sense of involving the activity of
God. Friedrich Schleiermacher (1768-1834), for example, held that
divine providence and causal law entirely coincide. Miracle is
but the religious name for event. God's immanent providential
activity raises humanity to higher levels of consciousness. Al-
brecht Ritschl (1822-1889) interpreted providence to be the immanent divine activity in history which elevated humanity to the

fullness of moral personality and to the achievement of a universal
moral society which is the Kingdom of God.

Thus it becomes clear that the liberal view of the divine
activity in the world was merely a simplified form of the traditional doctrine of primary and secondary causes with miracles de-
leted. God was seen to act in and through all finite actions and
processes and not apart from them, but how this was to be understood was never made clear. The liberal theologians wanted to
avoid the pantheism of identifying the divine and finite activity,
but the problem of the relation of the two was largely ignored.

The period of the dominance of liberal theology came to an
end with Karl Barth and the emergence of the dialectical or neo-
orthodox theology in the second quarter of this century. Central
in this theological movement was a strong emphasis on the freedom
and sovereignty of God's action in the world. Barth's interpretation of the divine activity in the world amounted to a reaffirmation and reinterpretation of the orthodox Protestant view described above.[4]

The impact of the neo-orthodox theology led in the 1940s
to the emergence of what has been called the "biblical theology
movement" which reaffirmed the centrality for faith and the church
of the biblical testimony to God's action in history as against
the interpretation of the Bible in the liberal theology.[5] This
brings us to the period covered by the selections in this book
which will now be introduced briefly.

The book *God Who Acts: Biblical Theology as Recital*[6] by G.
Ernest Wright (1909-1974), for many years professor of Old Testament at the Harvard Divinity School, is a volume of the series
Studies in Biblical Theology and is a classic of the biblical
theology movement. Its central thesis is that biblical theology
is the recital of the mighty acts of God, the historical events
in which God is active to elect, judge, and save the people of
God. "The central message of the Bible is a proclamation of the
Divine action. . . . Biblical faith . . . is first and foremost
a confessional recital of the gracious and redemptive acts of God."
[p.120]

Within this strong affirmation there is considerable obscurity
about the relation between observable historical events, the interpretation of these events by faith, and the divine action. Is
God's action located in the event or in the faithful interpretation? Is God active in all events whether or not they are seen by
faith? How is God's action related to the finite causal nexus?

This was one of several problematic features in the biblical theology movement which led to its demise in the early 60s.[7]

One of the most important critiques of the biblical theology
movement (and of Wright in particular) and especially its thesis
about the centrality of the action of God in history is the essay
written in 1961 by Longdon Gilkey, professor of theology at the
University of Chicago, entitled "Cosmology, Ontology, and the
Travail of Biblical Language." It was epochal in raising sharply
the fundamental theological issue of the movement which is also a
basic problem in modern theology.

Gilkey's thesis is that biblical theology and the neo-orthodox
theology allied with it, in which he included himself, is half orthodox and half modern. It speaks of the mighty acts of God attested in the Bible, but it also affirms the modern liberal proposition that God does not interrupt or intervene in the natural-
historical causal nexus. This leaves the concept of the act of
God empty or equivocal. The biblical theologians seemed to be
affirming that God acted in history, but when pressed they appeared
to affirm only that the Jews and the early Christians believed
that God acted in history. They denied that they understood the
activity of God in the world in a traditional or literal sense,
but they refused to say in what way they did understand it. Gilkey
concludes by calling for an ontology or philosophical theology
which would treat the relation of God's activity to ordinary events
and to the special events of salvation history.

One problem in Gilkey's essay is his assertion that modern
theologians assume the uninterruptable causal nexus. "Since they
participate in the modern world of science both intellectually and
existentially, they can scarcely do anything else." (p. 31)
[p. 195b] But assuming the causal nexus does not mean assuming
any particular metaphysical unification of the diverse and often
tentative sciences which describe such a nexus (such as subatomic
physics, molecular biology, and the varieties of psychology) let
alone a picture which makes divine influence impossible or unintelligible. Most of the neo-orthodox theologians, Barth and Brun-
ner, for example, were not liberal in the sense of denying divine
activity in the world or miracles. So the affirmation of an uninterruptable causal nexus is not a matter of accepting modern science but is rather a theological problem which Gilkey does not
explore.

Gilkey returned to this issue fifteen years later and posed
again the question of how we can understand the action of God in

history, of whether or not God can be understood to be a cause in
history. His answer is disappointingly vague. God can be understood as the ground of our being and becoming, as the ground of
the possibilities of history, and as the judgment and reconcilia-
tion of the estrangement of our history. But how God's action and
causality are to be understood is left unclear.[8]

In 1966 Frank B. Dilley, professor of philosophy at the University of Delaware, took up Gilkey's thesis and pursued it a few
steps further in his essay entitled "Does the 'God Who Acts' Really
Act?" He states that the biblical theologians attempted to stake
out a position which is an alternative to the liberal doctrine of
a God who is restricted to universal actions and the conservative
view of a God who performs outright miracles. He argues that their
position is a purely verbal or equivocal one without content and
not a real alternative since it simply dodges the question of the
relation of divine activity to the finite causal nexus.

Dilley takes up three possible ways of conceiving the divine
action in the world: the biblical view that God openly abridges
the natural order, a modern revision of that view which holds
that the divine activity is visible only to the eye of faith, and
the view that such acts are caused by God and creaturely causes
acting conjointly. He investigates each of these views and
finds all of them wanting. He concludes that the end of an era
has been reached, since it is now clear that there is no alternative between liberalism and conservatism on the issue of divine
activity in the world.

The difficulties in Dilley's essay are in his analysis of
the latter two views. He states that the second one is the only
real way of preserving the idea of the God who acts. One problem
he finds in it, however, is that "most moderns, even quite religious ones, *cannot* bring themselves to think in terms of miracles
anymore." (p. 54) [p. 76] But this is simply empirically false.[9]
Furthermore, he states that no one has tried to explain how miracles are possible in scientific terms and thus seems to be unaware
of the work of Pollard and Heim, for example.[10] Finally, his
criticism of the concept of the conjoint action of God and creatures does not take account of the traditional and highly subtle
treatment of this issue in terms of primary and secondary causes.

The main example offered by Dilley of the view which sees
God and finite causes acting conjointly in the same event is that
of Rudolph Bultmann (1884-1977) the distinguished German New
Testament scholar. In his essay "The Meaning of God as Acting"
Bultmann is responding to one of the charges against his program

of demythologizing the New Testament, namely, that he did not carry
out his program completely since any talk of God acting is mythological.

Bultmann's thesis is that mythological thinking sees God's
action as visible intervention in the finite chain of events, but
that his demythologized view interprets God's action as within the
finite events and visible only to the eye of faith. This is not a
general identity of divine and worldly action, as in pantheism,
but rather a paradoxical identity which is believed in the moment
of existential decision. "This is the paradox of faith, that faith
'nevertheless' understands as God's action here and now an event
which is completely intelligible in the natural or historical
connection of events." (p. 64)[p. 65] Thus God's action in the
world can be understood not as a cosmic action but on the analogy
of personal relations.

This is one of the main interpretations of the actions of
God in contemporary theology.[11] But several points remain unclear
in this view. Does God in fact act in the world, or is it only
that faith sees the world *as if* God were acting? Is there any
ontological difference between an event in which God is acting and
one in which God is not acting? How can we conceive of an act of
God which is real and yet which does not have any objective effect
on the finite causal nexus?[12]

In his essay "What Sense Does It Make to Say, 'God Acts in
History'?" Schubert M. Ogden, professor of theology at Perkins
School of Theology, Southern Methodist University, asserts that
Bultmann has made an important contribution to defining and re-
solving this problem. He agrees with Bultmann that the mythological
way of speaking of God's action represents God as another secondary
cause in the world and thus misrepresents the character of the
divine transcendence. He also agrees that the meaning of theological statements, such as those about God's activity, is existential, referring to the possibilities of human existence, rather
than objective or scientific. Ogden believes, however, that Bultmann's solution to the problem is problematic in that it is one-
sidedly existentialist and thus makes it impossible to speak directly of God, and also that Bultmann does not carry out his solution consistently, especially in regard to the act of God in
Christ.

In his own approach to the question of God's activity in the
world Ogden, following Hartshorne, proposes the analogy of the
relation of persons to their bodies. The action of God is also

to be understood on the analogy of the action of a person, especially the inner action by which the self constitutes itself. "The
primary meaning of God's action is the act whereby, in each new
present, he constitutes himself as God by participating fully and
completely in the world of his creatures." (p. 89) [p. 177]

Ogden concludes that there are two senses in which God may be
said to act in history. First, since all our bodily actions are
to some extent our actions, likewise every creature is to some extent God's act. Second, since humans can grasp the meaning of
reality and express it in symbolic speech and action, this action
can represent God and actually be God's action. It is not clear,
however, how the analogy of the inner act of self-constitution is
related to the self-body analogy.[13]

John B. Cobb, Jr., professor of theology at the Claremont
School of Theology and Graduate School, in his essay "Natural
Causality and Divine Action" uses the Aristotelian four causes to
interpret the ways in which God's activity in the world has been
interpreted in this century. Because various attempts to see God
as an efficient cause in the world have failed, theologians have
attempted to interpret God as formal cause (Wieman), as material
cause (Tillich), and as final cause (Pannenberg).

Believing these approaches to be inadequate Cobb considers
recent philosophical discussions of efficient causality and concludes that the most promising interpretation is that of actual
influence. Following Whitehead he suggests the analogy of the influence of one experience on another. As an experience of anger,
for example, influences subsequent events by constituting itself
as such, so God acts by constituting the divine reality in such a
way that other events, such as human experiences, take account of
God. Cobb believes that evidence for such a view of divine causality can be found in the experience of the lure toward new experience,
and that such an interpretation supports rather than threatens
human freedom.

The interpretation of divine power and activity in terms of
influence through being experienced is a radical departure from
the traditional doctrine. Although it offers a coherent view of
the divine activity, it raises fundamental questions about the
adequacy of the doctrine of God in process theology.[14]

In his essay "Relativism, Divine Causation, and Biblical
Theology" David R. Griffin, professor of the philosophy of religion
at the Claremont School of Theology, states that the most widely
accepted view of the relation between divine and non-divine

causation is the schema of primary and secondary causes. This
schema allows liberal biblical scholars, for example, as historians
to accept the claim that all events are intelligible in terms of
non-divine causes, and as people of faith to affirm divine providence or the view that God is the ultimate or primary cause of all
events. But Griffin argues that the schema is unintelligible, because it affirms two sufficient causes for one event, which is
contradictory.

Griffin also criticizes the primary-secondary cause schema because it leads to relativism in regard to faith. This is the result of locating the significance of divine revelation solely in
the receiver of revelation rather than in the divine revealer and
in the event in which revelation takes place. This leads to the
conclusion that the various religions are equally valid paths to
unity with God.

In the constructive part of his essay Griffin proposes that
Whitehead's process philosophy offers a way of speaking about the
relation of divine and non-divine causation which avoids these difficulties. According to Whitehead an event is to be explained by
the influence of previous events, by the influence of an initial
aim supplied by God, and by the event's own self-determination.
This makes it possible to articulate a view of the special action
of God in the world without breaking with the liberal conviction
that there are no interruptions of the normal course of events.
It is also possible on this basis to argue that, although God loves
all people equally, this love has been disclosed more decisively
in one tradition than in others, thus avoiding relativism. Griffin
concludes that on these grounds it should be possible for biblical
theologians to refer to divine influence as a causal factor in
history.[15]

Gordon D. Kaufman, professor of theology at the Harvard
Divinity School, in his essay "On the Meaning of 'Act of God'"
declares that the modern scientific view of nature is incompatible
with any idea of the activity of God as an interruption of the
natural order. He also disposes of the proposal to limit God's
action to the realm of history as distinct from nature. Finally,
he rejects the alternative of interpreting God in such a way that
divine activity is not implied.

According to Kaufman our basic difficulty with the idea of
the activity of God in the world is that we cannot conceive of an
event without prior finite causes. Thus the idea of an event with
a supernatural cause is literally inconceivable, self-
contradictory, and thus meaningless.

Kaufman then proposes that the concept of divine agency can
be reinterpreted in such a way as not to conflict with the modern
understanding of nature and history. Following the philosophy of
action he defines an act as involving the intention of an agent to
realize a goal. Drawing on an idea from John Macmurray, Kaufman
suggests that the whole course of history can be conceived as God's
act in the primary sense. Then certain aspects of cosmic history,
such as evolution, the emergence of human cultures, and the history
of Israel, can be understood as subordinate or subacts of God which
are steps in the achievement of the divine goal. In the march of
Jesus to the cross we see the only case of "a direct one-to-one
correspondence and coincidence of human activity with the divine."
Thus God can be understood as "working within and through the
closely textured natural and historical processes of our experience." (pp. 156, 157) [pp. 145, 147]

Although Kaufman begins his essay with a quote from Gilkey's
essay asking for "an ontology of events specifying what God's relation to ordinary events is like, and thus what his relation to
special events might be," he does not supply this. Rather he
finally settles for the liberal position that God somehow acts in
and through all the events and processes of nature and history to
achieve the divine goal but without explaining how this might be
understood. This liberal view seems to be in conflict with the
analogy of human action which implies an interruption of the causal
nexus. In fact the direction of Kaufman's thought seems to be to
give up on this issue. Not only is the idea of an event caused by
God self-contradictory, inconceivable, and meaningless, but also
in a note added later Kaufman suggests that it is not "logically
consistent with the meaning of 'God' to speculate on the means or
modes of his direct impingement on the world." (p. 159) [p. 129n][16]

Frank G. Kirkpatrick, associate professor of religion at
Trinity College, Hartford, Conn., in his essay "Understanding an
Act of God" develops his view in relation to Kaufman's by making
use of the analogy of human agency as clarified by the philosophy
of action. Like a human agent God can be understood as a singular
agent among others in a common world. Unlike human agents who act
through their bodies God can act directly on any point in the
world on the analogy of psychokinesis. Through an analysis of the
distinction between acts and events Kirkpatrick argues that there
is no conflict between causal law and divine action in the world.
Thus particular acts of God, such as that at the Red Sea, are as
intelligible as particular human acts.

The value of Kirkpatrick's essay lies in its detailed employment of the philosophy of action and the analogy of human agency
which is the primary analogy in the Bible, and in its dialogue
with many of the other views presented in this volume. The main
difficulties in the analogy of human action for divine action are
that it does not explain God's relation to ordinary events or those
in which God is not acting and that there is nothing in God corresponding to the body in human agency.[17]

Maurice Wiles, Regius Professor of Divinity at Oxford University, in his essay "Religious Authority and Divine Action" notes
the circular relation between the affirmation of the special action
of God in certain events and the acceptance of certain religious
authorities in history. This leads to the question of whether the
traditional conception of special divine activity is essential to
an understanding of Christian faith which holds the Bible to be
in some sense authoritative.

Taking Bultmann's view as his starting point Wiles dismisses
Dilley's criticism and makes his main proposal. To speak of God
acting in history is to speak of the varying human response which
is elicited by the unvarying divine presence in historical events.
This response arises from "experiencing what happens to us and
what we achieve as being in response to an overall purpose at work
in the world." (p. 185) [pp. 137-38] Just as some aspects of the
natural world have given rise more directly than others to the
apprehension of God's creativity, so certain historical events
have uniquely elicited the response of faith. It is especially in
Jesus Christ that God's action is decisively revealed through the
response it has evoked. Thus referring to certain events as special acts of God does not mean that there is any difference in the
relation of the divine action to these events but only a difference in the depth of the religious response to them.

Wiles admits that this involves a somewhat attenuated interpretation of the divine activity as truly personal action. He
associates his proposal with that of Ogden and the process theologians. But this is difficult to understand, since the process
view, especially as seen in the essays by Cobb and Griffin,
specifically involves a variety in the divine activity in relation
to various events. The chief difficulty with Wiles's proposal is
that it is not clear in what sense uniform activity can be purposive, and in what sense he is asserting any divine *activity* at
all, let alone special divine activity. Wiles offers no analogy
for his approach, but it is interesting to note that when

analogies are offered, they are impersonal.[18]

Austin Farrer (1904-1968), for many years warden of Keble
College, Oxford, states that the central chapters of his book
Faith and Speculation, from which the selections in this volume
are taken, deals with "the conceivability of divine action in the
world" in the fields of grace, nature, and history. He begins
with the analogy of human action for divine action. As against
Wiles he holds that general action is a meaningless notion and
that God's action is always particular. God acts through creaturely
agencies without either forcing them or competing with them. But
it is neither necessary nor possible to understand or conceive the
"causal joint" between finite and infinite action.

Farrer concludes with an extended discussion of the adequacy
of the mind-body analogy for the relation of God to the universe
and of the proper way to interpret it. The main problem in Farrer's
view of divine activity in the world is the tension between his
affirmation of double agency and his assertion that it is inconceivable in principle. It would seem that this might lead him to
explore other more conceivable interpretations of divine agency.[19]

Farrer stands generally in the Thomist tradition of which
one of the foremost modern interpreters is Etienne Gilson (1884-
1978) for many years director of studies at the Pontifical Insti-
tute of Medieval Studies in Toronto. His essay "The Corporeal
World and the Efficacy of Second Causes" is a classic statement
of the primary-secondary cause tradition deriving from Thomas
Aquinas. It is taken from his book *The Christian Philosophy of
St. Thomas Aquinas*[20] which is a translation of the fifth edition
of his well known volume *Le Thomisme* originally published in 1919.

On the basis of the fundamental Thomist distinctions of act
and potency, matter and form, and subject and accidents Gilson
develops the idea of God as the cause of the form, matter, and
act of being in all things and thus of their operations. He argues that this does not mean the dissolution of second causes into
the primary cause. "We must hold firmly to two apparently contradictory truths. God does whatever creatures do; and yet creatures themselves do whatever they do. It is a question of understanding how one and the same effect can proceed simultaneously
from two different causes: God and the natural agent which produces it." (p. 222) [p. 182]

Gilson offers the analogy of artisans and their instruments.
The axe and the worker both produce the whole effect, but they
do not produce it in the same manner. The worker is the first

and principal cause, while the axe is the second and instrumental
cause. Gilson notes the limitations of this anlogy in that God's
influence on the second cause penetrates far more deeply into it
than does the influence of the worker on the tool. He argues in
conclusion that this view of the relation of divine and finite
activity avoids the dual errors of seeing all causality deriving
from outside the creatures and seeing all causality deriving from
within them.[21]

NOTES

1. For the references in Augustine, see Eugene TeSelle,
Augustine the Theologian (New York: Herder and Herder, 1970),
pp. 219-23; and Langdon Gilkey, *Reaping the Whirlwind: A Christian
Interpretation of History* (New York: Seabury Press, 1976), ch. 7.

2. See, for example, Karl Rahner, *Foundations of Christian
Faith* (New York: Seabury Press, 1978), pp. 81-89.

3. Quoted by Heinrich Schmid, *The Doctrinal Theology of the
Evangelical Lutherine Church* (Philadelphia: Lutheran Publication
Society, 1876), p. 199.

4. See *Church Dogmatics*, III, 3 (Edinburgh: T. & T. Clark,
1960), pp. 90-154.

5. See Brevard S. Childs, *Biblical Theology in Crisis* (Philadelphia: Westminster Press, 1970), ch. 1, 2.

6. (London: SCM Press, 1952).

7. See Childs, *op. cit.*; and James Barr, "Biblical Theology,"
and "Revelation in History," *Interpreter's Dictionary of the
Bible*, Suppl. Vol. (Nashville: Abingdon, 1976).

8. See *Reaping the Whirlwind*, ch. 10.

9. See, for example, Andrew M. Greeley, *Religion in the
Year 2000* (New York: Sheed and Ward, 1969).

10. See the analysis of their views by Ian G. Barbour, *Issues
in Science and Religion* (Englewood Cliffs, N.J.: Prentice-Hall,
1966), ch. 13.

11. See, for example, Paul Tillich, *Systematic Theology*, 3
vols. (Chicago: University of Chicago Press, 1951-63), I:266-70.

12. For a parallel statement of the same argument see Rudolph
Bultmann, et al., *Kerygma and Myth: A Theological Debate*, ed.
Hans Werner Bartsch (New York: Harper & Brothers, 1961), pp.
196-211. For an excellent critique of Bultmann's approach, see
David R. Griffin, *A Process Christology* (Philadelphia: Westminster
Press, 1973), pp. 90-108; and also the essay by Ogden in this
volume.

13. For a critique of Ogden's essay see David Griffin, "Schubert Ogden's Christology and the Possibilities of Process

14   God's Activity in the World

Philosophy," in *Process Philosophy and Christian Thought*, ed. Delwin Brown, Ralph E. James, Jr., and Gene Reeves (Indianapolis: Bobbs Merrill Co., 1971).

14. For references to criticisms of process theology on this point, see John B. Cobb, Jr., and David Ray Griffin, *Process Theology: An Introductory Exposition* (Philadelphia: Westminster Press, 1976), p. 184.

15. For a further explication of Griffin's approach see his book *A Process Christology* (Philadelphia: Westminster Press, 1973), chs. 7, 9. For a rather different interpretation of God's activity in the world from a Whiteheadian point of view, see Daniel Day Williams, "How Does God Act?: An Essay in Whitehead's Metaphysics," in *Process and Divinity*, ed. William L. Reese and Eugene Freeman (Lasalle, Ill.: Open Court Publishing Co., 1964).

16. For analysis and criticism of Kaufman's essay see David R. Mason, "Can We Speculate on How God Acts?," *Journal of Religion* 57 (1977):16-32; F. Michael McLain, "On Theological Models," *Harvard Theological Review* 62 (1969):180-86; and David R. Griffin, "Gordon Kaufman's Theology: Some Questions," *Journal of the American Academy of Religion* 41 (1973):558-63.

17. For a similar approach see John J. Compton, "Science and God's Action in Nature," in *Earth Might Be Fair*, ed. Ian G. Barbour (Englewood Cliffs, N.J.: Prentice-Hall, 1972); and Horace Bushnell, *Nature and the Supernatural as Together Constituting The One System of God* (New York: Charles Scribner, 1858), pp. 251-68.

18. See James A. Pike, *A Time for Christian Candor* (New York: Harper & Row, 1964), chs. 7, 8; in which the analogies offered are that of volcanic eruption, oil-drilling, and steam heat. For a critique of Wiles's view see Brian L. Hebblethwaite, "Providence and Divine Action," *Religious Studies* 14 (1978):223-36; in which he is reproached for not considering Farrer's view. For Wiles's response, see his essay "Farrer's Concept of Double Agency," *Theology* 84 (1981):243-49; for the continuation of the discussion, see the essays by Wiles, Galilee, and Hebblethwaite, *Theology* 85 (1982):7-13.

19. For a critique of Farrer's position, see the essay by Wiles mentioned above.

20. (New York: Random House, 1956).

21. For a more recent and detailed presentation of this view in relation to questions raised by process theologians see John H. Wright, "Divine Knowledge and Human Freedom: The God Who Dialogues," *Theological Studies* 38(1977):450-77. For a detailed critique of this approach see the criticism of James F. Ross by David R. Griffin, *God, Power, and Evil: A Process Theodicy* (Philadelphia: Westminster Press, 1976), ch. 14. I regret that I was not able to find a selection by a Jewish author on divine activity in the world, but see Martin Buber, *Moses: The Revelation and the Covenant* (New York: Harper & Brothers, 1946), pp. 75-76.

2.   GOD WHO ACTS

G. Ernest Wright

In considering Biblical faith, it seems to me that the point
at which we must begin is not with the history of its evolving ideas
but with history in another sense.   It is history as the arena of
God's activity.   Biblical theology is first and foremost a theology
of recital, in which Biblical man confesses his faith by reciting
the formative events of his history as the redemptive handiwork
of God.   The realism of the Bible consists in its close attention
to the facts of history and of tradition because these facts are
the facts of God. . . .

At the centre of Israelite faith lay the great proclamation
that the God of the fathers had heard the cry of a weak, oppressed
people in Egypt.   They had been slaves, but then freed by mighty
acts which demonstrated God's power to the Egyptians and to the
world.   As slaves for whom the justice of the world made no pro-
vision, they were delivered by a most extraordinary exhibition of
Divine grace.   This was a sign, a wonder, not to be explained by
fortune or irrational chance, but solely by the assumption of a
personal Power greater than all the powers of this world.   This
was a God who could make the forces of nature serve him as well as
the recalcitrance of the heart of Pharaoh.   He was one who for
some reason had set his love on a defenceless people and had chosen
them for his own.

Israel's doctrine of God, therefore, was not derived from
systematic or speculative thought, but rather in the first instance
from the attempt to explain the events which led to the establishment of the nation.   While living in the world of natural religion,
they focussed their attention, not on nature and the gods of nature, but on the God who had revealed himself in an extraordinary
series of historical events.   The knowledge of God was an inference
from what actually had happened in human history.   The Israelite
eye was thus trained to take human events seriously, because in
them was to be learned more clearly than anywhere else what God
willed and what he was about.   Consequently, in all that happened
subsequently the Israelite simply interpreted the meaning of events

From G. Ernest Wright, *God Who Acts: Biblical Theology as Recital*
(London: SCM Press, 1952). Reprinted with permission.

15

by recognizing and acknowledging in them the God who had formed
the nation by the remarkable events at the Exodus and in the wilderness. The half-hearted, fearful and defeated attempt to break
into Canaan from Kadesh-barnea in the south was attributed to rebellion against God and lack of faith in his leadership (Num. 14;
Deut. 2.26-46). The long stay in the wilderness thus was seen to
be God's judgment upon the people for their sin. Yet subsequently
the successes of the conquest of Canaan were occasioned solely by
the powerful leadership of Yahweh. The initial defeat at Ai in
the tradition found ready explanation in Achan's violation of the
Divine command that all booty was to be 'devoted' to God and none
was to be taken for personal gain. The ideology of Holy War de-
picted in the books of Deuteronomy, Joshua and Judges was more than
a mere rationalization for the nation's wars. It was based on the
recognition that God who had saved Israel at the Exodus had a
historical purpose and programme. The battles of Joshua and the
Judges, therefore, were more than the mere fightings of men; they
were holy because they were God's war. According to an old fragment
of the law of this Holy War, a priest was required to explain to
the army whenever it was ready to go into battle: 'Hear, O Israel,
ye approach this day unto battle against your enemies. Let not
your hearts faint; fear not, and do not tremble, neither be ye
terrified because of them; for Yahweh your God is he that goeth
with you, to fight for you against your enemies, to save you'
(Deut. 20.3-4).[1]

When Israel settled in Canaan and attempted to make their
living from the soil, it was easy for many of them simply to interpret the agricultural pursuits in the same manner as their Canaanite
neighbours and teachers. Thus, we are told, they 'did evil in the
sight of Yahweh, and served Baalim. And they forsook Yahweh, God
of their fathers, who brought them out of the land of Egypt, and
followed other gods, of the gods of the people that were round
about them, and bowed themselves unto them, and provoked Yahweh
to anger' (Judg. 2.11-12). It was thus possible to interpret the
wars of the period of the Judges in this light. The judgment and
the grace of God were seen in the oppressions and deliverances,
and correlated with the idolatry, repentance and faith of the
people.

When Israel was caught up within the struggles of the world
powers during the first great empire-building epoch of history,
Yahweh was not lost within the events nor did he perish with the
state he had founded. On the contrary, he rescued a remnant as a
brand from the burning. For with what must have seemed to pagans

as infinite presumption Israel proclaimed that it was Yahweh himself who was directing these wars to his own ends, even though the
conquering armies did not know or acknowledge it. The Assyrian was
the 'rod of his anger' (Isa. 10.5); Nebuchadnezzar was his 'servant'
(Jer. 29.5); and Cyrus was his 'anointed' (Isa. 45.1). Let all the
nations be gathered together, said Second Isaiah; let them take
counsel and see if they can interpret either past or present (Isa.
43.8-9). Let them haste in the confusion of preparing their idols.
Let these gods 'bring forth and show us what shall happen; let
them show the former things, what they are, that we may consider
them and know the latter end of them, or declare us things to come.
Show us the things that are to come hereafter, that we may know
that ye are gods. . . . Behold, ye are as nothing, and your work
is of nought. An abomination is he that chooseth you' (Isa. 41.7,
21-24).[2] Yahweh alone is in charge of history. As one who had
met Israel in historical event, he thus was recognised as the Lord
of all events who was directing the whole course of history to his
own ends, for nothing happened in which his power was not acknowledged. . . .

From the above survey we are now in possession of the chief
clues to the theological understanding of the whole Bible. There
is, first, the peculiar attention to history and to historical traditions as the primary sphere in which God reveals himself. To be
sure, God also reveals himself and his will in various ways to the
inner consciousness of man, as in other religions. Yet the nature
and content of this inner revelation is determined by the outward,
objective happenings of history in which individuals are called to
participate. It is, therefore, the objectivity of God's historical
acts which are the focus of attention, not the subjectivity of inner, emotional, diffuse and mystical experience. Inner revelation
is thus concrete and definite, since it is always correlated with
a historical act of God which is the primary locus of concentration.
Mysticism in its typical forms, on the other hand, subtly turns
this concentration around, so that the focus of attention is on the
inner revelation, while the objectivity of God's historical acts
is either denied altogether or left on the periphery of one's vision. Important as Christian pietism has been in the Church, it
has not escaped this subtle inversion with the result that the
central Biblical perspective has been lost.

Secondly, the chief inference from this view of history as
revelation was the mediate nature of God's action in history: that
is, his election of a special people through whom he would

accomplish his purposes. This was a proper inference from the
Exodus deliverance; and the migration of Abraham to Canaan was believed to have been occasioned by a Divine call which involved
election. In Genesis the election is portrayed as the goal of
history and the Divine answer to the human problem. After the
Exodus, it formed the background for the interpretation of Israel's
life in Palestine and a central element in prophetic eschatology
and in the apocalyptic presentation of the Book of Daniel.

Thirdly, the election and its implications were confirmed and
clarified in the event of the covenant ceremony at Sinai. Israel's
sin was the breach of this covenant, which, therefore, enabled
the faithful to see that election was not unalterable. It could be
annulled by Israel herself. Consequently, covenant was something
that had to be periodically renewed by ceremonies of rededication.[3]
It involved the interpretation of the whole life of the people, in
the social, economic, political and cultic spheres. The law of the
society was the law of the covenant, given by God with the promise
of justice and security within the promised land. Consequently,
the central problem of Israel was envisaged as the problem of true
security in the midst of covenant violation and international up-
heaval. This security was seen by the prophets as only to be found
beyond the suffering and judgment of the Day of Yahweh. There would
be a revival of the community, but only after the elect people had
become scattered and dry bones (Ezek. 37).

These three elements are together the core of Israelite faith
and the unifying factor within it.[4] They have little abstract or
propositional theology within them. They are based on historical
events and the inferences drawn from them. They cannot be grasped
by the abstract rubrics of dogmatic theology. And these very same
elements are the centre and core of the faith of the early church.
For this reason the advent of Jesus Christ could not be understood
solely or chiefly as the coming of a teacher of moral and spiritual
truths. His coming was a historical event which was the climax of
God's working since the creation. All former history had its goal
in him because God had so directed it. All subsequent history will
be directed by him because God has exalted him as Lord. In so doing
he will fulfill the promises of God in the government of Israel,
assuming the royal office of David at the right hand of God and
providing the security which the sin of Israel made impossible of
achievement. The election of Israel as the agent of God in universal redemption is reaffirmed in the New Israel (e.g. I Pet. 2.9-10),
the Body of Christ, which is the partaker of the New Covenant in

Christ's blood. In Christ God has inaugurated the new age, fore-
seen of old; entrance into it is by faith and by the sharing of
Christ's cross, for in him our sins are forgiven and our alienation
from God done away. Thus God in Christ has completed the history
of Israel; he has reversed the work of Adam, fulfilled the promises
to Abraham, repeated the deliverance from bondage, not indeed from
Pharaoh but from sin and Satan, and inaugurated the new age and the
new covenant. To be sure, the world is unredeemed and the final
consummation is yet to appear. Yet Christ is the sign and seal of
its coming. Hence he is the climactic event in a unique series of
events, to be comprehended only by what has happened before him,
but at the same time the new event which marks a fresh beginning in
human history.

This, then, is the basic substance of Biblical theology. It
is true that we simply cannot communicate it without dealing with
the *ideas* of which it is composed. Yet to conceive of it primarily
as a series of ideas which we must arrange either systematically or
according to their historical development is to miss the point of
it all. It is fundamentally an interpretation of history, a confessional recital of historical events as the acts of God, events
which lead backward to the beginning of history and forward to
its end. Inferences are constantly made from the acts and are interpreted as integral parts of the acts themselves which furnish
the clue to understanding not only of contemporary happenings but
of those which subsequently occurred. The being and attributes
of God are nowhere systematically presented but are inferences from
events. Biblical man did not possess a philosophical notion of
deity whence he could argue in safety and 'objectivity' as to
whether this or that was of God. This ubiquitous modern habit of
mind which reasons from axioms and principles or universals to
the concrete would have been considered as faithless rebellion
against the Lord of history who used history to reveal his will
and purpose. Hence the nearest approach to atheism which the Old
Testament possesses is the fool who says in his heart there is
no God (Ps. 14.1; 53.1). Yet the Psalmist means by this, not a
theoretical atheism, but rather the practical atheism of a sinner
who calls God's works, not his being, into question.[5] Jeremiah
clarifies the point when he speaks of people in his day who refuse
to believe that the great events which then are happening are the
work of God. They thus 'have denied Yahweh and said: "It is not
he; neither shall evil come upon us; neither shall we see sword
nor famine"' (5.12). To refuse to take history seriously as the

revelation of the will, purpose and nature of God is the simplest
escape from the Biblical God and one which leaves us with an idol
of our own imagining.

    Consequently, not even the nature of God can be portrayed ab-
stractly. He can only be described *in relation to* the historical
process, to his chosen agents and to his enemies. Biblical theology
must begin, therefore, with the primary question as to why the
Bible possesses the historical nature that it does. It thus must
point in the first instance to this confessional recital of traditional and historical events, and proceed to the inferences which
accompanied those events, became an integral part of them, and
served as the guides to the comprehension of both past and future.
Biblical theology, then, is primarily a confessional recital in
which history is seen as a problem of faith, and faith a problem
of history. . . .[6]

    How do the various events align themselves together so as to
provide the structure for the Bible? In other words, what precisely has God done? This can best be discerned in the earliest
Christian preaching and in the Biblical confessions of faith.

    Professor Oscar Cullmann in his study of *The Earliest Christian
Confessions*[7] has singled out two formulae especially which were
the central elements of the confessions. These are 'Jesus Christ
is Lord' (I Cor. 12.3) and 'Jesus is the Son of God' (Acts 8.37;
Heb. 4.14; I John 4.15). Both of the statements, it may be noted,
are derived from what to the New Testament are historical acts of
God. The first refers to God's resurrection and exaltation of
Christ to be the reigning Lord of all creation. The second is the
same, though emphasizing by means of a Davidic or royal title drawn
from the Old Testament the special relationship existing between
God and Christ.[8] When these statements were expanded, the expansion was almost always in the form of additions from what to the
Christian were the facts of Jesus' life, death and resurrection.
The Apostle Paul in Phil. 2.6-11 quotes one of the earliest confessions preserved. It is a Christian psalm which speaks of Christ
emptying himself, taking the form of a servant, remaining obedient
unto death, and of God's exalting him to receive the worship of
all things 'that every tongue should confess that Jesus Christ is
Lord, to the glory of God the father'. Another common confession
used in preaching was probably that quoted by Paul in I Cor. 15.3-7,
which speaks of Christ's death for our sins, according to the
Scriptures, of his burial and resurrection, according to the
Scriptures, and of his various subsequent appearances on earth.

Rom. 1.1-3 affirms 'the gospel of God (which he had promised afore by his prophets in the holy scriptures), concerning his Son, who was born of the seed of David according to the flesh, and declared to be the Son of God with power, according to the spirit of holiness, by the resurrection from the dead: Jesus Christ our Lord'.

In New Testament times there were evidently a number of such formulae, differing in wording because of the differences in occasions and personalities involved in their construction. Most of them, says Cullmann,[9] contained only the one Christological article. To believe in Christ meant of necessity the belief in the God and Father of Jesus Christ and as well in the Holy Spirit. Definitely trinitarian confessions appear more commonly after about A.D. 150, presumably because of the necessity of clearing up all ambiguity for Gentile Christians exposed to Gnosticism and not well trained in the scriptures of the Old Testament. But the central emphasis continued to be the Christological, and our interest here is to point to its objective character. What is confessed is not an internal religious or mystical feeling, nor is it a series of spiritual or moral teachings, nor a system of propositional dogmatics. It is rather the work of God in the life and death of a historical person.

The substance of the early confessions was derived, of course, from the Gospel as preached by the early Church. Dr. C. H. Dodd in his study of *The Apostolic Preaching and its Developments* (London, 1936) has attempted to isolate the central elements of the earliest Christian preaching or proclamation (*kerygma*) from the letters of the Apostle Paul and from the sermons of the Apostles as presented to us in the first thirteen chapters of the Book of Acts. This common core of the proclamation he designates as the Jerusalem *kerygma*. It was composed of at least the following elements: (1) the new age, the time of fulfilment, which God foreshadowed by the mouth of the prophets, has actually been inaugurated by God in Christ; (2) God has accomplished this event through the ministry, death and resurrection of Jesus whose Messiahship, prophetic office (Acts 3.22), death and resurrection were all according to the Scriptures; (3) by virtue of the resurrection God has exalted Christ to his right hand as the Messianic Lord of the new Israel; (4) the actual existence and state of the Church is the proof of God's gift of the Spirit (cf. Joel 2.28 ff) and the sign of Christ's present power; (5) the Messianic age will shortly be consummated, according to God's word by the prophets,

in the return of Christ; (6) accordingly, it is incumbent upon
everyone to repent that God may forgive and send his Holy Spirit
upon him, for in Christ God has delivered men from sin into new
life.

The early preaching was thus purely confessional, possessing
an objective character, based upon the inferential interpretation
of the actual life and death of one who existed in history and of
one whose advent climaxed, culminated, and fulfilled God's work in
history. At the same time it inaugurated the beginning of a new
epoch in which the Christian now lives under Christ's Lordship
while awaiting the final victory which will take place at his return.

As Dodd further shows, this Jerusalem *kerygma* is the nerve
centre of the New Testament and followed the lines of the summary
of the preaching of Jesus as given in Mark 1.13-15: 'Jesus came
into Galilee, preaching the gospel of God, and saying, "The time
is fulfilled, and the kingdom of God is at hand: repent and believe
the gospel".' It is impossible, Dodd shows further, to find anything in the New Testament which is more primary than the *kerygma*.
We cannot think of the Gospels as the raw material from which the
preaching was constructed, because the actual situation is the
other way around. The Gospels themselves represent the expansion
of the *kerygma* from a number of sources of tradition. None of
them, therefore, are mere memoirs or biographies. They represent
a new literary form unknown in the pagan world; they are 'gospels',
i.e. confessional recital of historical events and traditions together with the inferences derived from the events and seen as an
integral part of them. The New Testament epistles, on the other
hand, are not primarily *kerygma*. They are addressed, not to pagans, but to Christians, and their concern is with the problems
which Christians faced in a pagan world. 'They have the character
of what the early Church called "teaching" or "exhortation".
They presuppose the preaching. They expound and defend the implications of the Gospel rather than proclaim it.'[10]

What were the chief events in the history of Israel to which
the New Testament most frequently refers as the preparatory background for God's work in Christ? It is interesting to note that,
while there are numerous citations, and allusions to, the Psalms
and the prophets, the events most often alluded to are the great
acts of God in the record beginning with Abraham and ending with
David. It is curious that the New Testament does not make use of
the destruction of Jerusalem, the exile, and the restoration, for

those events would have completed the typological comparison of
God's acts in Israelite history with his work in Christ. The
Jerusalem *kerygma*, however, was content to find references in the
prophets and Psalms which could be taken to refer to Jesus' death
and resurrection; it did not use the exile and restoration, probably because the literature of Israel and of Judaism did not concentrate on those events in the same sense that it did on the pre-
Davidic history. The tragedy of Jerusalem and Judah and the subsequent revival of a small post-Exilic community were interpreted
in prophecy as the beginning of the eschatological age when God
would establish his universal kingdom and redeem the whole of
creation. The delay in the arrival of that consummation became a
serious problem, particularly disillusioning in the failure of
Zerubbabel to become the Messiah of God. The hope continued to
live on and found expression in apocalyptic writings, but it was
Ezra's mission to re-establish the covenant nation and to turn the
people to a detailed attempt to live by the law. Prophecy as the
direct interpretation of God's work in historical events died out,
being replaced by apocalyptic writers, on the one hand, and
specialists in the law, on the other. The New Testament cuts in
behind this situation and adheres directly to the prophetic promise
of the new age, though employing apocalyptic materials in so doing.

The simplest summary of the central Biblical events as the
New Testament saw them is contained in the address attributed to
the Apostle Paul at Antioch in Pisidia (Acts 13.16 ff). It begins
in vv. 17-23 with a confessional summary of what God has done.
The following are the articles of faith which it proclaims:
(1) The God of Israel chose the fathers (Patriarchs); (2) he delivered their seed with uplifted arm from Egyptian slavery and
suffered them in the wilderness; (3) he directed the Conquest and
divided the land to them by lot; (4) after the judges, Samuel and
the rejected Saul, he raised up David to be their king, as a man
after his own heart who should do his will; (5) of whose seed, according to promise, he raised up a Saviour, Jesus.

The history, which this confession reviews, begins with the
Patriarchs and ends with David; from that point Paul passes immediately to Jesus Christ. He thus suggests that the events from
Abraham to David are the most significant history of the former
times and that Christ is the continuation, the clarification and
the fulfilment of the redemptive purpose of God within it. . . .

Numerous questions now present themselves, and to at least a
few of them we must here address ourselves. The contention thus

far has been that Biblical theology cannot be analyzed after the
manner of propositional dogmatics because it rests on a living,
changing, ever expanding and contracting attitude toward historical
events. Biblical man, living within a certain historical continuum, was aware that events were not really understood except as they
were searched for the revelation they contained of what God was
doing and what he willed. History thus could not be conceived as
a secular, naturalistic, cause-and-effect process in which events
are to be explained solely by the interplay of environment and
geography on individual and social organisms. Happenings become
history when they are recognized as integral parts of a God-planned
and God-directed working, extending from creation to the eschaton.
Each individual event has historical significance only when it is
taken into and used by this supra-individual, purposive activity.[11]

The clue to the meaning of history, as the Bible conceives it,
is a particular proclamation, a *kerygma*, of the great redemptive
acts of God which have been outlined above. Yet there is more to
history than the spectacular saving events which furnish security,
comfort and hope. History is also, perhaps more so, filled with
suffering, tragedy, death, defeat, war, destruction, insecurity and
disillusionment. Consequently, Biblical man recognized the anger
as well as the love of God, his function as Judge as well as Redeemer. Nevertheless, the *kerygma* proclaimed his saving acts as
the clue even to the meaning of tragedy, war, and suffering. History never escapes God's hand, its terrors never mean that he is
unjust; his anger never conflicts with his love. The grace of God
as affirmed in the *kerygma* was the inescapable inference from his
redemptive acts. Consequently, even war is a part of his gracious
activity; the 'day of Yahweh' is the first stage of redemption. He
uses sinful human agents as the instruments of his righteous judgment in history, though they may not recognize the fact that they
are his agents, so that the selfish imperialism of men is employed
by God to his own ends. Nevertheless, in the Biblical view this
does not mean that the responsibility of man for his own acts is
removed, nor does it mean that God is unrighteous. There is always
an element of mystery in God at this point, but Biblical man simply
recognized what to him were simple facts: namely, that the primary
acts of God were redemptive and reveal his saving purpose throughout all history (consequently, God is both Sovereign and good),
and that his acts of judgment were the just penalty on sin (consequently, man's response to God's will is a matter of responsible
choice).

The prophets were primarily interpreters of history in this light. They were not teachers of general religious truth; they were the heralds of God, and their 'Thus saith the Lord' explained God's intention and meaning in the events of their day. The source of their enlightenment was not from mystical experiences but from history itself and from the character and purpose of God revealed in both past and present. To be sure, Moses and Isaiah, like the Apostle Paul, had visions at the beginning of their careers, and these might be described in terms of religious experience; but such experiences were concerned with the call to a particular vocation which involved a complete change in their previous habit of life. They did not appeal subsequently to such experience as the source of their message. The Word which came to them interpreted events, and they were not concerned to deal publicly with their experience. The work of God which they expounded was more objective; it was exterior to that with which mystical experience customarily deals.

The Christian Church--especially those communions of the Church which trace their lineage to the Reformation--speaks of the Bible as 'the Word of God'. Yet when this phrase is interpreted to mean that the centre of the Bible is a series of divinely given teachings, then it is certainly a misconception and its use a disservice. The Bible indeed is filled with the words of God. The prophets proclaimed God's Word, not their own. The Word, however, is not an abstraction which can be presented in a systematic theology. It accompanies historical events. It is obvious that such events need interpretation before their true meaning can be understood. Consequently, when God acted, he also 'spoke' in numerous ways, but especially by chosen interpreters. Even the law as the Word of God was rooted in the Sinai covenant and was historically conditioned. It does not give timeless prescriptions for actions, as the casuistry of the Rabbinical Period in attempting to make the original laws fit every conceivable situation so vividly shows. The same is true of the prophetic Word, with the result that the great variety of attempts to apply it literally, especially in the apocalyptic wing of the Church, have always met with difficulty, since situations are never completely identical and since history never repeats itself in exactly the same way. Furthermore, if a prophet were accused of proclaiming a false Word, he could only rely upon the future action of God for confirmation (cf. I Kings 22.28; Jer. 28.5-9). The situation in the New Testament is quite similar. To speak of the Divine work in Christ as the Word of

God means that like the Evangelist John we must reinterpret radically what we mean by the Word. John's Gospel speaks of the Word
becoming flesh and dwelling among us. In other words, the Word is
a Person who lived in history, not a system of ideas or teachings,
nor even an abstract principle in the Greek sense. It is the occasion and the accompaniment of God's action in history, which attains
its ultimate form in the historical person of Christ.

        In dealing with Biblical theology, therefore, primary attention
must be given, not to abstractions concerning the nature of God,
but to history. This involves the use of all our tools for historical criticism, for if we fail to take history every bit as seriously as the Biblical writers, we shall not be expositors of Biblical faith. Yet history has a special sense in the Bible. While
dealing with actual events and traditions, Biblical history is
centred in its Creator and Director. By means of human agents God
provides each event with an accompanying Word of interpretation,
so that the latter is an integral part of the former, and both
together serve as the guide to the understanding of future events.
God is thus known by what he has done. The so-called 'attributes'
of God are inferences drawn from the way he has acted. His righteousness, justice, love, grace, jealousy, and wrath are not abstractions with which we are free to deal abstractly--that is,
apart from history. They are all descriptive of the way God has
directed history; and hence it is inferred that they all find
their unity in him. Unlike the Canaanite Baal who was the embodi-
ment of nature's cycle and thus could be acclaimed as alive only because during the summer he was dead, Yahweh is 'the living God'
because he is continually and eternally at work with his creation.
He is, therefore, external to the processes of his creation, while
at the same time revealing his purpose and will within them. He,
then, is God, not a creature, and consequently he is 'holy'. The
'attribute' of holiness simply refers to that mystery in the Divine
being which distinguishes him as God. It is possessed by creatures
and objects only in a derived sense, when these are separated by
God himself to a specialized function. Of all the Divine 'attributes' holiness comes the nearest to describing God's being rather
than his activity. Yet it is no static, definable 'quality' like
the Greek truth, beauty and goodness, for it is that indefinable
mystery in God which distinguishes him from all that he has created;
and its presence in the world is the sign of his active direction
of its affairs.

   Since God is known by what he has done, the Bible exists as a
confessional recital of his acts, together with the teaching accompanying these acts, or inferred from them in the light of specific situations which the faithful confronted.[12] To confess God
is to tell a story and then to expound its meaning. Is Biblical
theology solely concerned with abstractions of the meaning, or must
it be as primarily concerned with the story as were the Biblical
writers? Obviously, it must be both at the same time, for the abstractions cannot be separated from the history. They are inferences from the history and are always subject to deepening and correction in the light of the history. The nearest the Bible comes
to an abstract presentation of the nature of God by means of his
'attributes' is an old liturgical confession embedded in Exod.
34.6-7 and quoted in part in many other passages:[13]

> Yahweh, Yahweh, a compassionate and gracious God,
> slow to anger, abundant in *hesed* [gracious loyalty to the
> covenanted promises] and fidelity, keeping *hesed* for
> thousands, forgiving iniquity and rebellion and sin, though
> by no means acquitting (the guilty), visiting the iniquity
> of the fathers upon the children and upon the children's
> children unto the third, even the fourth (generation).

   The emphasis in this confession is upon the gracious, loyal
and forgiving nature of God, an emphasis which lies at the centre
of the Biblical *kerygma*. Yet this Divine grace is a two-edged
sword which appears in the human scene as a power working both for
salvation and for judgment that salvation may be accomplished. We
should note, however, that every statement of the confession is
inferential. We know God is like this because it is what we infer
from what he has done. Consequently, we may safely use these inferences in our struggle to understand what he will do in the time
to come.

                              NOTES

   [1]See further Gerhard von Rad, *Deuteronomium-Studien* (Göttingen,
1947), pp. 30-41; and *Der Heilige Krieg im alten Israel* (Zürich,
1951).

   [2]For discussion of these passages with references, see most
recently C. R. North, 'The "Former Things" and the "New Things"
in Deutero-Isaiah', *Studies in Old Testament Prophecy* (T. H.
Robinson Volume, ed. by H. H. Rowley; Edinburgh, 1950), pp. 111-126.

   [3]For a brief review of these ceremonies, see the writer in
The Old Testament Against its Environment, Chap. II. Form

criticism has led some scholars to the highly probable view that
in early Israel, at least, the ceremony of covenant renewal was a
yearly affair: see Gerhard von Rad, *Das formgeschichtliche Problem
des Hexateuchs* (Giessen, 1938), and Martin Noth, *Überlieferungs-
geschichte des Pentateuch* (Stuttgart, 1948), pp. 63 f.

[4]For the problem of the wisdom literature in this connection,
particularly Job, Proverbs and Ecclesiastes, see the treatment in
Chap. IV.

[5]Cf. Ludwig Köhler, *Theologie des Alten Testaments* (Zweite
Auflage; Tübingen, 1947), p. 1.

[6]An affirmation of Artur Weiser, *Glaube und Geschichte im
Alten Testament*, p. 19, here used in a somewhat different context.

[7]Translated by J. K. S. Reid, London, 1949.

[8]Later this title was understood, by means of the birth narratives, in another sense than it originally had.

[9]*Op. cit.*, pp. 35 ff.

[10]C. H. Dodd, *op. cit.*, p. 9.

[11]Cf. Artur Weiser, *Glaube und Geschichte im Alten Testament*,
p. 20. Weiser weakens his case, however, by his use of the word
'spiritual' for this supra-individual meaning; he thus unwittingly
throws his argument out of definite focus into a generalized,
diffuse, 'spiritual' continuum above the human sphere, which lacks
the driving, compelling solidity and definiteness of the Biblical
viewpoint.

[12]The wisdom literature and many of the Psalms do not fall into this description of the chief characterizing elements of Biblical
literature. Their relation to this statement will be dealt with
in Chapter IV.

[13]E.g. Exod. 20.5-6; Num. 14.18; Deut. 5.9-10; 7.9-10; II Chron.
30.9; Neh. 9.17, 31; Joel 2.13; Jonah 4.2; Ps. 86.15; etc. This
confession is one of the very few in the Bible which is not a
recital of events.

3. COSMOLOGY, ONTOLOGY, AND THE TRAVAIL OF BIBLICAL LANGUAGE

Langdon B. Gilkey

This is a paper on the intelligibility of some of the concepts of what we commonly call "biblical theology," or sometimes "the biblical point of view," or "the biblical faith." Although my remarks relate only to the Old Testament and at some points concern only two distinguished American representatives of the "biblical viewpoint," G. E. Wright and B. Anderson, the number of scholars of both testaments whose thoughts are based on the so-called "biblical view," and so who share the difficulties outlined below, is very great indeed. My paper stems not from a repudiation of that theological point of view. Speaking personally, I share it, and each time I theologize I use its main categories; but I find myself confused about it when I ponder it critically, and this paper organizes and states rather than resolves that confusion.

My own confusion results from what I feel to be the basic posture, and problem, of contemporary theology: it is half liberal and modern, on the one hand, and half biblical and orthodox, on the other, i.e., its world view or cosmology is modern, while its theological language is biblical and orthodox. Since this posture in two different worlds is the source of the difficulties and ambiguities which exist in current biblical theology, I had best begin with its elucidation.

Our problem begins with the liberal repudiation of orthodoxy. One facet of this repudiation was the rejection of the category "revelation through the special activity of God," what we now call "special revelation," "Heilsgeschichte," or popularly "the mighty acts of God." Orthodoxy, taking the Bible literally, had seen this special activity in the simple biblical twofold pattern of wondrous events (e.g., unexpected children, marvelous victories in battle, pillars of fire, etc.), on the one hand, and, on the other hand, a divine voice that spoke actual words to Abraham, to Moses, and to their prophetic followers. This orthodox view of the divine self-manifestation through special events and actual voices offended the liberal mind on two distinct grounds: (1) In understanding God's

Reprinted from *The Journal of Religion* 41 (1961): 194-205 by permission of The University of Chicago Press.

acts and speech literally and univocally, the orthodox belief in
special revelation denied the reign of causal law in the phenomenal
realm of space and time, or at least denied that that reign of law
had obtained in biblical days. To the liberals, therefore, this
orthodox view of revelation represented a primitive, prescientific
form of religion and should be modernized. (2) Special revelation
denied that ultimately significant religious truth is universally
available to mankind, or at least in continuity with experiences
universally shared by all men. On these two grounds of causal
order and universality liberalism reinterpreted the concept of revelation: God's acts ceased to be special, particular, and concerned
with phenomenal reality (for example, the stopping of the sun, a
visible pillar of fire, and audible voices). Rather, the divine
activity became the continual, creative, immanent activity of God,
an activity which worked through the natural order and which could
therefore be apprehended in universal human experiences of dependence, of harmony, and of value--experiences which in turn issued
in developed religious feeling and religious consciousness. The
demands both of world order and of universality were thus met by
this liberal reconstruction of religion: The immanent divine activity was now consistent throughout experience, and whatever special activity there was in religious knowledge was located sub-
jectively in the uniquely gifted religious leader or culture which
possessed deeper insight and so discovered deeper religious truth.

Against this reduction of God's activity to his general influence and of revelation to subjective human insight, neo-orthodoxy,
and with it biblical theology, reacted violently. For them,
revelation was not a subjective human creation but an objective
divine activity; God was not an inference from religious experience
but he who acts in special events. And Hebrew religion was not
the result of human religious genius or insight into the consistent
continuity of God's activity; rather, biblical religion was the
response of faith to and the recital of the "mighty acts of God."
Both contemporary systematic and contemporary biblical theology are
in agreed opposition to liberalism in emphasizing that revelation
is not a possibility of universal human experience but comes through
the objective, prior, self-revelation of God in special events in
response to which faith and witness arise. Whether or not this
self-understanding is accurate is a question we shall try to answer.

Contemporary systematic and biblical theology have, however,
often failed to note that in repudiating the liberal emphasis on
the universal and immanent as against the special and objective

activity of God, they have *not* repudiated the liberal insistence
on the causal continuum of space-time experience. Thus contemporary theology does not expect, nor does it speak of, wondrous
divine events on the surface of natural and historical life. The
causal nexus in space and time which Enlightenment science and
philosophy introduced into the Western mind and which was assumed
by liberalism is also assumed by modern theologians and scholars;
since they participate in the modern world of science both intellectually and existentially, they can scarcely do anything else.

Now this assumption of a causal order among phenomenal events,
and therefore of the authority of the scientific interpretation of
observable events, makes a great difference to the validity one
assigns to biblical narratives and so to the way one understands
their meaning. Suddenly a vast panoply of divine deeds and
events recorded in Scripture are no longer regarded as having
actually happened. Not only, for example, do the six days of
creation, the historical fall in Eden, and the flood seem to us
historically untrue, but even more the majority of divine deeds
in the biblical history of the Hebrew people become what we choose
to call symbols rather than plain old historical facts. To mention
only a few: Abraham's unexpected child; the many divine visita-
tions; the words and directions to the patriarchs; the plagues
visited on the Egyptians; the pillar of fire; the parting of the
seas; the verbal deliverance of covenantal law on Sinai; the stra-
tegic and logistic help in the conquest; the audible voice heard
by the prophets; and so on--all these "acts" vanish from the plane
of historical reality and enter the never-never land of "religious
interpretation" by the Hebrew people. Therefore when we read what
the Old Testament seems to say God did, or what precritical commentators said God did (see Calvin), and then look at a modern
interpretation of what God did in biblical times, we find a tremendous difference: the wonder events and the verbal divine com-
mentaries, commands, and promises are gone. Whatever the Hebrews
believed, *we* believe that the biblical people lived in the same
causal continuum of space and time in which we live, and so one
in which no divine wonders transpired and no divine voices were
heard. Nor do we believe, incidentally, that God could have done
or commanded certain "unethical" deeds like destroying Sodom and
Gomorrah or commanding the murder of the Amalekites. The modern
assumption of the world order has stripped bare our view of the
biblical history of all the divine deeds observable on the surface
of history, as our modern humanitarian ethical view has stripped
the biblical God of most of his mystery and offensiveness.

     Put in the language of contemporary semantic discussion,
both the biblical and the orthodox understanding of theological
language was univocal. That is, when God was said to have "acted,"
it was believed that he had performed an observable act in space
and time so that he functioned as does any secondary cause; and
when he was said to have "spoken," it was believed that an audible
voice was heard by the person addressed. In other words, the
words "act" and "speak" were used in the same sense of God as of
men. We deny this univocal understanding of theological words.
To us, theological verbs such as "to act," "to work," "to do,"
"to speak," "to reveal," etc., have no longer the literal meaning
of observable actions in space and time or of voices in the air.
The denial of wonders and voices has thus shifted our theological
language from the univocal to the analogical. Our problem is,
therefore, two fold: (*a*) We have not realized that this crucial
shift has taken place, and so we think we are merely speaking the
biblical language because we use the same words. We do use these
words, but we use them analogically rather than univocally, and
these are vastly different usages. (*b*) Unless one knows in some
sense what the analogy means, how the analogy is being used, and
what it points to, an analogy is empty and unintelligible; that is,
it becomes equivocal language. This is the crux of our present
difficulty; let us now return to biblical theology to try to show
just how serious it is.

     We have said that there is a vast difference between our-
selves and the Bible concerning cosmology and so concerning the
concrete character of the divine activity in history and that this
difference has changed biblical language from a univocal to an
analogical form. If, then, this difference is there, what effect
has it had on the way we understand the narratives of Scripture,
filled as they undoubtedly are with divine wonders and the divine
voice? A perusal of such commentators as Wright and Anderson will
reveal that, generally speaking, there has been a radical reinterpretation of these narratives, a reinterpretation that has been
three fold. First, the divine activity called the "mighty deeds
of God" is now restricted to one crucial event, the Exodus-covenant
complex of occurrence. Whatever else God may not have done, we
say, here he really acted in the history of the Hebrew people, and
so here their faith was born and given its form.

     Second, the vast panoply of wonder and voice events that
preceded the Exodus-convenant event, in effect the patriarchal
narratives, are now taken to be Hebrew interpretations of their

own historical past based on the faith gained at the Exodus. For
us, then, these narratives represent not so much *histories* of what
God actually did and said as *parables* expressive of the faith the
post-Exodus Jews had, namely, belief in a God who was active, did
deeds, spoke promises and commands, and so on. Third, the biblical accounts of the post-Exodus life--for example, the proclamation and codification of the law, the conquest, and the prophetic
movement--are understood as the covenant people's interpretation
through their Exodus faith of their continuing life and history.
Having known God at the Exodus event, they were able now to understand his relation to them in terms of free covenant and law and
to see his hand in the movement of their subsequent history. In
sum, therefore, we may say that for modern biblical theology the
Bible is no longer so much a book containing a description of God's
actual acts and words as it is a book containing Hebrew interpretations, "creative interpretations" as we call them, which, like
the parable of Jonah, tell stories of God's deeds and man's response to express the theological beliefs of Hebrew religion.
Thus the Bible is a book descriptive not of the acts of God but of
Hebrew religion. And though God is the subject of all the verbs
of the Bible, Hebrew religious faith and Hebrew minds provide the
subjects of all the verbs in modern books on the meaning of the
Bible. Incidentally, we avoid admitting these perennial human
subjects by putting our verbs in the passive voice: "was seen to
be," "was believed to be," etc. For us, then, the Bible is a book
of the acts Hebrews believed God might have done and the words he
might have said had he done and said them--but of course we recognize he did not. The difference between this view of the Bible
as a parable illustrative of Hebrew religious faith and the view
of the Bible as a direct narrative of God's actual deeds and words
is so vast that it scarcely needs comment. It makes us wonder,
despite ourselves, what, in fact, do we moderns think God *did* in
the centuries preceding the incarnation; what *were* his mighty acts?

        The nub of this problem is the fact that, while the object of
biblical recital is God's acts, the object of biblical theological
inquiry is biblical faith--that is to say, biblical theology is,
like liberalism, a study of Hebrew religion. Thus while the language of biblical theology is God-centered, the whole is included
within gigantic parentheses marked "human religion." This means
that biblical theology is fundamentally liberal in form and that
without translation it provides an impossible vehicle for biblical-
theological confession, since it is itself a witness to Hebrew

religion and not to the real acts of God. For of course the real
action and revelation of God must precede and be outside these
great parentheses of Hebrew faith if the content of that faith--
as a response to God's acts--be not self-contradictory and illu-
sory, beguiling but untrue, like the poetic religion in Santayana's
naturalism.

As we noted, most modern Old Testament commentators reduce the
mighty acts of God to one event: the Exodus-covenant event. Let
us, therefore, look at our understanding of this event, for around
it center the problems we see in biblical theology. Here, we are
told, God acted, and in so doing, he revealed himself to the Hebrew
people and established his covenant relation to them. Since current
biblical theology is, like most contemporary theology, passionately
opposed to conceptions of God based on natural theology or on general religious experience, we may assume that before this initial
divine deed there was no valid knowledge of God at all: if knowledge of God is based only on his revelatory acts, then prior to
those acts he must have been quite unknown. Exodus-Sinai, then,
is the pivotal point of biblical religion.

Now this means that the Exodus event has a confessional as
well as a historical interest for us. The question of what God did
at Sinai is, in other words, not only a question for the scholar
of Semitic religion and theology, it is even more a question for
the contemporary believer who wishes to make his witness today to
the acts of God in history; and so it poses a question for the
systematic theologian who wishes today to understand God as the
Lord who acted there. We are thus not asking merely the historical
question about what the Hebrews believed or said God did--that is
a question for the scholar of the history of religions, Semitic
branch. Rather, we are asking the systematic question, that is,
we are seeking to state in faith what *we* believe God actually did.
For, as biblical scholars have reminded us, a religious confession
that is biblical is a direct recital of God's acts, not a recital
of someone else's belief, even if it be a recital of a Hebrew
recitation. If, therefore, Christian theology is to be the recitation in faith of God's mighty acts, it must be composed of confessional and systematic statements of the form: "We believe that
God did so and so," and not composed of statements of biblical
theology of the form: "The Hebrews believed that God did so and
so."

If we had asked an orthodox theologian like Calvin this confessional and systematic question: "What do you believe God did

at the Exodus?" he would have given us a clear answer.   "Look at the
book of Exodus," he would have answered, "and see what it says that
God did."   And in his commentary he recites that deed of God just
as it appears on the pages of Scripture; that is, his confessional
understanding of the event includes the divine call heard by Moses,
all the plagues, the pillar of fire, the parting of the seas, the
lordly voice booming forth from Sinai, and the divinely proclaimed
promises and legal conditions of the covenant.   At the Reformation,
therefore, statements in biblical theology and in systematic theology coalesced because the theologian's understanding of what God
did was drawn with no change from the simple narratives of Scripture, and because the verbs of the Bible were thus interpreted
univocally throughout.   Thus in Reformation theology, if anywhere,
the Bible "speaks its own language" or "speaks for itself" with a
minimum of theological mediation.

When, however, one asks Professors Wright or Anderson the
systematic or confessional question: "What did God actually do in
the Exocus-Sinai event, what actually happened there?" the answer
is not only vastly different from the scriptural and orthodox accounts, but, in fact, it is extremely elusive to discover.
Strangely enough, neither one gives the questions "What did God
really do?" "What *was* his mighty act?" much attention.   First of
all they deny that there was any miraculous character to the event,
since "the Hebrews knew no miracles."   They assert, therefore,
that outwardly the event was indistinguishable from other events,[1]
revelation to the Hebrews always being dependent on faith.   And
finally they assert that probably there was a perfectly natural
explanation of the objective side of the event.   As Anderson puts
it, the rescue of the Hebrews resulted "probably from an East wind
blowing over the Reed Sea";[2] and in a single sentence Wright makes
one mysterious reference to "certain experiences that took place
at the Holy mountain . . . which formed the people into a nation."[3]
Considering that each writer clearly feels that the Bible is about
the real acts of God, that our religion is founded thereon, and
that Christian theology must recite these acts of God, this uncon-
cern with the character of the one act that God is believed actually
to have done is surprising.

In any case, this understanding of the event illustrates the
uneasy posture in two worlds of current biblical theology and thus
its confusion about two types of theological language.   When modern
biblical writers speak *theologically* of the revelatory event,
their attention focuses on the prior and objective event, and they
speak in the biblical and orthodox terms of a God who speaks and

acts, of divine initiation and human response, and of revelation
through mighty, divine deeds in history. When, however, they function as *scientific* historians or archeologists and ask what actually happened, they speak of that same prior event in purely naturalistic terms as "an ordinary though unusual event," or as "an
East wind blowing over the Reed Sea." Thus they repudiate all the
concrete elements that in the biblical account made the event itself unique and so gave content to their theological concept of a
special divine deed. In other words, they continue to use the
biblical and orthodox theological language of divine activity and
speech, but they have dispensed with the wonders and voices that
gave univocal meaning, and thus content, to the theological words
"God acts" and "God speaks."

This dual posture in both biblical orthodoxy and modern cosmology, and the consequent rejection of univocal meanings for our
theological phrases, raises our first question: "Are the main
words and categories in biblical theology meaningful?" If they are
no longer used univocally to mean observable deeds and audible
voices, do they have any intelligible content? If they are in fact
being used as analogies (God acts, but not as men act; God speaks,
but not with an audible voice), do we have any idea at all to what
sort of deed or communication these analogies refer? Or are they
just serious-sounding, biblical-sounding, and theological-sounding
words to which we can, if pressed, assign no meaning? Note I am
not making the empiricist or positivist demand that we give a
naturalistic, empirically verifiable meaning to these theological
words, a meaning outside the context of faith and commitment. I
am asking for a confessional-theological meaning, that is, a meaning based on thought about our faith concerning what we mean by
these affirmations of faith. The two affirmations I especially
wish to consider are, first, "God has acted mightily and specially
in history for our salvation, and so God is he who acts in history." And second, "Our knowledge of God is based not on our discovery of him but on God's revelation of himself in historical
events." My point is that, when we analyze what we mean by these
theological phrases, we can give no concrete or specifiable content so that our analogies at present are empty and meaningless.
The result is that, when we push the analysis of these analogical
words further, we find that what we actually mean by them contra-
dicts the intent of these theological phrases.

Let us take the category of "mighty act" first. Perhaps the
most important theological affirmation that modern biblical

theology draws from the Scripture is that God is he who acts, meaning by this that God does unique and special actions in history. And yet when we ask: "All right, what has he done?" no answer can apparently be given. Most of the acts recorded in Scripture turn out to be "interpretations by Hebrew faith," and we are sure that they, like the miracles of the Buddha, did not really happen at all. And the one remaining objective act, the Exodus, becomes on analysis "the East wind blowing over the Reed Sea," that is, an event which is objectively or ontologically of the same class as any other event in space and time. Now if this event is validly to be called a mighty act of God, an event in which he really did something special--as opposed to our just believing he did, which would be religious subjectivism and metaphysical naturalism--then, ontologically, this must in some sense be more than an ordinary run-of-the-mill event. It may be epistemologically indistinguishable from other events to those without faith, but for those of faith it must be objectively or ontologically different from other events. Otherwise, there is no mighty act, but only our belief in it, and God is the God who in fact does not act. And then our theological analogies of "act" and "deed" have no referent, and so no meaning. But in current biblical theology such an ontologically special character to the event, a special character known perhaps only by faith but really "out there" nevertheless, is neither specified nor specifiable. For in the Bible itself that special character was understood to be the very wonders and voices which we have rejected, and nothing has appeared in modern biblical thought to take their place. Only an ontology of events specifying what God's relation to ordinary events is like, and thus what his relation to special events might be, could fill the now empty analogy of mighty acts, void since the denial of the miraculous.

Meanwhile, in contemporary biblical theology, which dares to stray into the forbidden precincts of cosmology and ontology only far enough to deny miracles, all that can be said about the event leaves the analogy of the mighty act quite empty. We deny the miraculous character of the event and say its cause was merely an East wind, and then we point to the unusual response of Hebrew faith. For biblical theology, that which remains special about the event, therefore, is only its subjective result, namely, the faith response. But if we then ask what this Hebrew response was *to*, what God did, we are offered merely an objectively natural event. But this means merely that the Hebrews, as a religious people, were unusual; it does not mean that the event to which they responded

was unusual. One can only conclude, therefore, that the mighty act
of God is not his objective activity in history but only his inward
incitement of a religious response to an ordinary event within the
space-time continuum. If this is what we mean, then clearly we
have left the theological framework of "mighty act with faith response" and returned to Schleiermacher's liberalism, in which
God's general activity is consistent throughout the continuum of
space-time events and in which special religious feeling appre-
hends the presence of God in and through ordinary finite events.
Thus our theological analogy of the mighty act seems to have no
specifiable referent or meaning: like the examples of God's
speaking, the only case turns out on analysis to be an example, not
of God's activity at all, but of Hebrew insight based on their
religious experience.

A similar problem arises when we ask what is meant by "revelation" in a modern mighty acts theology. The correlation of ordinary event and faith response is basic for contemporary theology:
no event, we say, becomes revelatory (i.e., is known to be revelatory) unless faith sees in it the work of God. Now this correlation of ordinary event with discerning faith is intelligible enough
once the covenant relation between God and his people has been established: then God is already known, faith has already arisen,
and so God's work can be seen by faith in the outwardly ordinary
events of Hebrew existence. But can the rule that revelatory events
are only discerned by faith be equally applied to the event in
which faith takes its origin? Can it, in other words, provide a
theological understanding of *originating* revelation, that is, of
God's original self-manifestation to man, in which man does not
discern an already known God but in which God reveals himself to
men who know nothing of him? Certainly it is logical to contend
that faith cannot be presupposed in the event which purportedly
effects the origination of faith.

When we consider the description that biblical theology makes
of the origination of faith, moreover, the problems in this view
seem vast indeed. Theologically it is asserted that God is not
known through general, natural, historical, or inward experience.
Thus presumably the Hebrews fled from Egypt uncognizant of God,
having in their minds no concepts at all of the transcendent,
active, covenant deity of later Hebrew religion. How, then, did
they come to know this God? The answer of contemporary theology,
of course, is that at this point the East wind over the Red Sea
rescued the Hebrew people from the Egyptians, and so, according to

Wright, their faith arose as the only assumption that could make
sense of this great stroke of good fortune: "They did not have the
power themselves (to effect the rescue); there was only one explanation available to them. That was the assumption that a great
God had seen their afflictions, had taken pity on them. . . ."[4]
Thus Hebrew faith is here presented as a human hypothesis, a religious assumption arising out of intuition and insight into the
meaning of an unusual and crucial experience.

One can only wonder at this statement. First of all in what
sense can one speak of *revelation* here? Is this not a remarkably
clear example of natural religion or natural theology? The origination of Hebrew faith is explained as a religious assumption
based on an unusual event but one which was admittedly consistent
with, of the same order as, other events within the nature-history
continuum. In what way does this faith come from God and what he
has done rather than from man and what he has discovered, or even
just poetically imagined? It seems to be only the religious insight and imagination of the Jews that has created and developed
this monotheistic assumption out of the twists and turns of their
historical experience. And second, why was there "only one explanation available" to them? Why was this response so inevitably
tied with this event as to make us feel that the response was revealed in the event? Why could not the Hebrews have come to believe in a god of the East Wind, or a benevolent Fate, or any of
the thousands of deities of unusual events that human religion has
created? Surely on neo-orthodox principles, the theological concept or religious assumption *least* available to the imagination of
men who knew not God was that of the transcendent, covenant God
of history--exactly the assumption now called "inevitable" when
an East wind had rescued them.

Furthermore, we should recall that for biblical theology the
entire meaning of the concept of revelation through divine activity
rather than through subjective experience or insight hangs on this
one act of divine revelation. Thus the admission at this vital
point that Hebrew faith was a daring human hypothesis based on a
natural but unusual event is very puzzling. For it indicates that
despite our flowery theological language, our actual understanding
of Hebrew religion remains inclosed within liberal categories.
When we are asked about what actually happened, and how revelation
actually occurred, all we can say is that in the continuum of the
natural order an unusual event rescued the Hebrews from a sad fate;
from this they concluded there must be somewhere a great God who

loved them; thus they interpreted their own past in terms of his
dealings with them and created all the other familiar character-
istics of Hebrew religion: covenant, law, and prophecy. This
understanding of Hebrew religion is strictly "liberal": it
pictures reality as a consistent world order and religious truth
as a human interpretation based on religious experience. And yet
at the same time, having castigated the liberals, who at least knew
what their fundamental theological principles were, we proclaim
that our real categories are orthodox: God acts, God speaks, and
God reveals. Furthermore, we dodge all criticism by insisting
that, because biblical and Christian ideas of God are "revealed,"
they are, unlike the assumptions and hypotheses of culture and of
other religions, beyond inspection by the philosophical and moral
criteria of man's general experience.

What has happened is clear: because of our modern cosmology,
we have stripped what we regard as "the biblical point of view" of
all its wonders and voices. This in turn has emptied the Bible's
theological categories of divine deeds and divine revelations of
all their univocal meaning, and we have made no effort to understand what these categories might mean as analogies. Thus, when
we have sought to understand Hebrew religion, we have unconsciously
fallen back on the liberal assumptions that do make some sense to
us. What we desperately need is a theological ontology that will
put intelligible and credible meanings into our analogical categories of divine deeds and of divine self-manifestation through
events.

Our point can perhaps be summarized by saying that, without
such an ontological basis, the language of biblical theology is
neither univocal nor analogical but equivocal, and so it remains
empty, abstract, and self-contradictory. It is empty and abstract
because it can provide us with no concrete cases. We say the
biblical God acts, but we can give neither concrete examples nor
an analogical description; we say he speaks, and no illustrative
dialogues can be specified. What has happened is that, as modern
men perusing the Scriptures, we have rejected as invalid all the
innumerable cases of God's acting and speaking; but as neo-orthodox
men looking for a word from the Bible, we have induced from all
these cases the theological generalization that God is he who acts
and speaks. This general truth about God we then assert while
denying all the particular cases on the basis of which the generalization was first made. Consequently, biblical theology is left

with a set of theological abstractions, more abstract than the
dogmas of scholasticism, for these are concepts with no known concreteness. Finally, our language is self-contradictory because,
while we use the language of orthodoxy, what we really mean is
concepts and explanations more appropriate to liberal religion.
For if there is any middle ground between the observable deed and
the audible dialogue which we reject, and what the liberals used
to call religious experience and religious insight, then it has
not yet been spelled out.

In the cases both of the mighty act of God and of the speech
of God, such a spelling-out is an enterprise in philosophical
theology. While certainly this enterprise cannot be unbiblical,
it must at least be ontological and philosophical enough to provide theological meaning to our biblical analogies of divine deeds
and words, since today we have abandoned the univocal, literal
meanings of these words. One example may illustrate. Commenting
on the "biblical view," Wright says: "He [God] is to be known by
what he has done and said, by what he is now doing and saying; and
he is known when we do what he commands us to do."[5] Unless we can
give some analogical meaning to these concepts "do," "say," and
"command," we are unable to make any confessional sense at all of
this sentence, since every actual case of doing, saying, or commanding referred to in the Scripture has for us vanished into subjective Hebrew religious experience and interpretation. One might
almost conclude that without a theological ontology, biblical
theology is in danger of becoming a version of Santayana's poetic
view of religion, in which believing man paints the objective flux
of matter in the pretty subjective pictures of religious language
and myth.

Two changes in our thinking can, I believe, rescue us from
these dilemmas. First of all, biblical theology must take cosmology
and ontology more seriously. Despite the undeniable but irrelevant fact that the Hebrews did not think much about cosmology,
cosmology does make a difference in hermeneutics. When we say "God
acts," we mean something different cosmologically than the writers
of JED and P, or even than Calvin, did. Thus the modern discipline
of "biblical theology" is more tricky than we perhaps assumed when
we thought we could just lift out theological abstractions (God
speaks, God acts) from the narratives of Scripture and, calling
them "the biblical point of view," act as if they were the only
theology we needed. If in doing this we pretend that we are "just
letting the Bible speak for itself," we are fooling no one but

ourselves. Actually we are translating the biblical view into
our own, at least in rejecting its concrete content of wonders and
voices and so changing these categories from univocal concepts to
empty analogies. But we have done this translating without being
aware of the change we have made and thus without thinking out the
problems in which this shift in cosmology and the resultant translation of biblical language involve us. Hence the abstractness and
self-contradictory character of our categories in present "biblical
theology." To speak the biblical word in a contemporary setting
is a difficult *theological* task as well as a difficult existential
task.

This means in turn that two very different enterprises must be
distinguished in Christian theology, for they cannot be confused
without fatal results. First there is the job of stating what the
biblical writers meant to say, a statement couched in the Bible's
own terms, cosmological, historical, and theological. This is
"biblical theology," and its goal is to find what the Bible truly
says--whether what in specific instances the Bible says seems to
us in fact to be true or not. Then there is the other task of
stating what that Word might mean for us today, what *we* believe
God actually to have done. This is confessional and systematic
theology, and its object is what *we* believe the truth about God
and about what he has done to be. To use Wright's language, we
must distinguish between *Hebrew* recital (biblical theology) and
our recital (confessional or systematic theology) if our confessions are to make any sense at all. To confuse the two, and to
try to make a study of what the biblical writers said also and at
the same time an attempt to say what we believe to be true about
God, is fatal and leads to the kind of confusions we have outlined.

Second, it is clear that throughout this paper our central
problem has been that, in the shift of cosmology from ancient to
modern, fundamental theological concepts have so changed their
meaning as almost to have lost all reference. The phrases "God
acts" and "God speaks," whatever they may ultimately mean to us,
do not signify the wonders and voices of ancient days. As we have
seen, it is no good repeating the abstract verbs "to act" and "to
speak," if we have no intelligible referents with which to replace
the vanished wonders and voices; and if we use these categories
as analogies without any discussion of what we mean by them, we
contradict ourselves over and over. When we use the analogies
"mighty act," "unique revelatory event," or "God speaks to his
people," therefore, we must also try to understand what we might

mean in systematic theology by the general activity of God. Unless
we have some conception of how God acts in ordinary events, we can
hardly know what our analogical words mean when we say: "He acts
uniquely in this event" or "this event is a special divine deed."
Thus if we are to give content to the biblical analogy of a mighty
act, and so to our theological concepts of special revelation and
salvation, we must also have some understanding of the relation of
God to general experience, which is the subject of philosophical
theology. Put in terms of doctrines, this means that God's special
activity is logically connected with his providential activity in
general historical experience, and an understanding of the one assumes a concurrent inquiry into the other. For this reason, while
the dependence of systematic and philosophical theology on biblical
theology has long been recognized and is obvious, the dependence
of an intelligible theology that is biblical on the cosmological
and ontological inquiries of believing men, while now less universally accepted, is nonetheless real. There is no more primary
discipline in the life of the church, for all of us--biblical
scholars and theologians--live and think in the present and look
for the truth in documents from the past. And for all of us, a
contemporary understanding of ancient Scriptures depends as much
on a careful analysis of our present presuppositions as it does on
being learned in the religion and faith of the past.

NOTES

1. G. E. Wright, *Books of the Acts of God* (Garden City,
N.Y.: Doubleday & Co., 1959), p. 18.

2. B. Anderson, *Understanding the Old Testament* (Englewood
Cliffs, N.J.: Prentice-Hall, Inc., 1957), pp. 47-49.

3. Wright, *op. cit.*, p. 86.

4. *Ibid.*, p. 73.

5. *Ibid.*, p. 32.

4. DOES THE "GOD WHO ACTS" REALLY ACT?

Frank B. Dilley

The modern "Biblical Theologian" is in a quandary about what
to say. His view of man and of history centers upon his assertion
of a "God Who Acts," yet he seems unable to communicate what it
is that he means by the actions of God. Unwilling to endorse the
conservative view of a God Who Acts through outright miracles or
the liberal doctrine of a God restricted to universal actions, he
speaks about a God who acts specially in history, but without
giving any concrete content to his assertions, and he seems unable
to distinguish his position from that of the liberalism he rejects.
In short, though he tries to stake out an alternative to conservatism and liberalism, he does not do so, except verbally.

His plight is not a happy one. If he says that God does interfere in the workings of nature and history, then he violates
his understanding of modern science and the validity of scientific
explanation. He does not believe that people walk on water or
that corpses rise into the air. If, on the other hand, he maintains that God does *not* interfere, then he has to give up the Biblical notion of a God who acts specially in history. He speaks
then of "acts of God" in terms of east winds and visions, using
Biblical language to assert liberal content. He refuses to be
explicit as to what he means, perhaps because any explication would
make clear that there is no alternative to conservatism and liberalism except a merely verbal one. In short, unless he equivo-
cates he is lost.

As a case in point, what is said about the central doctrine
of the resurrection of Christ? The conservative says quite unequivocally that the body of Jesus actually rose from the grave
leaving an empty tomb behind, that it ate and drank and stayed on
earth for forty days. The liberal also unequivocally asserts that
the body of Jesus stayed right where it had been placed after the
crucifixion, unless someone stole it away. Any appearances were
visions or spiritualistic phenomena.

The Biblical theologian is unwilling to affirm either of
these alternatives, the first because he cannot accept such

From *The Anglican Theological Review* 47 (1965): 66-80. Reprinted
with permission.

interruptions of normal causality, the second because he feels
that such phenomena as liberals affirm do not really constitute a
resurrection. Therefore he states, quite equivocally, that Jesus
rose bodily from the grave, but that of course he did not literally
"rise," and it was not exactly a "body" either, the empty tomb
stories being legendary in all probability. He is sure that the
liberal's version is not true either, but he is unable to indicate
how his position differs other than verbally from the liberal one.
Thus, he asserts a resurrection while negating all affirmations
about the what of resurrection, giving rise to the suspicion that
he is using mere formulas. Neither in his analysis of past history
nor in his analysis of present history has the Biblical theologian
been able to "cash in" his concepts in terms of stating concretely
the what of God's actions.[1]

The analysis in this paper proceeds as follows: after a brief
examination of crucial passages from the writings of some Biblical
theologians in order to document the claim that there is considerable equivocation, an attempt is made to sketch the various alternatives available within the general framework of this tradition. No attempt has been made to document every assertion about
the positions discussed. The material is familiar enough to stu-
dents of contemporary theological movements. The subject of the
paper is the claim that God acts *particularly*, for this is the
central emphasis of the "God Who Acts" school. Beyond what would
be described as the general working of God in creation, in sustaining the universe, in inspiring men to seek after truth and
goodness, there are events in which God acts in special ways,
events in which God in some sense "interferes" with the general
order of things. When the activity of God is referred to, it is
this active "intervention" to which reference is being made.

I.   The "Action" of the God Who Acts

For many reasons, some having to do with science and some
having to do with theology, modern Biblical scholars have concluded
that as Biblical tradition has developed a heightening of the
miraculous has taken place. By well-known processes of accumula-
tion, traditions concerning key people have been embroidered in the
continued retelling which preceded the writing down of Biblical
narratives.

The center of controversy is how much of the Biblical record
ought to be explained as mythical and legendary accretion. Very

conservative theologians would tend to insist that all is fact,
none myth. Less conservative theologians might admit some accretion, but would hold to an underlying core of miracle, saying that
God really did intervene in history to push back the waters of the
"Red Sea" for example. More liberal theologians would assert that
what took place was only a particularly fortunate natural event,
or might describe it as an instance of the general cosmic activity
of God. The questions requiring exploration are these: Which of
these alternatives, if any, is accepted by those who are known as
Biblical theologians? And, what alternatives could they *possibly*
defend within the general framework of their tradition? Crucial
passages in representative textbooks and monographs will be examined in an attempt to find an answer.

　　G. Ernest Wright, author of the monograph "God Who Acts," has
argued in his various writings that Biblical faith arose in connection with the Sinai event, and that all Israel's re-working of
primitive myth and borrowed religious and national institutions
reflects a belief that there is a God who acts purposefully in
history.[2] This belief came into being in connection with the
events surrounding the flight from Egypt and the covenant on the
holy mountain. His constant theme is that Israel's faith is a
Sinai faith, to be understood in terms of this mighty act.

　　That a mighty God was acting to rescue them was "the only
one explanation available to them" that could make sense of what
had taken place.[3] Wright notes also that modern investigators
have shown that even the covenant relation "was borrowed from the
social and political law of the day,"[4] and that this covenant form
included a recitation of the mighty acts of the one offering the
covenant.[5] Thus the covenant form was itself borrowed from near-
Eastern culture. The views of the prophets resulted from the
application of this faith to subsequent historical events, later
codes of law were its implementation in the life of the sacred
people, and Israel awaited a future in which the relationship between people and God begun at Sinai would be consummated in a
Messianic age of righteousness and peace.

　　Since *all* centers upon the Exodus and Sinai, one might expect
to find in Wright's monographs and books some detailed discussion
of the mighty events which took place there. However one searches
in vain for any clear description of what God actually did. He
asserts *that* God acted but never does he attempt to say what concretely took place in that Divine act.

That he intends to affirm that God really did act is shown by
his assertion that in Biblical faith everything depends upon
whether the central events are really *facts* or not.[6] Instead of
providing a description of what really took place, he speaks only
of "certain experiences" at the Holy Mountain.[7] That certain
natural and human events took place is clear, but what is meant
when we say that a Divine event took place is not clear, "thus the
covenant at Sinai is clearly a human event, but is it a Divine act
in history? The deliverance of Israel from Egyptian slavery at
the time of Moses is a fact, but is it also a historical fact that
God had chosen Israel for his special possession?"[8] The context
indicates that Wright holds that the latter is a fact, that Sinai
is a divine act in history, but here is no discussion as to *how*
this event is both a human event and a Divine act, no discussion
as to what exactly God did and how.

Similarly, Bernhard Anderson's account of the Exodus leaves
his readers in doubt as to what he means to affirm. After explaining that of course the burning bush was not a photographable
event, that quails and manna have appeared often on the Sinai
peninsula, that the crossing of the "Red Sea" (probably Lake Tim-
sah), was made possible by an east wind which drove back the
waters--an event which has occurred at other times as well--he
concludes his description of the mighty "act of God" by saying
merely that "the miracle was that it happened at a particular
time and with a particular meaning."[9] He is silent on the important issue, the issue as to whether God really intervened to cause
it or whether it just happened fortuitously while the Israelites
were on their way to Sinai. The phrase "act of God" has either
meaning in common English usage, and Anderson's account seems to
trade on the essential ambiguity of that phrase.

If he means to use the Biblical language to communicate a
non-Biblical world view, if he is masking a liberal metaphysic,
then this ought to be admitted openly. If he is not, then there
is an obligation to provide some clear statement as to what he
does mean. If one is to speak of a God who acts he must be prepared to offer some description of the mechanics of Divine action,
particularly if he rejects both the conventional liberal and the
conventional conservative views.

The problem is intensified when the question of the resurrection is considered, and the position of Biblical theology becomes
even more bewildering. In the case of the Exodus and Mt. Sinai,
some clue is provided as to what actually happened in history; at

least it is stated that a wind dried up the waters temporarily,
allowing the Israelites to pass over with safety. One looks in
vain, however, for any concrete description of the resurrection
beyond the mere assertion that God raised Jesus of Nazareth.

Reginald Fuller says that no more can be said than that "the
disciples underwent certain experiences which gave them the conviction that God had raised their master from the dead."[10] He
does not say that Jesus really did rise from the dead; he merely
says that certain experiences caused the disciples to have this
conviction. He goes on to affirm that "it was as both risen and
exalted that he was apprehended by the disciples in their post-
Easter experiences" (suggesting that the tradition gradually separated the resurrection and the ascension) and that this "series of
encounters" may have taken place at their common meals. However
this is *all* that he says positively about the resurrection, and
what is said above is unquestionably evasive. Were the experiences
veridical? Was the apprehension objective? Was the conviction
true? The reader is allowed to supply an interpretation in terms
of miracle or of no miracle as he sees fit. If Fuller means to
say that *no* objective event took place except some visions, then
he ought to say so; if he does not then he should say what he
does mean in addition to that.

Howard Kee and Franklin Young provide an account of the resurrection which is just as empty of concrete detail. Beginning with
the assertion that the only explanation for the sudden change of
spirit among Jesus' followers is that "the community had become
convinced that Jesus had been victorious over death and was
alive,"[11] they go on to supply only the following details: a discussion (inconclusive) as to whether the empty tomb stories were
part of the earliest tradition, a claim that the Hebrews thought
in terms of resurrection rather than immortality of the soul, a
rejection of theories that the disciples had mistakenly gone to
the wrong tomb or had merely invented another dying-and-rising-god
story; but then they stop. They quite obviously mean to convey to
the reader that they affirm the resurrection, but they also leave
the impression that they are unwilling to affirm even a single
detail about it.

In the case of the Exodus and Sinai, Biblical theologians are
able to supply an east wind and some water, and can give an account
of what a secular historian would have seen had he been present.
In the case of the resurrection, nothing factual is ever cited.
Would the unbeliever have seen a body which occupied space? No

answer. Was the tomb really empty? No answer. Would the unbeliever
have seen merely a group of ecstatic disciples, as at Pentecost observers saw people who seemed to be filled with new wine? No
answer. Apparently these theologians are unwilling to have it
either way, either the Biblical way or the liberal way, but they
are also unable to supply any third way.

G. Ernest Wright dodges the issue very neatly. Once he almost
speaks to the crucial point, but he turns his attention to other
matters at once, as though he realizes the impending danger. He
states *that* the resurrection was not an objective event of history
in the same sense as was the crucifixion. It turns out, however,
that what he is talking about is merely a matter of methodology
and does not provide any clue as to his own position on the matter. He means that "Christ as risen was not seen by everyone, but
only by the few. . . . That is not an area where a historian can
operate. Facts available to all men are the only data with which
he can work, the facts available to . . . a few are not objective
history in the historian's sense."[12] Thus he dodges the question,
using as his pretext the perfectly valid point that no historians
were present when these events took place. What Wright's readers
want to know is, was the resurrection a fact, not what modern
historians can legitimately say about it. What would ancient
historians have said had they been with the disciples at the time
of the resurrection appearances? Did the disciples really touch
anything? What are the natural phenomena corresponding to the
east wind and water in the Exodus event? And, if these can be
supplied, how were these phenomena caused?

When an admitted liberal refers to the resurrection it is to
be understood that he does *not* mean the raising of a physical body,
and when a conservative speaks it is clear that he *does* mean a
body which occupies space and can be touched. A photograph would
have shown a real body according to conservatives, and would have
been blank according to a liberal. What would a Biblical theologian expect to see on a photograph?

The verbal nature of the utterances of Biblical theology is
shown in the following set of assertions. Having denounced such
modern theologians as Rudolf Bultmann and Reinhold Niebuhr for
having compromised the Biblical notion that God really acts,[13]
and having defended the claims that the Bible is the "story of
what God once did"[14] and that in Biblical faith everything depends
upon whether the central events are really facts or not,[15] Wright
presents the following account of the resurrection:

The process, the how of Christ's transition from death to

> the living head of the new community, and the language used
> to describe that transition ("raised the third day," . . .)
> --these are products of the situation. They are the temporal
> language of the first-century Christians. To us, they
> are symbols of deep truth and nothing more, though they
> are symbols that are difficult to translate.[16]

What is this language symbolic of? If it is symbolic of the
raising of a physical body, then the language is really literal
and not merely symbolic. If the event does not involve the
raising of a body then what does it involve? And how does one
justify the retention of the symbol "resurrection" for what took
place if there was no body? Surely Wright must offer some clue
as to what he is describing if he is to justify speaking of the
resurrection as a *fact* and as an act of God. What is resurrection
that is only symbolically a raising, a resurrected body which can
only symbolically be called a body? If the Biblical content is
to be negated in this way, then some other content must be supplied. Wright is silent as to this other content, except to reject every particular specifiable content suggested by anyone else.

The Biblical theologians' lot is not a happy one, for he is
confronted only by alternatives which are unacceptable to him. He
cannot bring himself to affirm real miracles, nor can he bring
himself to affirm a world without miracles. He cannot say that a
physical body rose from the grave, went up into the sky where it
waits for a time when it will descend again leading hosts of angels; nor will he say that no objective occurrence beyond the
creation of a new fellowship and some visions took place. He is
silent, affirming *that* a resurrection took place but not *what* it
is that took place, using the words while denying all the concrete
meanings of those words. That he can say nothing specific ought
to be taken as evidence that there is nothing specific to be said,
that Biblical Theology is a purely verbal position. Once content
is supplied, either conservatism or liberalism enters in.

II. Alternative Ways of Conceiving God's Action

What are the available alternative ways of conceiving special
acts of God? In the first place, one could take the Biblical view
that God openly and obviously abridges the natural order, that he
predicts and produces spectacular events which should convince
everyone but the fool that there is a God. Or, one could take
instead a modern revision of that view. Divine actions are not
spectacular to the external eye but closely resemble events which
sometimes happen for more ordinary reasons. Recognition of Divine
causality is limited to those to whom God reveals himself. A

third possibility is that such special acts are caused both by
God and by nature simultaneously, a view which has the advantage
of preserving the natural order intact, thus avoiding the idea of
"interference" so jarring to modern minds. On either of the former views, the causal order is broken at times, and therefore, on
those occasions, scientific accounts provide pseudo-explanations.
The analysis of these three alternatives proceeds as follows:

   1. The Bible's view quite clearly is that God is the supernatural cause of certain special events. The prophets are "seers"
of these Divine actions, both predicting their occurrence and interpreting their theological meaning. Interpretation is usually
given in terms of reward and punishment for Israel's deeds, though
not always.

   At times the conclusion is drawn that God is the sole cause
of such events, even when they seemingly fall in the realm of human
decision. Paul is perhaps the first to state this systematically,
but the doctrine seems a necessary corollary to the affirmation
that these events are Divinely caused. If God causes them, then
man does not. There are the familiar passages dealing with God's
hardening of Pharaoh's heart, with Isaiah's mission of making the
hearts of the people fat "lest they hear and repent," with Assyr-
ia's role of being unknowingly the rod of God's anger against
Israel. There are also passages which make even Israel's sin to
be God's work. A passage seldom commented on records a prophet's
lament, "O LORD, why dost thou make us err from thy ways and
harden our heart, so that we fear thee not?" (Isaiah 63:17) The
prophet goes on to lament that "Thou art our Father; we are the
clay, and thou art our potter; we are all the work of thy hand,"
(Isaiah 64:8) ascribing the plight of Israel to God's decree not
merely in the usual sense but in the further sense that the hard-
ness of heart which brought on the calamities is also directly
God's work. When Paul later systematically states this tradition,
ascribing all activity to God and even explaining why the heart of
Israel has been hardened by God, this is merely making explicit
a tradition which has been an undercurrent all along. The doctrine
of predestination seems inevitable if one holds the notion that
prophets can predict future human actions, and that the acts of
human beings are really the acts of God. If human actions are the
actions of God, then freedom in the usual sense of the word is
denied. That no escape from this dilemma is possible is shown by
the history of the predestination controversy. Were Divine causation and human freedom compatible then surely someone would have
solved the problem by now.

This Biblical view is troublesome to moderns for two reasons,
its predestinationist implications undercut the freedom of individual action and thereby the moral meaning of history, but also
it implies that God is a being working in history alongside other
beings, a notion which seems both theologically and scientifically
unsatisfactory to modern theologians. The trouble is not merely
with notions of walking on water and sending fire out of heaven to
consume wet sacrifices but also with an anthropomorphic God who
works in such ways. Biblical theology exists partly because moderns have found the Biblical notions unsatisfactory on these two
accounts.

2. The difficulties mentioned above can be reduced if one is
willing to allow certain modifications in the Biblical view. The
resulting theology might still allow for special actions of God,
but depart from the above views at two points. One can hold that
God acts merely in nature, never interfering with human decisions,
thus avoiding the problems of predestination. And one can hold
that instead of being spectacular the acts of God are ordinary, so
that God is "hidden" in his actions. Attempts are made at times
to derive this second notion from the first on the grounds that if
the miracles of God were as obvious as the Bible says they were,
man would be coerced into obedience.[17]

There is no *a priori* objection to considering God in such
terms, as a higher sort of being, even a creator, who acts on the
world by interfering in its processes occasionally, as a man might
interfere in the world of an amoeba or an electron. Modern theology
is temperamentally averse to such suggestions, but they must not
be eliminated from serious consideration for that reason.

What is being discussed here is the God that Tillich decries
as the God of personalistic theism, the God that William James suggested is a finite God working alongside man. Such a God is a
superior being who has created nature outside himself, and who
works in and with the world that he has created, guiding its working, taking steps to correct man's evil, punishing and rewarding
with storms and gentle rains where appropriate, and quite capable
of aiding a band of fugitive slaves with an east wind. Such a God
is the sort which the man on the street worships, although it is
not the God of the theologians and philosophers, and one would
probably have to look to science fiction to find an imaginative
presentation of such views.

A finite God of this sort is not the Biblical God as presented
by theologians, although a good case can be made that it is the
Biblical God presented by the Biblical writers themselves.

Biblical theologians do not seem to find such views very attractive although in this writer's judgment they do present the
only real way of preserving the tradition of the God who acts.
In addition to theological objections to such a God, there are at
least two troublesome difficulties created. In the first place,
such a God does interfere in natural processes, and this is not
congenial to modern theology. John Bennett has well stated this
objection:

> We do not observe that God even intervenes with an occa-
> sional miracle as He was believed to do in the days of the
> Bible. It would not tempt a responsible religious commen-
> tator on events to attribute the calm sea and fog on the
> English Channel that facilitated the evacuation of Dunkirk
> to a divine miracle as the plague that defeated the hosts of
> Sennacherib before the gates of Jerusalem was interpreted
> as a miracle.[18]

If this point of view is accepted then it is also questionable
whether ancient theologians were justified in thinking in terms
of miracles.

This difficulty does not seem to be merely one of prejudice;
it is more troublesome than that. The difficulty seems to be that
most moderns, even quite religious ones, *cannot* bring themselves
to think in terms of miracles anymore. The categories of scientific explanation have replaced those of theological explanation
for modern religious men, and there seems to be no rolling back
the clock. Even those people who do still affirm miracles do not
seem to be able to provide any accounting for them. Defenders of
miracles ought to be bringing forth real explanations, in terms
of physics for example, of how it is that God acts. There should
be a Christian physics and a Christian mathematics, not in the
attenuated sense of being Christian by opposing evolution but in
the sense of showing in science itself how it is that God acts,
where he is, what means he uses, and so on. One should be attempting to show that in some cases the actual distribution of
physical forces is changed in unnatural ways. This sort of en-
deavor seems to have been abandoned, and perhaps should have been.
However, it indicates that the category of miracle is rather empty
of concrete content even among those who use it. One cannot com-
bat Bultmann merely by pointing out that his world-view is not the
Christian one; one must show how the Christian world-view can possibly be maintained, given what we now know scientifically. That
this is not being done would seem to show that it cannot be done.

The second difficulty is that even a modified version of the
God who acts creates enormous problems for theodicy, for it makes

God responsible for every preventable natural evil. If God could
send an east wind to rescue the people of Israel, then he could
have sent one to melt the iceberg that sank the Titanic, and he
could have sent a disease germ to destroy Hitler as he sent a plague
to rout the armies of Sennacherib. It would take very little interference to make the world considerably better. Liberalism, by
confining God's actions to general ones, reduced the problem of
theodicy considerably by affirming that there are many evils which
result from the general order and hence are not preventable. Once
it is said that God can act selectively, then it is legitimate to
raise the question "why" about every preventable natural evil, and
many preventable human evils. The standard answers in terms of
the usefulness of diseases and earthquakes to remind men of their
frailty somehow do not seem very persuasive to moderns who stand
in a post-Bomb and post-Dachau world.

    This modified Biblical position, then, would be resisted by
Biblical theologians on two grounds, (1) its use of miracle as a
problem for theodicy, and (2) the difficulties of a highly anthropomorphic view of God as a being alongside other beings. The
second kind of objection does not seem compelling to this writer,
however the first kind does. Anthropomorphism is better than most
other morphisms, although our inability to "cash in" the notion of
Divine actions does constitute a serious problem. It is just this
problem that causes Biblical theology to reject the more conservative traditions and to attempt to find a middle-ground between it
and liberalism, and if these objections are still compelling, and
if, as will not be argued, there is no genuine middle ground, then
a liberal theology is the only answer.

    3. Neither of the foregoing alternatives being acceptable,
the Biblical theologian seems to be offering a third option, one
which would solve the major problems, if only it were feasible.
For if it could be held that both God and man (plus nature) act
conjointly in the events spoken of as "acts of God" then the
problems presented by modern cosmology would be solved. One could
then say that history makes sense when viewed secularly, that is
that events really do follow one another in closed natural sequence. One could also say that history makes sense when viewed
religiously, since these events are at the same time the work of
God. One meaning of history is seen by those who lack faith, but
another meaning--the only full meaning--is seen by the man to
whom God's supernatural activity has been disclosed. Both theological and naturalistic explanations are true, religion and

science do not interfere with each other, there is no problem of
miracles yet there is activity of God, and everyone can be happy.
What science understands, correctly, as the product of antecedent
natural causes, theology understands also correctly, as the act of
God.

Rudolf Bultmann seems to be proposing this solution when he
states that:

> The only way to preserve the unworldly, transcendental char-
> acter of the divine activity is to regard it not as an
> interference in worldly happenings, but something accom-
> plished *in* them in such a way that the closed weft of history
> as it presents itself to objective observation is left un-
> disturbed. To every other eye than the eye of faith the
> action of God is hidden. Only the 'natural happening' is
> generally visible and ascertainable. In it is accom-
> plished the hidden act of God.[19]

Unfortunately, however, it does not take much reflection to perceive that although this theory may be very attractive, it is impossible to make it really work.

The conditions which would have to be satisfied to make this
option plausible would be these: there must be two active agents,
God on the one hand, and man and nature on the other, both actually
carrying out the same action independently, in such a way that
both parties are free, and neither produces the other's action.
There must be a continual perfect coincidence of action by two
sets of free causes, and this seems inconceivable. This incon-
ceivability accounts for the fact that predestination had to be
accepted by the classical theological tradition in order to explain
how events could happen according to Divine will. One is confronted by an either/or, either divine action or human action, and
the tradition preferred the former.

There are several ways of conceiving the action of two sets
of causes which might at first glance seem to satisfy the necessary conditions, but examination indicates that these fail for one
of two reasons. Either the freedom of one of the parties is denied, or else the work must be divided up, one part being done by
one party, the other part being done by the other, in order to
preserve the freedom of both. What is required, however, is that
the *same* act be done by two sets of causes operating freely. If
God does one part and man the rest, then each is doing part of the
act, and they are not both doing the same act at the same time.
In addition, to say that God does part of the act would be to say
that he does act in nature to "interfere."

One type of example involves a violation of mutuality of action in order to preserve mutuality of freedom. This is accomplished when the labor is divided. For example, if God tells man
what to do and man does it, even though the wills of both God and
man are fulfilled it is obvious that only one part--in this case
man--is actually acting. God calls Moses, Moses responds and leads
the people out, then God sends an east wind to help them escape.
In this case the freedom of all parties is preserved, but only one
party is active in each part of the act. It is the action of God
and man only in that each one contributes something to a combined
act. In no single part of the action are both actively involved
in the same deed.

The other type of example sacrifices mutuality of freedom to
mutuality of action. Suppose it is said that the mind wills the
arm to move, and that when the arm moves the self is involved in
motion. But only one party is active in such a case, the mind
which wills the arm to move. If we were to attribute freedom to
the arm the same situation would obtain, only in reverse. In such
a case only the arm would really be the cause, the self would be
passive.[20]

In short, the dilemma is this: if there is genuine unity of
action, two parties doing exactly the same act at the same time,
then there is no duality of causes; and if there is duality of
causes, then there is no unity of action. The only kind of unity
there can be is unity of will, the sharing of a will to the same
result, but in such cases each party acts separately, each does
his part, but they do not do the same thing. If it is not possible
to conceive of two sets of free causes operating conjointly in
exactly the same action, then it is not possible to satisfy the
conditions by which one would be able to say that *both* naturalistic
(and human) and theological explanations are valid. One can say
that one *or* the other is valid for any particular case, or that
each contributes a part to the total action, but further than this
one cannot go. Hence the seeming plausibility of the joint-cause
solution breaks down. The alternative to conservatism and
liberalism turns out to be a delusion.

The end of an era has been reached. For a while it seemed
possible to stake out a middle ground between conservatism and
liberalism, to find some place for asserting that there are miracles which are not really miraculous, which are fully part of the
natural order and yet are supernatural at the same time. The
case seemed hopeful until it was noticed that advocates of this

position really have nothing concrete to say about their "acts of
God" as historical events. They willingly affirm that God acts,
and they point to Biblical events as instances of that action, but
they deny the concrete contents of the Biblical record of those
events, and all that they affirm are facts perfectly consistent
with naturalistic explanation. In short, they provide no justification in terms of concrete detail for calling such events special
acts of God. No effort is being made to "cash in" the concept of
a "God Who Acts."

Perhaps because the anthropology of this tradition was so
exciting, its failure as a theology in the strict sense of that
word was not noticed as clearly as it should have been. Perhaps
under the cover of a much-needed heightened view of sin--even as
an instrument in recovering that sense of man's depravity which
events in modern history have forced on religious understanding
again--a theology affirming the special actions of God received
wide acceptance even though its promise as theology could never be
fulfilled.

Once again, as before, it becomes increasingly obvious that
the alternatives are only two: either a conservative tradition
affirming miraculous acts of God, whether spectacular or "hidden,"
or a God who acts solely through the general orders and processes
of nature and history. The former alternative runs counter to
the anti-miracle tradition in modern thought, to our unwillingness
and inability to cash in miracles, as well as counter to our theological distrust of a God who is a being beside other beings. If
the times can be reversed and men can think miraculously once again,
then there is still place for a God Who Acts. If he cannot, then
a God who is conceived as a general cosmic process (perhaps personal), who works universally rather than specially, is the only
hope. Such a God might produce unique currents of history through
variability of human response to him, but not through variability
of his own action. Perhaps someone with one eye on Whitehead and
the other on the Bible will bring in the next era in theology.

NOTES

[1]Langdon Gilkey pointed this out in his "Cosmology, Ontology
and the Travail of Biblical Language," *Journal of Religion*, July,
1961, and his points have not been successfully refuted. He there
called for a reexamination of the concept of the action of God, and
it is that examination that this paper attempts to supply among
other things.

[2]The following abbreviations will be used. *GWA* and *BAG* stand for *God Who Acts* and *The Book of the Acts of God*, by G. Ernest Wright, the second work in collaboration with Reginald H. Fuller. *UOT* and *UNT* stand for *Understanding the Old Testament* and *Understanding the New Testament*, by Bernhard Anderson and by Howard Clark Kee and Franklin W. Young, respectively.

[3]*BAG*, p. 70.

[4]*Ibid.*, p. 87.

[5]Wright here presents a valuable weapon to adversaries of the God Who Acts tradition. The tendency in the past has been for some theologians to point to Israel's covenantal understanding of history as something unique, perhaps to be explained only in terms of Divine revelation. How could this new understanding have occurred? God must have given it. Now, however, it is clear that the covenant form in its fullness had been there to be used prior to Moses' application of it to Israel's relationship with God. A successful migration, some favorable weather, perhaps even a whole succession of fortuitous circumstances are enough to account for the application of covenant to history. This concept, once adopted, is enough to account for the modification of borrowed forms which took place in Israel's later development. Thus the final stone in a liberal or even a naturalistic account of Israel's religion falls into place. My point here is not that of suggesting that this explanation is the correct one but merely that of pointing out that it is a possible one.

[6]*GWA*, p. 127.

[7]*BAG*, p. 84.

[8]*GWA*, p. 117.

[9]*UOT*, p. 48.

[10]*BAG*, p. 288.

[11]*UNT*, p. 177.

[12]*BAG*, p. 141.

[13]*GWA*, p. 124.

[14]*BAG*, p. 15.

[15]*Ibid.*, p. 127.

[16]*Ibid.*, p. 14.

[17]The reasoning here seems to me to be faulty. The argument that obvious miracles would be coercive hence contrary to faith fails to observe the distinction between believing that God exists and believing in him to faith. According to tradition both Satan and Adam believed in God, but they chose to rebel against him. What is being said here applies also to the argument that proofs for the existence of God cannot be valid because they would undercut faith. No proof could ever force one to trust in God, all it could do is to prove that God exists.

[18]John C. Bennett, *Christian Realism*, p. 34.

[19]Rudolf Bultmann, *Kerygma and Myth*, p. 197.

[20]One of the great merits of Charles Hartshorne's *The Divine Relativity* is the clarity with which it makes this point. If man is free, and if his experience enters into God's own awareness, then the Divine is *passive* in this repsect. God, Hartshorne says, is supreme "yet indebted to all." The classical tradition, in recognition of this point and in order to save the impassibility of God had to deny not only man's freedom but also the reality of God's relatedness to man. St. Thomas is driven to deny both that God is related to the world and that God knows the world directly-- seemingly strange conclusions to a position which is built upon proofs of God's existence arising out of the need for a First Cause.

5. THE MEANING OF GOD AS ACTING

Rudolph Bultmann

•1•

It is often said that it is impossible to carry through de-
mythologizing consistently, since, if the message of the New Testament
is to be retained at all, we are bound to speak of God as acting.
In such speech there remains a mythological residue. For is it not
mythological to speak of God as acting? This objection may also
take the form that, since de-mythologizing as such is not consistent
with speaking of God as acting, Christian preaching must always remain mythological as was the preaching of the New Testament in general. But are such arguments valid? We must ask whether we are
really speaking mythologically when we speak of God as acting. We
must ask in what case and under what conditions is such speaking
mythological. Let us consider how God's action is understood in
mythological thinking.

In mythological thinking the action of God, whether in nature,
history, human fortune, or the inner life of the soul, is understood
as an action which intervenes between the natural, or historical, or
psychological course of events; it breaks and links them at the same
time. The divine causality is inserted as a link in the chain of the
events which follow one another according to the causal nexus. This
is meant by the popular notion that a miraculous event cannot be
understood except as a miracle, that is, as the effect of a supernatural cause. In such thinking the action of God is indeed conceived
in the same way as secular actions or events are conceived, for the
divine power which effects miracles is considered as a natural power.
In fact, however, a wonder in the sense of an action of God cannot be
thought of as an event which happens on the level of secular (worldly)
events. It is not visible, not capable of objective, scientific
proof which is possible only within an objective view of the world.
To the scientific, objective observer God's action is a mystery.

The thought of the action of God as an unworldly and transcendent action can be protected from misunderstanding only if it is
not thought of as an action which happens between the worldly actions
or events, but as happening within them. The close connection between natural and historical events remains intact as it presents

itself to the observer. The action of God is hidden from every eye
except the eye of faith. Only the so-called natural, secular
(worldly) events are visible to every man and capable of proof. It
is *within* them that God's hidden action is taking place.

If someone now insists that to speak in this sense of God as
acting is to speak mythologically, I have no objection, since in
this case myth is something very different from what it is as the
object of de-mythologizing. When we speak of God as acting, we do
not speak mythologically in the objectifying sense.

·2·

Now another question arises: If faith maintains that God's
hidden action is at work within the chain of secular events, faith
may be suspected of being pantheistic piety. As we reflect on this
problem, we can further clarify the sense in which we must understand God's action. Faith insists not on the direct identity of
God's action with worldly events, but, if I may be permitted to put
it so, on the paradoxical identity which can be believed only here
and now against the appearance of non-identity. In faith I can
understand an accident with which I meet as a gracious gift of God
or as His punishment, or as His chastisement. On the other hand,
I can understand the same accident as a link in the chain of the
natural course of events. If, for example, my child has recovered
from a dangerous illness, I give thanks to God because He has saved
my child. By faith I can accept a thought or a resolution as a
divine inspiration without removing the thought or the resolution
from its connection with psychological motivation. It is possible,
for example, that a decision which seemed insignificant when I made
it, is seen later on to have marked a decisive and fruitful "turn-
ing point" in my life. Then I give thanks to God who inspired the
decision. The creedal belief in God as creator is not a guarantee
given in advance by means of which I am permitted to understand
any event as wrought by God. The understanding of God as creator
is genuine only when I understand myself here and now as the creature of God. This existential understanding does not need to express itself in my consciousness as explicit knowledge. In any
case the belief in the almighty God is not the conviction given in
advance that there exists an almighty Being who is able to do all
things. Belief in the almighty God is genuine only when it actually
takes place in my very existence, as I surrender myself to the
power of God who overwhelms me here and now. Once more this does
not mean that the belief must express itself in my consciousness

as explicit knowledge; it does mean, however, that the statements
of belief are not general statements. For example, Luther's statement *terra ubique domini* is not genuine as a dogmatic statement but
only here and now when spoken in the decision of my very existence.
This distinction, I think, can be best understood today by one for
whom the dogmatic statement has become doubtful, that is, in the
misery of imprisonment in Russia.

We may conclude that pantheism is indeed a conviction given in
advance, a general world-view (*Weltanschauung*), which affirms that
every event in the world is the work of God because God is immanent
in the world. Christian faith, by contrast, holds that God acts on
me, speaks to me, here and now. The Christian believes this because he knows that he is addressed by the grace of God which meets
him in the Word of God, in Jesus Christ. God's grace opens his
eyes to see that "in everything God works for good with those who
love him" (Rom. 8:28). This faith is not a knowledge possessed
once for all; it is not a general world-view. It can be realized
only here and now. It can be a living faith only when the believer
is always asking what God is telling him here and now. God's actions generally, in nature and history, is hidden from the believer
just as much as from the non-believer. But in so far as he sees
what comes upon him here and now in the light of the divine word,
he can and must take it as God's action. Pantheism can say "there
divinity is working" with regard to any event, whatever it may be,
without taking into account the importance of what happens for my
personal existence. Christian faith can only say, "I trust that
God is working here and there, but His action is hidden, for it is
not directly identical with the visible event. What it is that He
is doing I do not yet know, and perhaps I never shall know it, but
faithfully I trust that it is important for my personal existence,
and I must ask what it is that God says to me. Perhaps it may be
only that I must endure and be silent."

What follows from all this? In faith I deny the closed connection of the worldly events, the chain of cause and effect as
it presents itself to the neutral observer. I deny the interconnection of the worldly events not as mythology does, which by
breaking the connection places supernatural events into the chain
of natural events; I deny the worldly connection as a whole when
I speak of God. I deny the worldly connection of events when I
speak of myself, for in this connection of worldly events, my self,
my personal existence, my own personal life, is no more visible
and capable of proof than is God as acting.

    In faith I realize that the scientific world-view does not
comprehend the whole reality of the world and of human life, but
faith does not offer another general world-view which corrects
science in its statements on its own level. Rather faith acknowl-
edges that the world-view given by science is a necessary means for
doing our work within the world. Indeed, I need to see the worldly
events as linked by cause and effect not only as a scientific observer, but also in my daily living. In doing so there remains no
room for God's working. This is the paradox of faith, that faith
"nevertheless" understands as God's action here and now an event
which is completely intelligible in the natural or historical connection of events. This "nevertheless" is inseparable from faith.
This "nevertheless" (the German *dennoch* of Ps. 73:23; and Paul
Tillich's *in spite of*) is inseparable from faith. Only this is
real faith in wonder. He who thinks that it is possible to speak
of wonders as of demonstrable events capable of proof offends
against the thought of God as acting in hidden ways. He subjects
God's action to the control of objective observation. He delivers
up the faith in wonders to the criticism of science and in so
doing validates such criticism.

    ·3·

    Here another question arises. If God's action must be thought
of as hidden, how is it possible to speak of it except in purely
negative statements? Is the conception of transcendence an exclusively negative conception? It would be if to speak of God did
not also mean to speak of our personal existence. If we speak of
God as acting in general, transcendence would indeed be a purely
negative conception, since every positive description of transcendence transposes it into this world. It is wrong to speak of God
as acting in general statements, in terms of the formal analysis
of man's existence. It is precisely the formal, existentialist
analysis of human existence which shows that it is indeed impossible
to speak of our personal existence in general statements. I can
speak of my personal existence only here and now in the concrete
situation of my life. To be sure, I can explicate in general
statements the meaning, the sense of the conception of God and of
God's action in so far as I can say that God is the power which
bestows upon me life and existence, and in so far as I can describe
these actions as the encounter which demands my own personal decision. By doing so I acknowledge that I cannot speak of God's action
in general statements; I can speak only of what He does here and

now with me, of what He speaks here and now to me. Even if we do
not speak of God in general terms but rather of His action here
and now on us, we must speak in terms of general conceptions, for
all of our language employs conceptions, but it does not follow
that the issue in hand is a general one.

   ·4·

      Now we may ask once more whether it is possible to speak of
God as acting without falling into mythological speech. It is often asserted that the language of the Christian faith must of necessity be mythological language. This assertion must be examined
carefully. First, even if we concede that the language of faith
is really the language of myth, we must ask how this fact affects
the program of de-mythologizing. This concession is by no means a
valid argument against de-mythologizing, for the language of myth,
when it serves as the language of faith, loses its mythological
sense. To speak, for example, of God as creator, no longer involves
speaking of His creatorship in the sense of the old myth. Mythological conceptions can be used as symbols or images which are perhaps necessary to the language of religion and therefore also of
the Christian faith. Thus it becomes evident that the use of
mythological language, far from being an objection to de-mythologizing, positively demands it.
      Second, the assertion that the language of faith needs the
language of myth can be validated only if a further qualification
is taken into account. If it is true that mythological conceptions
are necessary as symbols or images, we must ask what it is that is
now expressed by such symbols or images. Surely it is impossible
that their meaning within the language of faith should be expressed
in terms of mythological conceptions. Their meaning can and must
be stated without recourse to mythological terms.
      Third, to speak of God as acting does not necessarily mean to
speak in symbols or images. Such speech must be able to convey its
full, direct meaning. How, then, must we speak of God as acting
if our speech is not to be understood as mythological speech? God
as acting does not refer to any event which can be perceived by me
without myself being drawn into the event as into God's action,
without myself taking part in it as being acted upon. In other
words, to speak of God as acting involves the events of personal
existence. The encounter with God can be an event for man only
here and now, since man lives within the limits of space and time.
When we speak of God as acting, we mean that we are confronted with

God, addressed, asked, judged, or blessed by God. Therefore, to
speak in this manner is not to speak in symbols or images, but to
speak analogically. For when we speak in this manner of God as
acting, we conceive God's action as an analogue to the actions
taking place between men. Moreover, we conceive the communion between God and man as an analogue to the communion between man and
man.[*] It is in this analogical sense that we speak of God's love
and care for men, of His demands and of His wrath, of His promise
and grace, and it is in this analogical sense that we call Him
Father. We are not only justified in speaking thus, but we must do
so, since now we are not speaking of an idea about God, but of God
Himself. Thus, God's love and care, etc., are not images or symbols:
these conceptions mean real experiences of God as acting here and
now. Especially in the conception of God as Father the mythological
sense vanished long ago. We can understand the meaning of the term
Father as applied to God by considering what it means when we speak
to our fathers or when our children speak to us as their fathers.
As applied to God the physical import of the term father has disappeared completely; it expresses a purely personal relationship.
It is in this analogical sense that we speak of God as Father.

     From this view of the situation some important conclusions fol-
low. First, only such statements about God are legitimate as express
the existential relation between God and man. Statements which speak
of God's actions as cosmic events are illegitimate. The affirmation
that God is creator cannot be a theoretical statement about God as
creator mundi in a general sense. The affirmation can only be a
personal confession that I understand myself to be a creature which
owes its existence to God. It cannot be made as a neutral statement, but only as thanksgiving and surrender. Moreover, statements
which describe God's action as cultic action, for example, that He
offered His Son as a sacrificial victim, are not legitimate, unless
they are understood in a purely symbolic sense. Second, the so-
called images which describe God as acting are legitimate only if
they mean that God is a personal being acting on persons. Therefore, political and juridical conceptions are not permissible, unless they are understood purely as symbols.

     ·5·

     At this point a really important objection arises. If what we
have said is correct, does it not follow that God's action is deprived of objective reality, that it is reduced to a purely

---

*See the discussion of analogy by the late Erich Frank in his
Philosophical Understanding and Religious Truth (New York, 1945).

subjective, psychological experience (*Erlebnis*); that God exists
only as an inner event in the soul, whereas faith has real meaning
only if God exists outside the believer? Such objections are
brought forward again and again, and the shades of Schleiermacher
and Feuerbach are conjured up in this controversy. *Erlebnis* (psychological experience) was indeed a popular catchword in German
theology before the first World War. Faith was often described as
Erlebnis. It was on this catch-word that Karl Barth and the so-
called dialectical theologians made an all-out attack.

When we say that to speak of God means to speak of our own
personal existence, the meaning is a totally different one. The
objection which I have just summarized suffers from a psychological
misunderstanding of the life of the soul. From the statement that
to speak of God is to speak of myself, it by no means follows that
God is not outside the believer. (This would be the case only if
faith is interpreted as a purely psychological event.) When man
is understood in the genuine sense as an historical being which has
its reality in concrete situations and decisions, in the very encounters of life,* it is clear, on the one hand, that faith, speaking of God as acting, cannot defend itself against the charge of
being an illusion, and, on the other hand, that faith does not mean
a psychologically subjective event.

Is it enough to say that faith grows out of the encounter with
the Holy Scriptures as the Word of God, that faith is nothing but
simple hearing? The answer is yes. But this answer is valid only
if the Scriptures are understood neither as a manual of doctrine
nor as a record of witnesses to a faith which I interpret by sympathy and empathy. On the contrary, to hear the Scriptures as the
Word of God means to hear them as a word which is addressed to me,
as *kerygma*, as a proclamation. Then my understanding is not a
neutral one, but rather my response to a call. The fact that the
word of the Scriptures is God's Word cannot be demonstrated objectively; it is an event which happens here and now. God's Word
is hidden in the Scriptures as each action of God is hidden everywhere.

I have said that faith grows out of the encounters which are
the substance of our personal lives as historical lives. Its
meaning is readily understood when we reflect upon the simple
phenomena of our personal lives. The love of my friend, my wife,
my children, meets me genuinely only here and now as an event.
Such love cannot be observed by objective methods but only by

*Man is an historical being not only in so far as he is enmeshed
in the course of the world-history, but particularly in so far as
he has a personal history of his own.

personal experience and response. From the outside, for example,
by psychological observation, it cannot be perceived as love, but
only as an interesting detail of psychological processes which are
open to different interpretations. Thus, the fact that God cannot
be seen or apprehended apart from faith does not mean that He does
not exist apart from faith.

We must remember, however, that the affirmations of faith in
its relation to its object, to God, cannot be proved objectively.
This is not a weakness of faith; it is its true strength, as my
teacher Wilhelm Herrmann insisted. For if the relation between
faith and God could be proved as the relation between subject and
object in the worldly situations can be proved, then He would be
placed on the same level as the world, within which the demand for
proof is legitimate.

May we then say that God has "proved" Himself by the "facts of
redemption" (Heilstatsachen)? By no means. For what we call facts
of redemption are themselves objects of faith and are apprehended
as such only by the eye of faith. They cannot be perceived apart
from faith, as if faith could be based on data in the same way as
the natural sciences are based on data which are open to empirical
observation. To be sure, the facts of redemption constitute the
grounds of faith, but only as perceived by faith itself. The principle is the same in our personal relationship as persons with
persons. Trust in a friend can rest solely on the personality of
my friend which I can perceive only when I trust him. There cannot
be any trust or love without risk. It is true, as Wilhelm Herrmann
taught us, that the ground and the object of faith are identical.
They are one and the same thing, because we cannot speak of what
God is in Himself but only of what He is doing to us and with us.

· 6 ·

Now another question can be answered. If we hold that God's
action is not visible, not capable of proof; that the events of
redemption cannot be demonstrated, that the spirit with which the
believers are endowed is not an object visible to objective observation; if we hold that we can speak of all such matters only when
we are concerned with our personal existence, then it can be said
that faith is a new understanding of personal existence. In other
words, God's action bestows upon us a new understanding of ourselves.

The objection may be raised that in this case the event of
God's revelation is nothing but the occasion which gives us

understanding of ourselves and that the occasion is not recognized
as an action which occurs in our actual lives and transforms them.
In short, revelation is not recognized as a wonder. Then, the objection goes on, nothing happens but understanding or consciousness
of the self; the content of the self-understanding is a timeless
truth; once perceived it remains valid without regard to the occasion, namely, revelation, which has given rise to it.

This objection is based on a confusion to which I have referred above (p. 64), i.e., self-understanding of personal existence
is confused with the philosophical analysis of man. The existential
understanding (*das Existentielle*) is confused with the existentialist
understanding (*das Existential*). Of philosophical analysis it may
well be said that its statements are statements of timeless truth,
not answers to the questions of the actual moment. But it is precisely this philosophical analysis of man, the *existentialist* understanding, which shows that the self-understanding--the existential
understanding--becomes realized only here and now as my own self-
understanding. Philosophical analysis shows what existence in the
abstract means. By contrast, existential, personal self-understanding does not say what existence means in the abstract, but
points to my life as a concrete person in the here and now. It is
an act of understanding in which my very self and the relationships
in which I am involved are understood together.

Such existential, personal understanding need not take place
on the level of consciousness, and this, indeed, is rare. But such
personal self-understanding, albeit unconscious, dominates, or
exercises a powerful influence upon, all our sorrows and cares,
ambitions, joys and anxieties. Moreover, this personal self-understanding is put to the test, is called into question (*ist in Frage
gestellt*) in every situation of encounter. As my life goes on, my
self-understanding may prove inadequate or it may become clearer
and deeper as the result of further experiences and encounters.
This change may be due to radical self-examination or it may occur
unconsciously, when, for example, my life is led out of the darkness of distress into the light of happiness or when the opposite
experience comes to me. Entering into decisive encounters I may
achieve a totally new self-understanding as a result of the love
which is bestowed upon me when, for example, I marry or make a new
friend. Even a little child unconsciously manifests such self-
understanding in so far as he realizes that he is a child and that
he therefore stands in a special relationship to his parents. His
self-understanding expresses itself in his love, trust, feeling of
security, thankfulness, etc.

In my personal existence, I am isolated neither from my environment nor from my own past and future. When for example, I achieve through love a new self-understanding, what takes place is not an isolated psychological act of coming to consciousness; my whole situation is transformed. In understanding myself, I understand other people and at the same time the whole world takes on a new character. I see it, as we say, in a new light, and so it really is a new world. I achieve a new insight into my past and my future. I recognize new demands and am open to encounters in a new manner. My past and future become more than pure time as it is marked on a calendar or timetable. Now it should be clear that I cannot possess this self-understanding as a timeless truth, a conviction accepted once and for all. For my new self-understanding, by its very nature, must be renewed day by day, so that I understand the imperative self which is included in it.

Mutatis mutandis we may here apply the saying, "if we live by the Spirit, let us also walk by the Spirit" (Gal. 5:25). For indeed the saying is applicable to the self-understanding of faith, which is a response to our encounter with the word of God. In faith man understands himself anew. As Luther says in his interpretation of the Epistle to the Romans, "God going out from Himself brings it about that we go into ourselves; and making Himself known to us, He makes us known to ourselves." In faith man understands himself ever anew. This new self-understanding can be maintained only as a continual response to the word of God which proclaims His action in Jesus Christ. It is the same in ordinary human life. The new self-understanding which grows out of the encounter of man with man can be maintained only if the actual relation between man and man is maintained. "The kindness of God is new every morning"; yes, provided I perceive it anew every morning. For this is not a timeless truth, like a mathematical statement. I can speak of the kindness of God which is new every morning only if I myself am renewed every morning.

These considerations in turn throw light on the paradoxical juxtaposition of indicative and imperative in Paul to which I just referred above (Gal. 5:25). We now see that the indicative calls forth the imperative. The indicative gives expression to the new self-understanding of the believer, for the statement "I am freed from sin" is not a dogmatic one, but an existential one. It is the believer's confession that his whole existence is renewed. Since his existence includes his will, the imperative reminds him that he is free from sin, provided that his will is renewed in obedience to the commandment of God.

·7·

A further objection which may arise is that the future action
of God is eliminated by de-mythologizing. I reply that it is precisely de-mythologizing which makes clear the true meaning of God
as acting in the future. Faith includes free and complete openness
to the future. Philosophical analysis of existence shows that openness to the future is an essential feature of man's existence. But
can philosophical analysis endow the concretely existing man with
the openness? By no means. It can no more do this than it can
bestow existence upon us. Philosophical analysis, as Heidegger
has shown, can do no more than explain that man, if he is willing
to exist in a full personal sense, must be open to the future. It
can call attention to the effect, stimulating or frightening, of
this perception when it affirms that for philosophical analysis the
future cannot be characterized otherwise than as nothing.

Therefore, free openness to the future is freedom to take
anxiety upon ourselves (*Angstbereitschaft*), i.e., to decide for it.
If it is true that the Christian faith involves free openness to
the future, then it is freedom from anxiety in the face of the
Nothing. For this freedom nobody can decide of his own will; it
can only be given, in faith. Faith as openness to the future is
freedom from the past, because it is faith in the forgiveness of
sins; it is freedom from the enslaving chains of the past. It is
freedom *from* ourselves as the old selves, and *for* ourselves as the
new selves. It is freedom from the illusion, grounded in sin, that
we can establish our personal existence through our own decision.
It is the free openness to the future which Paul acclaims in saying
that "death is swallowed up in victory" (I Cor. 15:54).

·8·

Here a final and crucial question arises. If we must speak
of God as acting only in the sense that He acts with me here and
now, can we still believe that God has acted once for all on behalf of the whole world? Are we not in danger of eliminating this
"once for all" of Paul's (Rom. 6:10)? Are we not in danger of
relegating the divine dispensation, the history of salvation, to
the dimension of timelessness? It should be clear from what we
have said that we are not speaking of an idea of God but of the
living God in whose hands our time lies, and who encounters us here
and now. Therefore, we can make our answer to the objection in
the single affirmation that God meets us in His Word, in a concrete

word, the preaching instituted in Jesus Christ. While it may be
said that God meets us always and everywhere, we do not see and
hear Him always and everywhere, unless His Word supervenes and
enables us to understand the moment here and now, as Luther so often
insisted. The idea of the omnipresent and almighty God becomes real
in my personal existence only by His Word spoken here and now. Accordingly it must be said that the Word of God is what it is only
in the moment in which it is spoken. The Word of God is not a
timeless statement but a concrete word addressed to men here and
now. To be sure God's Word is His eternal Word, but this eternity
must not be conceived as timelessness, but as His presence always
actualized here and now. It is His Word as an event, in an encounter, not as a set of ideas, not, for example, as a statement
about God's kindness and grace in general, although such a statement
may be otherwise correct, but only as addressed to me, as an event
happening and meeting me as His mercy. Only thus is it the *verbum
externum*, the word from the outside. Not as a knowledge possessed
once for all, but precisely as meeting me over and over again is
it really the *verbum externum*.

From this it follows that God's Word is a real word spoken to
me in human language, whether in the preaching of the Church or
in the Bible, in the sense that the Bible is not viewed merely as
an interesting collection of sources for the history of religion,
but that the Bible is transmitted through the Church as a word addressing us. This living Word of God is not invented by the human
spirit and by human sagacity; it rises up in history. Its origin
is an historical event, by which the speaking of this word, the
preaching, is rendered authoritative and legitimate. This event is
Jesus Christ.

We may say that this assertion is paradoxical. For what God
has done in Jesus Christ is not an historical fact which is capable
of historical proof. The objectifying historian as such cannot see
that an historical person (Jesus of Nazareth) is the eternal Logos,
the Word. It is precisely the mythological description of Jesus
Christ in the New Testament which makes it clear that the figure
and the work of Jesus Christ must be understood in a manner which
is beyond the categories by which the objective historian understands world-history, if the figure and the work of Jesus Christ
are to be understood as the divine work of redemption. That is the
real paradox. Jesus is a human, historical person from Nazareth in
Galilee. His work and destiny happened within world-history and
as such come under the scrutiny of the historian who can understand

them as part of the nexus of history. Nevertheless, such detached historical inquiry cannot become aware of what God has wrought in Christ, that is, of the eschatological event.

According to the New Testament the decisive significance of Jesus Christ is that he--in his person, his coming, his passion, and his glorification--is the eschatological event. He is the one "who is to come," and we are not to "look for another" (Matt. 11:3). "When the time had fully come, God sent forth his Son" (Gal. 4:4). "This is the judgment, that the light has come into the world" (John 3:19). "The hour is coming, and now is, when the dead will hear the voice of the Son of God, and those who hear will live" (John 5:25). All these sayings declare that Jesus Christ is the eschatological event. The crucial question for de-mythologizing is whether this understanding of Jesus Christ as the eschatological event is inextricably bound up with the conceptions of cosmological eschatology as it is in the New Testament, with the single exception of the Fourth Gospel.

In the Fourth Gospel, as we have seen, the cosmological eschatology is understood, from our point of view, as an historical eschatology. We have also seen that for Paul the believer is already a new creation, "the old has passed away, behold, the new has come" (II Cor. 5:17). We must, therefore, say that to live in faith is to live an eschatological existence, to live beyond the world, to have passed from death to life (cf. John 5:24; I John 3:14). Certainly the eschatological existence is already realized in anticipation, for "we walk by faith, not by sight" (II Cor. 5:7). This means that the eschatological existence of the believer is not a worldly phenomenon, but is realized in the new self-understanding. This self-understanding, as we have seen before, grows out of the Word. The eschatological event which is Jesus Christ happens here and now as the Word is being preached (II Cor. 6:2; John 5:24) regardless of whether this Word is accepted or rejected. The believer has passed from death to life, and the unbeliever is judged; the wrath of God rests upon him, says John (John 3:18, 36; 9:39). The word of the preaching spreads death and life, says Paul (II Cor. 2:15f.).

Thus, the "once for all" is now understood in its genuine sense, namely, as the "once for all" of the eschatological event. For this "once for all" is not the uniqueness of an historical event but means that a particular historical event, that is, Jesus Christ, is to be understood as the eschatological "once for all." As an eschatological event this "once for all" is always present in the

proclaimed word, not as a timeless truth, but as happening here and
now. Certainly the Word says to me that God's grace is a prevenient
grace which has already acted for me; but not in such a way that I
can look back on it as an historical event of the past. The acting
grace is present now as the eschatological event. The word of God
is Word of God only as it happens here and now. The paradox is that
the word which is always happening here and now is one and the same
with the first word of the apostolic preaching crystallized in the
Scriptures of the New Testament and delivered by men again and
again, the word whose content may be formulated in general statements. It cannot be the one without the other. This is the sense
of the "once for all." It is the eschatological once-for-all because the word becomes event here and now in the living voice of
the preaching.

The word of God and the Church belong together, because it is
by the word that the Church is constituted as the community of the
called, in so far as the preaching is not a lecture comprised of
general propositions but the message which is proclaimed by author-
ized, legitimate messengers (II Cor. 5:18-20). As the word is
God's word only as an event, the Church is genuine Church only as
an event which happens each time here and now; for the Church is
the eschatological community of the saints, and it is only in a
paradoxical way identical with the ecclesiastical institutions which
we observe as social phenomena of secular history.

.9.

We have seen that the task of de-mythologizing received its
first impulse from the conflict between the mythological views of
the world contained in the Bible and the modern views of the world
which are influenced by scientific thinking, and it has become
evident that faith itself demands to be freed from any world-view
produced by man's thought, whether mythological or scientific. For
all human world-views objectivize the world and ignore or eliminate
the significance of the encounters in our personal existence. This
conflict shows that in our age faith has not yet found adequate
forms of expression; that our age has not yet become aware of the
identity of its ground and object; that it has not yet genuinely
understood the transcendence and hiddenness of God as acting. It
is not yet aware of its own "nevertheless," or of its "in spite
of"; over and over again it yields to the temptation to objectivize
God and His action. Therefore, the criticism of the mythological
world-view of Biblical and ecclesiastical preaching renders a

valuable service to faith, for it recalls faith to radical reflection on its own nature. The task of de-mythologizing has no other
purpose than to take up this challenge. The invisibility of God
excludes every myth which tries to make God and His action visible;
God withholds Himself from view and observation. We can believe in
God only in spite of experience, just as we can accept justification only in spite of conscience. Indeed, de-mythologizing is a
task parallel to that performed by Paul and Luther in their doctrine
of justification by faith alone without the works of law. More
precisely, de-mythologizing is the radical application of the doctrine of justification by faith to the sphere of knowledge and
thought. Like the doctrine of justification, de-mythologizing destroys every longing for security. There is no difference between
security based on good works and security built on objectifying
knowledge. The man who desires to believe in God must know that
he has nothing at his own disposal on which to build this faith,
that he is, so to speak, in a vacuum. He who abandons every form
of security shall find the true security. Man before God has always empty hands. He who gives up, he who loses every security
shall find security. Faith in God, like faith in justification,
refuses to single out qualified and definable actions as holy actions. Correspondingly, faith in God, like faith in creation, refuses to single out qualified and definable realms from among the
observable realities of nature and history. Luther has taught us
that there are no holy places in the world, that the world as a
whole is indeed a profane place. This is true in spite of Luther's
"the earth everywhere is the Lord's" (*terra ubique Domini*), for
this, too, can be believed only in spite of all of the evidence.
It is not the consecration of the priest but the proclaimed word
which makes holy the house of God. In the same way, the whole of
nature and history is profane. It is only in the light of the proclaimed word that what has happened or is happening here or there
assumes the character of God's action for the believer. It is precisely by faith that the world becomes a profane place and is thus
restored to its true place as the sphere of man's action.

Nevertheless, the world is God's world and the sphere of God
as acting. Therefore, our relation to the world as believers is
paradoxical. As Paul puts it in I Cor. 7:29-31, "Let those who
have wives live as though they had none, and those who mourn as
though they were not mourning, and those who rejoice as though they
were not rejoicing, and those who buy as though they had no goods,

and those who deal with the world as though they had no dealings
with it." In terms of this book, we may say, "let those who have
the modern world-view live as though they had none."

6. WHAT SENSE DOES IT MAKE TO SAY,
"GOD ACTS IN HISTORY"?

Schubert M. Ogden

The question is often asked, "Can one make sense of the statement 'God acts in history'?" Here I would like to reformulate the
question and ask instead, "What sense does it make to say, 'God
acts in history'?" Since the differences between the two questions
are slight, I need to explain why I nevertheless think them
important.

First of all, the question as I have formulated it already assumes an affirmative answer to the original question; and this assumption seems appropriate to the present discussion. I certainly
do not want to presume too much, and I recognize there are many for
whom the original question may seem better just because it does
not make this assumption. But, for my part, the real issue is not
whether the statement "God acts in history" makes sense, but *what*
sense it makes. Furthermore, it belongs to the very nature of the
theologian's work that the possibility of speaking of God's acting
in history is not the question he must consider. It is true that
he would not ask even the reformulated question unless such speaking
were in some sense problematic. He asks this question only because
he recognizes that not all the ways in which his fathers in the
faith have spoken of God's action are relevant possibilities for
men today. Indeed, it is probably just because some one or other
of these traditional ways has now shown itself to be no longer
relevant that he, too, is tempted to ask whether one can really
speak of God's acting at all. But he ought to resist this tempta-
tion--so long, at least, as he continues to profess the Christian
faith and, at some level or other, engages in trying to explicate
that faith in an adequate Christian theology. Thus precision in
formulating the question I have to consider seems to me to require
the changes I have made.

But there is a second reason for these changes. If I understand the lesson to be learned from what Frederick Ferré has called

Chapter VI. "What Sense Does It Make To Say, 'God Acts in History'?"
(pp. 164-187) in *The Reality of God and Other Essays* by Schubert
M. Ogden. Copyright 1963 by Schubert M. Ogden. Reprinted by permission of Harper & Row, Publishers, Inc.

"contemporary linguistic philosophy,"[1] the question whether "God
acts in history" *can* make sense is a somewhat old-fashioned question.   According to Ferré, the development of linguistic philosophy
falls into two more or less distinct phases: a first phase characterized by "verificational analysis" and a more recent phase in
which the emphasis has been on "functional analysis."[2]   In the
earlier period, which was dominated by the logical positivists and
their so-called "verification principle," the question under discussion was precisely whether theological statements can make sense;
and the positivists gave a resoundingly negative answer to the question.   But subsequent discussion has made clear that their answer
was based less on a careful analysis of the actual uses of religious
and theological language than on certain *a priori* assumptions that
reflected, as one historian has written, "an extreme respect for
science and mathematics" and "an extreme distaste for metaphysics."[3]
Later linguistic philosophers, by contrast, have tended to proceed
more cautiously.   Instead of asking whether theological statements
can make sense, they have attempted to determine what sense such
statements in fact *do* make by analyzing their function in actual
religious and theological speech.   If this shift in approach is, as
I believe, fortunate, it presumably has a bearing on the procedure
of the theologian.   It suggests he will do better not to pronounce
on the question *whether* "God acts in history" makes sense, except
insofar as an attempt to show *what* sense it makes implies an answer
to that question.   If his attempt to explain the sense of the
statement is successful, then, of course, one can make sense of it;
for *ab esse ad posse valet consequentia.*   If, on the other hand,
his attempt should fail, the possibility will still exist for someone else to show that, and how, the statement makes sense.

The following discussion is divided into two main parts.   In the
first, I shall try to clarify the problem as I understand it and
indicate briefly the more important resources available for solving
it.   In the second, I shall attempt to point the way to a constructive solution.

1

It may be claimed without exaggeration that no Protestant
theologian of our century has given more sustained and self-conscious
attention to the meaning of theological statements than Rudolf
Bultmann.   Unlike many of his contemporaries, Bultmann has continued
to be sensitive to the difficulties posed by traditional theological language for anyone whose outlook has been shaped by

the scientific world picture and a distinctively modern understanding of human existence. One could wish, perhaps, that Bultmann's resources for dealing with these difficulties were not so
exclusively limited to those of Continental theology and philosophy
and that he was more knowledgeable than he is of the work done on
the logic of theological language by Anglo-Saxon philosophers and
theologians. Certainly for any of us who live in the Anglo-Saxon
world and are sympathetic with Bultmann's basic approach, there is
an obligation, which I myself feel with increasing intensity, to
enter into discussion with English-speaking thinkers who are concerned primarily to clarify the meaning of theological language.
But, granting the limitations of Bultmann's work, I would insist
that the meaning of theological statements has been the focus of
all his systematic efforts and that his contribution toward defining
this problem and attempting to solve it is of fundamental importance
for the rest of us who also have the problem.

As is well known, Bultmann maintains that the language of
Christian theology, both in Holy Scripture and in the church's tradition, is for the most part and in its central elements "mythical"
or "mythological" language. By this he means that the statements
in which theology has usually spoken of God and his action in history have the same "objectifying" character as the statements of
empirical science. Although the "intention" of such mythological
statements--or, as the functional analyst would say, their "use"
or function--is quite different from that of scientific statements,
their linguistic form is essentially the same. Like scientific
statements, they "objectify" the existential reality of which they
speak and thus represent it in terms of space, time, causality, and
substance--or, in a word, in the Kantian forms of sensibility and
categories of understanding that Bultmann takes to be determinative
for all empirical knowledge. The result is that God and his action
are represented as though God were but one more secondary cause in
the chain of secondary causes and his action but one more action
alongside those of other causal agents.[4]

It should be clear from even this brief summary that Bultmann
does not so define "myth" (or "mythology") as to make it inclusive
of all analogical discourse about God.[5] He holds, rather, that
"myth" refers to only one way in which God may be spoken about in
language otherwise used to speak of the nondivine. As we shall see
further below, he distinguishes a "mythological" way of speaking
of God and his action from another way that he refers to as "analogy"; and this distinction can be understood only if the restricted

scope of his definition of "myth" is carefully observed. The
specific difference of myth is not that it speaks of God in terms
also applicable to the nondivine, but that its terms are "objectifying" in a manner appropriate only to ordinary empirical knowledge
and its refinement by the various special sciences.

Bultmann maintains that such mythological language makes for
a double difficulty. First, because mythological statements have
the linguistic form of scientific statements, they are open to
scientific criticism, with results that are devastating. Given the
thoroughgoing development of scientific thinking as we find it in
the method of modern natural science, mythology seems to be merely
a primitive attempt to think scientifically which is no longer
credible or relevant. The scientist, as Laplace said, has no need
of the "God hypothesis" to perform his particular task. His continuum of secondary causes does not include the cause represented
by myth as God, nor does he reckon with the action of such a being
in his scientific explanations. Because this critical attitude
toward myth has come to determine our whole contemporary cultural
consciousness, the problem inevitably arises--for those of us who
share in that consciousness--how the statement "God acts in history"
makes any sense. We realize that it certainly cannot make *scientific* sense, since the logic of scientific discourse simply leaves
no room for it in its traditional mythological form.

But there is a second and, Bultmann argues, more fundamental
difficulty. It may be equally doubted whether mythological statements make *theological* sense--or, better said, whether they are an
appropriate way of expressing the sense or meaning that theological
statements are supposed to express. Just because mythology ob-
jectifies God and his action and thus represents them in the terms
and categories appropriate solely to empirical knowledge, it
seriously misrepresents the divine transcendence as understood by
Christian faith. Instead of preserving "the infinite qualitative
difference" between God and the world, myth so represents God that
he seems to be but one more item within the world. Thus, for example, the mythological way of speaking of God as the Creator represents his creative act as though it were simply the temporally
prior action in the whole series of causal actions. Myth thereby
obscures faith's understanding that God's act as Creator is presupposed by *all* actions in the series, including the temporally
first, if, indeed, there ever was any first action. Similarly, the
mythological representation of God as the Redeemer or Consummator
(in the manner, say, of apocalyptic eschatology) pictures his

action as though it were the temporally last in the causal series. Myth thus fails to make clear that God's redemptive action fulfills or consummates *all* actions, including the temporally last, insofar as one may meaningfully speak of a last action.

Bultmann insists that the first difficulty of myth's evident incompatibility with the thinking of science but provides the occasion for focusing this more fundamental difficulty of myth's inappropriateness as the language of Christian faith. It forces us to ask for the true meaning of theological statements, and whether there is not some other, nonmythological way in which their meaning can be expressed.[6]

Bultmann's answers to these questions are given in his project of "existentialist interpretation." He holds that the true meaning of theological statements is not scientific but "existential" and that the existentialist analysis of the early Martin Heidegger provides an alternative conceptuality in which this meaning can be given nonmythological expression.

In holding that theological statements really have an existential intention or use, Bultmann means that they function to present a certain possibility for understanding human existence, summoning us directly or indirectly to realize this possibility. This is the true intention, he argues, even of the mythological statements, which, on the face of it, seem to have a scientific or pseudoscientific use. Although such statements have the linguistic form of objectifying assertions, their function is not to provide scientific information, but to express an understanding of man's existence as a historical being who must continually decide how he is to understand himself in the world. Thus, to take the same examples considered above, the mythological statement that God is the Creator is "in its fundamental intention not the statement of a cosmological theory that seeks to explain the origin of the world, but rather man's confession to God as his Lord--the Lord to whom the world belongs, whose power and care sustain and preserve it, and to whom man himself owes obedience."[7] To affirm that God is Creator, then, is in reality to affirm a certain possibility for understanding one's historical existence; it is to affirm the utter dependence of one's self and his world on the existential reality of God's power and love, which are the ultimate ground of all created things. Likewise, the real use of mythological statements about God's final redemption of the world is very different from that, say, of modern scientific theories about the eventual "running down" of the physical universe. Their true intention, Bultmann says, is to remind

us that "the fulfillment of life cannot be the result of human effort, but is rather a gift from beyond, a gift of God's grace."[8]
Hence, to affirm such statements is really to affirm an understanding of one's existence in which one renounces every attempt at self-
contrived security and utterly opens himself to the security of
God's love, wherein all things find an ultimate acceptance.

Bultmann proposes to solve the problem of the meaning or sense
of all theological statements in the way illustrated by these two
examples. He believes that the intention of such statements is
throughout existential and that the task of theology is to recognize
this and to give their intention appropriate expression. As indicated above, he regards Heidegger's existentialist analysis as
making available the philosophical concepts in which this may be
done. The reason for this is that Heidegger has provided in a conceptually clear and precise analysis of the phenomenon of human
existence, which quite avoids objectifying this phenomenon either
in the manner of mythology or in the manner of the special sciences.

My position is that the problem of theological meaning is the
general problem Bultmann clarifies and that his proposed solution
to it is essentially the correct solution. I, too, would say that
the use of theological statements is existential and that the sense
of the statement "God acts in history" is therefore an existential
sense. And yet, while agreeing with Bultmann's analysis of the
general problem and the direction of his proposal for solving it,
I would urge that his solution itself is problematic, so that the
problems it raises define, as it were, the specific differences of
the general problem as I myself understand it. In particular, his
solution poses two problems that must also be taken into account
and solved in any tenable answer to the question of this essay.

There is, first, what I will call somewhat hesitatingly the
one-sidedly existentialist character of his solution. As the term
"existentialist interpretation" already suggests, Bultmann proposes
to treat all theological statements as statements about man and
his possibilities for understanding his existence. Thus, in pref-
acing the interpretation of Paul in his *Theology of the New Testament*, he argues that, for Paul, "every assertion about God is simultaneously an assertion about man and vice versa" and that, therefore, "Paul's theology can best be treated as his doctrine of man."[9]
The difficulty with this argument is that its conclusion is one-
sided. If the premise is correct--that, for Paul, all statements
about God are statements about man *and vice versa*--then one could
just as well conclude that Paul's theology can best be presented as

the doctrine of *God*. But Bultmann is reluctant to accept this second conclusion. For reasons I cannot give here,[10] he displays a
marked unwillingness to speak directly of God and his action and
prefers instead to speak of them only indirectly by speaking of man
and his possibilities of self-understanding. Add to this, then,
his repreated defenses of the theological adequacy of Heidegger's
existentialist analysis, in which God does not so much as figure,
and what I mean by his one-sided existentialism will be obvious.[11]

Other critics have remarked this same one-sidedness and have
even gone so far as to say that Bultmann so interprets Christian
faith that it is in danger of becoming indistinguishable from a
merely human self-understanding utterly lacking in any divine basis
or object.[12] But this is to go too far. Both in practice and in
theory, Bultmann makes clear that he has no intention of reducing
faith simply to a human attitude or persepctive. His view may fairly
be said to be one-sided and less than fully secure against a reduc-
tive or restrictive existentialism. Yet the existentialist interpretation he actually practices and, to a limited extent, also
theoretically justifies is ampler than it sometimes seems to be
from certain of his statements.

The chief evidence of this is the attention he has given in
his more recent writings, beginning with his reply to his critics
of 1952, to what he speaks of as "analogy."[13] Although he unfortunately fails to develop exactly what he means by "analogy," he
does state that, while mythology can have no place in an existentialist theology, analogical speaking of God can and must have a
place in it. Furthermore, he makes clear that the specific difference of analogy from mythology is that it represents God, not in
the objectifying categories of empirical knowledge, but in the non-
objectifying "existentials" (*Existenzialien*) of Heidegger's philosophy. Analogy thus represents God's action as analogous to human
action and the relation between God and man as analogous to the
relation of men with one another. In this way, analogy, unlike
mythology, preserves God's hiddenness or transcendence because it
represents him as "a personal being acting on persons."[14]

In brief, Bultmann's theory of analogy, however fragmentary
and undeveloped, makes clear that he has no intention of excluding
by his existentialist interpretation a direct speaking of God and
his action such as Christian faith requires. Demythologizing there
must be, and it must be radical and thoroughgoing. But the positive
alternative to mythology is not existentialist interpretation alone,
but existentialist interpretation *plus* analogy--or, better said,

existentialist interpretation as inclusive of an analogical speaking
of God and his action.

    Nevertheless, because Bultmann's treatment of analogy is so
fragmentary and because his aversion to direct speaking of God is
so marked, his position does have a certain one-sidedness that
requires correction. And here is where I see the great importance
of Charles Hartshorne's philosophical theology. I believe it can
be shown that Hartshorne's dipolar view of God provides a virtually
exact counterpart to Heidegger's existentialist analysis of man.
By attempting to take seriously "the religious idea of God" and
working out a conception of the divine in strict analogy to personal
existence, Hartshorne presents in its fullness what is barely more
than postulated as Bultmann's fragmentary remarks on analogy. He
thus provides a means for correcting Bultmann's one-sided existentialism by offering a precise philosophical conceptuality in which
God as well as man can be appropriately spoken about in nonmythological terms. My view is that Bultmann's existentialist solution
to the problem of the meaning of theological statements can be fully
justified, in accordance with his own intention in proposing it,
only when Heidegger's existentialist analysis is complemented or
supplemented by something like Hartshorne's dipolar theism.[15]

    I have spoken of Bultmann's existentialist one-sidedness only
with certain misgivings. This is because I profoundly share his
conviction that all theological statements are, directly or indirectly, existential statements and that there are serious dangers
in speaking as though only *some* such statements are existential,
while others have to do not with man but with God and his action.
I fear my proposal just now to supplement Bultmann's position with
Hartshorne's--or, rather to bring the two positions together into
one integrated position--is open to just this misunderstanding. I
would stress, therefore, that in calling for the correction of
Bultmann's one-sided existentialism by Hartshorne's fully developed
theism, I in no way intend to abandon the position that *all* theological statements are existential statements. That no such abandonment is logically required seems evident to me because, for
Hartshorne, no less than for Bultmann, to speak of God and his action here and now is also always to speak of man and his possibilities of self-understanding, and, of course, *vice versa*.[16]

    The second problem posed by Bultmann's project of existentialist
interpretation--or, rather, by his own execution of that project--
arises from his failure consistently to carry it out. I have argued
at length elsewhere[17] that he stops short of a thoroughgoing

existentialist interpretation of theological statements in the central matter of christology. In the manner of the radically "christocentric" theology that is one main strand in the Protestant tradition, he claims that authentic human existence is factually possible solely in consequence of God's unique act in Jesus Christ. Although all men simply as men have the "possibility in principle" of authentic life, this possibility becomes a "possibility in fact" for them exclusively in the event of Jesus' crucifixion, or in the proclamation of the Christian church in which that event is again and again re-presented. But, as I have sought to show, this claim as such is mythological, by Bultmann's own definition, and therefore stands in need of demythologizing, which is to say, existentialist interpretation.

In one sense, Bultmann himself recognizes this, and his existentialist interpretation of the christological statements of the New Testament and of the theological tradition is an attempt to express the existential meaning of Jesus Christ. Yet he refuses to accept the implication that the significance of Jesus is simply that he decisively manifests or re-presents man's universal possibility of authentic existence in and under the love of God. Jesus not only decisively *reveals* God's love, he claims, but actually *constitutes* it as an event, so that apart from him (or the witness of the church that proclaims him), man cannot actually realize his authentic life.

In making this claim, however, Bultmann falls back into the very mythology he wants to overcome. By saying that God acts to redeem mankind *only* in the history of Jesus Christ, he subjects God's action as the Redeemer to the objectifying categories of space and time and thus mythologizes it. Therefore, I argue, the only course open to one who wishes to follow Bultmann in his intention is to carry out his existentialist interpretation with a consistency he himself fails to display. The claim "only in Jesus Christ" must be interpreted to mean, not that God acts to redeem only in the history of Jesus and in no other history, but that the only God who redeems any history--*although he in fact redeems every history*--is the God whose redemptive action is decisively represented in the word that Jesus speaks and is.

But this position obviously has its own complex of problems and, in particular, raises the question of the sense, if any, in which one can still say with the historic Christian community that the event of Jesus Christ is the decisive act of God. Since I understand this question to be the crux of the problem before us here, it is toward answering it that the second and constructive part of the essay must be directed.

2

If one proposes to deal with the sense of theological statements in the way I have indicated, he is immediately faced with the
question of analogy. It is well known that this question has been
and still is perhaps the most complex and difficult question the
theologian faces. Its difficulty is felt with particular force today because it is widely believed by contemporary philosophers and
theologians that the classical theory of analogy cannot be maintained, since it fails to solve the problem it purports to solve.
Intended to provide a middle way between univocality and equivo-
cality--or between anthropomorphism and agnosticism--it actually
does nothing but oscillate uneasily between the two extremes, caught
in an inescapable dilemma.[18] Thus Ferré argues persuasively that
"it is no longer possible . . . to hold that the logic of analogy,
as it has normally been interpreted, is cogent" and proposes that
it be reassigned a purely "formal" instead of a "material" function
in "the manifold logic of theism."[19]

While recognizing the complexity and difficulty of this question, I, too, hold that the classical theory of analogy is untenable. Instead of solving the problem it is intended to solve, it
but reflects and perpetuates the problem in the way its modern
critics have so often pointed out. But I also hold that the problematic character of the classical theory of analogy is entirely of
a piece with the problems posed by classical theism generally and
is, indeed, but a particularly clear evidence of the indefensibility
of this theological position. Because classical theism is the impossible attempt to synthesize the personalistic view of God of
Holy Scripture with the substance ontology of classical Greek
philosophy, the theory of analogy it develops to rationalize its
procedures cannot but be an inconsistent and untenable theory.

Still, to grant that the classical theory of analogy is untenable is not to concede the untenability of all theories of
analogy--any more than to reject a classical theistic position as
indefensible is to say that no theistic position can be defended.
On the contrary, Hartshorne has amply demonstrated that a consistent logic of analogy can be developed and that the ancient dilemma
of anthropomorphism and agnosticism can be resolved without in any
way prejudicing the claims of Christian faith.[20] That he does this
only by taking the dilemma by the horns and working out a frankly
"anthropomorphic" view of God must be admitted. But he also con-
vincingly shows that the traditional prejudices against such a view

spring, not from commitment to the understanding of God attested
by Scripture (with which understanding, on the contrary, this view
is perfectly compatible), but rather from the tacit assumption of
the premises of classical metaphysics.[21]

The crucial insight of the neoclassical theism Hartshorne has
pioneered in developing is that God is to be conceived in strict
analogy with the human self or person. The force of the word
"strict" is that God, as Whitehead says, is not to be treated as an
exception to metaphysical principles, but rather is to be understood as exemplifying them.[22] Thus, for example, if to be a self
is possible only by being related to and dependent on others, and
most directly on the others that constitute one's body, then God
also can be conceived only as related to and dependent on the others
that constitute his body, which is to say, the whole world of
created beings. On the other hand, the word "analogy" reminds us
that God is not a self in univocally the same sense as man--that,
as Whitehead puts it, God is not simply *an* exemplification of metaphysical principles, but is their *"chief"* exemplification.[23] So,
whereas the human self is effectively related only to a very few
others--indeed, only to a very few others within the intimate
world of its own body--the divine Self is effectively related to
all others in such a way that there are no gradations of intimacy
of the various creatures to it. God is not located in a particular
space and time, but rather is omnipresent and eternal, in the sense
that he is directly present to all spaces and times and they to
him.

Or, to take another illustration of the same point, God's dependence on his world, which is a real and not merely verbal dependence, is by no means simply the same as man's dependence on his
world or body. We are dependent on our bodies not only for whether
we shall be in this actual state or that, but also for whether we
shall be in any actual state at all. Ours is, we may say, a dependence both for actuality and for existence. In the case of God,
however, there is no existential dependence, but only an actual
dependence. *That* God is, in some actual state or other, or in relation to some actual world, is dependent on nothing whatever and
is in the strictest sense necessary. The only thing that is contingent (and that only in part) is *what* God is, what actual state
of the literally infinite number of states possible for him is in
fact actualized; and this depends both on his own contingent or
free decisions and on the free decisions of the creatures who constitute his world.[24]

But, if God is thus to be conceived in strict analogy to the
human self, his action must be understood in strict analogy to the
action of man. In saying this, however, one must take pains to
clarify exactly what is meant by man's action. We ordinarily understand a human act to be a specific word or deed whereby, through
the instrumentality of the body and its various members, the self
undertakes to carry out its particular purposes or projects. Thus
I may be said to be acting in any attempt by means of the written
word to communicate my understanding of the issues of the present
discussion. And yet this ordinary meaning of the words "human act"
is certainly not their only or even primary meaning. Both Heidegger
and Hartshorne, each in a different way, remind us that human action is also to be understood in another and more fundamental sense
as the action whereby the self as such is constituted. Behind all
its public acts of word and deed there are the self's own private
purposes or projects, which are themselves matters of action or
decision. Indeed, it is only because the self first acts to constitute itself, to respond to its world, and to decide its own inner being that it "acts" at all in the more ordinary meaning of the
word; all its outer acts of word and deed are but ways of expressing
and implementing the inner decisions whereby it constitutes itself
as a self.

These decisions by which the human self acts to constitute its
own inner being may take one or the other of two basic forms--or,
as we may also say, the self is always confronted with two basic
possibilities for understanding itself in relation to its world.[25]
Either it can open itself to its world and make its decisions by
sensitively responding to all the influences that bear upon it, or
it may close itself against its world and make its decisions on the
basis of a much more restricted sensitivity than is actually possible for it. In other words, man can act either as a self who
loves and thus participates as fully and completely as he can in
his own being and in the being of others, or he can act as a self
who hates and thus is estranged both from the more intimate world
of his own bodily life and the larger world of fellow selves and
creatures. In the first case, all his outward acts of word and
deed will be in function of the inner act whereby he constitutes
himself as one who loves--just as in the second case, by contrast,
all his "acts" in the more ordinary sense of the word will but express or implement the primal act of a self who hates.

Now, if God's action is to be understood by strict analogy to
the action of man, what is meant by man's action is, first of all,

this inner act whereby the human self as such is constituted, and constituted, moreover, as a self who loves. According to the central claim of the Christian witness of faith, the being of God is a being of "pure unbounded love" (Charles Wesley). I take this to imply that the primary meaning of God's action is the act whereby, in each new present, he constitutes himself as God by participating fully and completely in the world of his creatures, thereby laying the ground for the next stage of the creative process. Because his love, unlike ours, is pure and unbounded, his relation to his creatures and theirs to him is direct and immediate. The closest analogy--and it is but an analogy--is our relation to our own bodily states, especially the states of our brains. Whereas we can act on other persons and be acted on by them only through highly indirect means such as spoken words and bodily actions, the interaction that takes place between our selves or minds and our own brain cells is much more intimate and direct. We respond with virtual immediacy to the impulses that come from our brains, and it is over our brains (or their individual cells) that our decisions as selves or minds exercise a virtually direct power or control. I hold with Hartshorne that the interaction between God and the world must be understood analogously to this interaction between our own minds and bodies--with the difference that the former interaction takes place, not between God and a selected portion of his world (analogous to our own brain cells and central nervous system), but between God and the whole world of his creatures. Because his love or power of participation in the being of others is literally boundless, there are no gradations in intimacy of the creatures to him, and so there can be nothing in him corresponding to our nervous system or sense organs. The whole world is, as it were, his sense organ, and his interaction with every creature is unimaginably immediate and direct.

It is in terms of this conception, in which God's action is conceived by strict analogy to man's, that I believe one may appropriately interpret the Christian faith in God as Creator and Redeemer and the traditional theological statements in which that faith has found expression. On this conception, to say that God acts as the Creator is not merely to say that both I and my world are utterly dependent on his power and love and that I am bound to be obedient to his will as it pertains to myself and my world. That this existential meaning is the *indirect* meaning of the statement is to be readily granted. But what it *directly* says is that the ultimate ground of every actual state of the world is

not just the individual decisions of the creatures who constitute
its antecedent states, but rather these decisions as responded to
by God's own decision of pure unbounded love. In a similar way,
to say that God acts as Redeemer is to say more than that I now
have the possibility of that radical freedom from myself and openness to my world that constitutes the authentic existence of love.
It is also to say--and that directly--that the final destiny both
of myself and of all my fellow creatures is to contribute ourselves
not only to the self-creation of the subsequent worlds of creatures,
but also the self-creation of God, who accepts us without condition
into his own everlasting life, where we have a final standing or
security that can nevermore be lost.

I cannot now explore the ramifications of this basic conception
or show how it might be used to provide a nonmythological interpretation of all the claims implicit in the Christian understanding
of God. But I hope even this brief outline will make clear what
is meant by saying that an adequate existentialist interpretation
of theological statements must be understood to include an analogi-
ical speaking of God and his action. I have tried to show that,
although all theological statements directly or indirectly have an
existential significance, the direct reference of *some* theological
statements is not to man and his possibilities of decision, but to
God and his action as Creator and Redeemer.

I now turn directly to the question, "What sense does it make
to say, 'God acts in history'?" It may appear that the line of
thought just developed is a strange preparation for answering this
question. The force of the preceding argument is to affirm that
God's action, in its fundamental sense, is not an action in history
at all. Although his action as Creator is related to history--in-
deed, is the action in which all historical events are ultimately
grounded--his creative action as such is not an action *in* history,
but an action that *transcends* it--just as, by analogy, our own inner decisions as selves are not simply identical with any of our
outer acts of word and deed, but rather transcend or lie behind
them as the decisions in which our words and deeds are gounded and
to which they give expression. Likewise, God's action as the Redeemer cannot be simply identified with any particular historical
event or events. As the act whereby he ever and again actualizes
his own divine essence by responding in love to all the creatures
in his world, it is an act that transcends the world as the world's
ultimate consequence--just as, again by analogy, the acts whereby
we constitute our own selves by responding to our worlds can never

be identified with any of the things within these worlds to which
we respond. Yet, if this conception is valid, it may seem to make
any statement that God acts *within* history impossible. Does it
not, in fact, completely rule out all such statements by representing God's act as something necessarily timeless and unhistorical?

I respond, in the first place, by suggesting that such words
as "timeless" and "unhistorical" do not conduce to clarity in
grasping the fundamental issue. If the viewpoint set forth here
is correct, there is a real sense--namely, an analogical sense--in
which God as well as man is a temporal and historical being. Because God is to be understood in strict analogy to the human self
or person, one must distinguish in him, no less than in man, between what he essentially is and the contingent acts or states in
which his essence is again and again actualized. God is not the
timeless Absolute of classical metaphysics, who may be said to act
only in some Pickwickian sense that bears no real analogy to anything we know as action. Instead, he is the living dynamic God of
Holy Scripture, to whom the temporal distinctions of past, present,
and future may be properly applied and whose being is the eminent
instance of historical being. And yet, because God's historicity
is an *eminent* historicity, it must never be confused with the
ordinary historicity of man or of the other creatures. God acts,
and he acts in the strict sense of the word; but his action is
his action, and it cannot be simply identified with the action of
ordinary historical beings.

Is there no sense, then, in which God may be meaningfully
said to act *in* history? There are, I believe, two senses in which
this may be said.

If we recall the basic insight that God is to be conceived by
strict analogy to the human self and that, in particular, his relation to the world is to be viewed as analogous to our own relation to our bodies, then we may say that every creature is to some
extent God's act--just as, by analogy, all our bodily actions are
to some extent our actions as selves. There is, to be sure, a
certain freedom on the part of the creatures so that they are the
result not only of God's action but also of their own; in part, at
least, they are self-created. Still, this creaturely freedom has
definite limits ultimately grounded in God's own free decisions,
and in this sense every creature has its basis in God's creative
action. Although the acts whereby God actualizes his essence are
his acts and not the acts of the creatures, each creature is what

it is only by partly reflecting or expressing in its being God's
free decisions.

This is the first sense in which God may be meaningfully said
to act in history. But there is also a second sense in which this
may be said, and with it we come to the crux of our problem.

It is the distinct prerogative of the uniquely human being
that it not only is, but also knows or understands that it is. Man
has the capacity of consciousness or of self-consciousness, with
the result that he is uniquely the creature of meaning. He is able
to understand himself and his fellow creatures and the divine
reality in which they have their origin and end and, through his
thought and language, is able to bring all this to unique expression. As *logos* himself, he is able to grasp the *logos* of reality
as such and to represent it through symbolic speech and action.

This capacity to discern meaning and to give it symbolic expression is what lies behind the whole complex phenomenon of human
culture. Thus it also lies behind the particular cultural expression ordinarily designated "religion." What constitutes religion
as one form of culture alongside of others is man's attempt to
express the ultimate meaning of his existence by grasping the
divine *logos* that he encounters in his experience and re-presenting
it through appropriate symbolic means. All the various historical
religions are so many such attempts, and each of them implicitly
or explicitly makes the claim that through it man is decisively
confronted with the word that reveals the ultimate truth about his
existence.

This is to say that man as the being who can understand his
existence and express its meaning symbolically through word and
deed can, at least in principle, also re-present or speak for the
divine. Insofar as what comes to expression through his speech
and action is the gift and demand signified by God's transcendent
action as Creator and Redeemer, he re-presents not only his own
understanding of God's action, but, through it, the reality of
God's action itself. As a matter of fact, one may even say that,
in this case, man's action actually *is* God's action--just as, in
our case, our outer acts of word and deed may be said to be ours
just because or insofar as they give (or are understood to give)
expression to the inner actions whereby we constitute our existence
as selves.

In one sense, of course, all our bodily actions, including the
actions of all our organs and cells, are our actions because they
are to some extent the result of the inner decisions by which we

actualize our selves or persons. And we have just seen that there
is something analogous to this in the case of God, that every
creature in his body or world is to some extent his action because
it is created by him by being ultimately grounded in the decisions
through which he realizes his own divine essence. Yet I think
we all recognize that, although all our actions are equally ours,
some of them are peculiarly ours in a way that the others are not,
especially in our relations with other persons. This is particularly true of those distinctively human actions in which, through
word and deed, we give symbolic expression to our own inner beings
and understandings. Such actions are, as we say, our "characteristic" actions, since, in them or through them, the persons we are,
are uniquely re-presented or revealed to others. Each of us is
known to other persons through such acts, and all the other things
that we may be and do are interpreted by our fellows in terms of
what they understand to be typically *our* statements and actions.

Thus, to take a specific example, my understanding of my wife,
and of myself in relation to her, is based upon certain of her
words and deeds in a way that it is not based on the many other
things that she is and says and does. Who she is for me is who I
understand her to be in terms of certain quite particular events,
having a "once-for-all" historical character, that I take to be
revelatory of her person and attitude as they relate to me. It is
true that my understanding of her is to some extent constantly
changing in the light of new "revelations" of her being and that I
can never be absolutely certain she really is as I understand her
to be. Even so, not everything she says and does is equally important in revealing her to me, and I always think of her in terms of
certain actions that are hers in a sense that the other things
she does are not.

It is because we all commonly understand one another in this
way that we are occasionally even led to deny that someone has done
something he has in fact done because the action in question is
understood to be so untypical or out of character. Thus it is not
unusual to find ourselves saying such things as, "Why, John
wouldn't do that!"

In short, some of our outer acts of word and deed either are
in fact or at least are understood to be *our* acts in a way that
others are not. Because certain of our actions give peculiarly
apt expression to what we are (or are rightly or wrongly believed
to be by others), these actions *are* our actions (or are believed
to be our actions) in a special sense.

A strictly analogous statement can be made about the actions
of God. Although every creature, as we have seen, is in one sense
his act, certain creaturely happenings may be said to be his act
in another and quite special sense. Wherever or insofar as an
event in history manifests God's characteristic action as Creator
and Redeemer, it actually *is* his act in a sense in which other
historical events are not.

It will be obvious from what has been said that the possibility of being such a special act of God is peculiarly open to those
uniquely human events in which man expresses his understanding of
the ultimate meaning of his existence through symbolic speech and
action. Because man, at least in principle, can grasp and express
the ultimate truth about his life, his words and deeds always carry
within themselves, so to speak, the possibility of becoming an act
of God. It is also possible, naturally, that they will not become
God's act, that the understanding to which they give expression
will not re-present the divine *logos* or will re-present it only in
a fragmentary or distorted way. The existence of the several
historical religions is a constant reminder that this possibility
is in fact actualized; for given the quite different and conflicting understandings of existence expressed in these religions,
they cannot all be true and so cannot all be genuine revelations or
acts of God. But wherever or insofar as particular religious
symbols appropriately re-present God's action as Creator and Redeemer, they actually are or become his act in a sense strictly
analogous to the sense in which some of our own symbolic actions
are our acts in a way others are not.

Of course, it is not such intentionally symbolic actions alone
that have the possibility of being special acts of God. Any event,
whether intended by anyone as symbolic or not, can become such an
act of God insofar as it is received by someone as a symbol of
God's creative and redemptive action. Because man is distinctively
the creature of meaning, there is no event he experiences that
cannot become for him such a symbol. The objective ground of this
possibility is that, by the "analogy of being" (*analogia entis*),
not only man himself, but also every event or creature is in some
sense the image or reflection of the transcendent God and therefore
expresses God's being and action in its own creaturely nature. It
may be argued that one can discern this symbolic meaning in any
event only in the light of some intentionally symbolic action such
as a human word or deed through which the meaning of God's action
is re-presented. The truth in this argument is that man is the

creature of meaning and his encounter with reality and understanding of it are ordinarily mediated by such intentionally symbolic
structures as concepts and language. But it would be wrong to
assign such intentional symbols any absolute priority. After all,
they themselves are the products of man's immediate encounter with
reality, and so are not original but derived. If we must decide
the question of priority as between the symbolic meaning of events
themselves and the intentionally symbolic meaning of our own words
and deeds, the former is undoubtedly prior. The various religions,
like human culture generally, all have the character of a response
to something more original than themselves. They are human attempts
in face of the actual events of existence to discern the divine
word or meaning of which these events are understood to be the symbols.

And yet, because man is the creature of meaning and ordinarily
understands and expresses his existence through the intentionally
symbolic actions of human words and deeds, such actions are uniquely
adapted to become acts of God. Therefore, what is meant when we
say that God acts *in* history is primarily that there are certain
distinctively human words and deeds in which his characteristic
action as Creator and Redeemer is appropriately re-presented or
revealed. We mean that there are some human actions, some specific
attempts to express the ultimate truth of our existence through
symbolic words and deeds, that are vastly more than merely human
actions. Because through them nothing less than the transcendent
action of God himself is re-presented, they are also acts of God,
that is, they *are* acts of God analogously to the way in which our
outer acts *are* our acts insofar as they re-present our own characteristic decisions as selves or persons.

Against this background, I may now answer the question raised
at the end of the first part of the essay. I asked there how one
can overcome Bultmann's own inconsistency in carrying out his
project of existentialist interpretation while still affirming with
the Christian community that the history of Jesus of Nazareth is
the decisive act of God.[26] If the preceding argument is correct,
to say of any historical event that it is the "decisive" act of
God can only mean that, in it, in distinction from all other historical events, the ultimate truth about our existence before God
is normatively re-presented or revealed. The decisiveness of the
event, in other words, lies in its power to decide between all the
different and conflicting historical claims to reveal the divine
logos or meaning everywhere discernible to our experience. In

this sense, a decisive act of God is the "revelation of revelations" or, in Paul Tillich's word, the "final" revelation that
provides the criterion by which all putative revelations are at
once judged and fulfilled.[27]

That any event ever becomes such a decisive act of God is,
naturally, also a function of its being received and understood by
someone as having decisive revelatory power. A revelation is not
only a revelation *of something* (or someone), but also a revelation
to somebody--just as analogously, in the example above, certain of
my wife's words and deeds reveal her being for me both because
they in fact express her inner attitude toward me and because I receive them as having such expressive power by understanding her and
myself in relation to her in the way they concretely make possible.
Indeed, this second or "subjective" component in the revelatory
correlation is existentially fundamental. No event can become a
decisive act of God for us unless we receive it as determinative
of our self-understanding; and, as has been indicated, we may receive events as thus decisive, and so as final revelations of God's
being and action, which in fact do not re-present his gift and demand as they actually confront us. This is the reason Luther can
say in the statement so often quoted from the *Large Catechism* that
"the trust and the faith of the heart alone make both God and an
idol. . . . For these two belong together, faith and God. That to
which your heart clings and entrusts itself, is, I say, really your
God."[28]

On the other hand, Luther also recognizes that there is a
"wrong" as well as a "right" faith and that it is only when "your
faith and trust are right" that "your God is the true God."[29] What
constitutes such "right" faith he subsequently explains when he
says that God "wishes to turn us away from everything else, and to
draw us to himself, because he is the one eternal good."[30] In
other words, there is an "objective" as well as a "subjective" component in the revelatory correlation, and this means that an event
is a decisive revelation of God only insofar as it truly re-presents
the existential gift and demand of "the one eternal good." This
it can do only to the extent that its form or structure is such
that the possibility of self-understanding it expresses is in fact
the true or authentic understanding of human existence.

To say with the Christian community, then, that *Jesus* is the
decisive act of God is to say that in him, in his outer acts of
symbolic word and deed, there is expressed *that* understanding of
human existence which is, in fact, the ultimate truth about our

life before God; that the ultimate reality with which we and all
men have to do is God the sovereign Creator and Redeemer, and that
in understanding ourselves in terms of the gift and demand of his
love, we realize our authentic existence as men.

Presupposed by this argument is the conviction that the entire
reality of Jesus' history--at any rate, as it is presented to us
in the Gospels--is simply a transparent means of representing a
certain possibility for understanding human existence.[31] Not only
Jesus' preaching and acts of healing, but also his fellowship with
sinners and (perhaps unintentionally) his eventual death on the
cross are so many ways of expressing symbolically an understanding
of our existence *coram deo*. They are a single witness to the truth
that all things have their ultimate beginning and end solely in
God's pure unbounded love and that it is in giving ourselves wholly
into the keeping of that love, by surrendering all other securities,
that we realize our authentic life. In relation to this understanding of human existence and to the one task of giving it appropriate
symbolic expression through word and deed, everything in Jesus'
history is strictly instrumental. He knows no other work than to
reveal the love of the Father in all its radical meaning as gift and
demand, and he neither makes nor tolerates any claims other than
those that this love itself makes or implies (cf. e.g., Luke 11:27
f.; Mark 3:31-35; Matt. 7:21).

But if this understanding of existence that Jesus re-presents
is true, if we really are created and redeemed by God's sovereign
love, then, in a real sense, Jesus himself *is* God's decisive act in
human history. For in him, in the word that he speaks and is,
God's action as Creator and Redeemer is expressed with utter decisiveness; and this can only mean, for the reasons given above, that
he actually *is* God's decisive act.

We may also say, of course, that if Jesus is God's decisive
act, then the ultimate truth about our existence--indeed, about
every man's existence--is that we are created and redeemed by God's
love, and that in abandoning ourselves wholly to him we realize
our true life. It is the nature of the decision of Christian faith
that it resolves this hypothetical statement into a categorical
confession by affirming its antecedent and thus also affirming its
consequent. My conviction, to which this discussion has tried to
give support, is that both of these affirmations are valid and may
be so understood as to make sense. So far from being incompatible,
the two statements that God's act is, in one sense, not a historical
act at all, while, in another sense, it is precisely the act of

Jesus' history, mutually require and support one another. Just
when we take with complete seriousness the utter transcendence of
God's action as sovereign Creator and Redeemer, the historical
event of Jesus' life and ministry is seen to be God's decisive act
in human history. For the whole meaning of this event is to express or reveal God's transcendent love as the sole basis of our
authentic existence; and just in this fact it stands before us as
itself God's act in a sense that we both can and must affirm.[32]

NOTES

[1]*Language, Logic, and God,* New York: Harper & Row, 1961, p.
vii.

[2]*Ibid.,* pp. 8, 58.

[3]G. J. Warnock, *English Philosophy Since 1900,* London: Oxford
University Press, 1958, p. 44.

[4]See, e.g., Rudolf Bultmann, "On the Problem of Demythologizing," *Journal of Religion,* April, 1962, pp. 96-102.

[5]See my discussion in *Christ Without Myth: A Study Based on
the Theology of Rudolf Bultmann,* New York: Harper & Row, 1961,
pp. 24-31, 90-93, 146 ff., 166-70.

[6]See Rudolf Bultmann, *Jesus Christ and Mythology,* New York:
Charles Scribner's Sons, 1958, pp. 83 ff.

[7]Rudolf Bultmann, *Das Urchristentum im Rahmen der antiken
Religionen,* Zürich: Artemis Verlag, 1949, p. 11 (English translation by R. H. Fuller in Rudolf Bultmann, *Primitive Christianity in
Its Contemporary Setting,* New York: Meridian Books, Inc., 1956,
p. 15).

[8]*Glauben und Verstehen,* Vol. III, Tübingen: J. C. B. Mohr,
2d ed., 1962, p. 88.

[9]*Theology of the New Testament,* trans. Kendrick Grobel, New
York: Charles Scribner's Sons, 1951, p. 191.

[10]See, however, my essay in William L. Reese and Eugene Freeman
(eds.), *Process and Divinity: The Hartshorne Festschrift,* La Salle,
Ill.: Open Court Publishing Co., 1964, pp. 493-513.

[11]One such defense of Heidegger's philosophy is made in *Jesus
Christ and Mythology,* pp. 57 ff.

[12]See, e.g., John Macquarrie, *An Existentialist Theology: A
Comparison of Heidegger and Bultmann,* London: SCM Press Ltd., 1955,
especially pp. 240-46.

[13]H. W. Bartsch (ed.), *Kerygma und Mythos,* Vol. II, Hamburg:
Herbert Reich-Evangelischer Verlag, 1952, pp. 196 f. (English
translation by R. H. Fuller in H. W. Bartsch [ed.], *Kerygma and*

Myth, New York: Harper & Row, 2d ed., 1961, pp. 196 f.). Cf.
Jesus Christ and Mythology, pp. 60-70; and "On the Problem of De-
mythologizing," *Journal of Religion*, April, 1962, p. 101. Cf. also
my discussion in *Christ Without Myth*, pp. 90-93, 146 f., 169 f.

[14]*Jesus Christ and Mythology*, p. 70; cf. p. 68.

[15]This view is more fully worked out in the essay referred to
above in n. 10.

[16]See, e.g., Hartshorne's statement that "self-knowledge and
knowledge of God are apparently inseparable" and that "neither is
clear unless both are somehow clear" ("The Idea of God--Literal
or Analogical?" *Christian Scholar*, June, 1956, p. 136).

[17]*Christ Without Myth*, pp. 111-26.

[18]See, e.g., Frederick C. Copleston, *Contemporary Philosophy*,
London: Burns & Oates, 1956, p. 96.

[19]*Op. cit.*, pp. 76 f., 154.

[20]In addition to Hartshorne's essay referred to above in n. 16,
see his arguments in *Man's Vision of God and the Logic of Theism*,
New York: Harper & Brothers, 1941, especially pp. 174-205, and
*The Logic of Perfection and Other Essays in Neoclassical Metaphys-
ics*, La Salle, Ill.: Open Court Publishing Co., 1962, especially
pp. 133-47.

[21]See especially *Man's Vision of God*, pp. 85-141.

[22]Alfred North Whitehead, *Process and Reality: An Essay in
Cosmology*, New York: The Macmillan Co., 1929, p. 521. Another way
of explaining what is meant by "strict" is made clear by Hartshorne
when he argues that there must be a literal as well as an analogical
sense in which fundamental concepts refer to God ("The Idea of God--
Literal or Analogical?" *Christian Scholar*, June, 1956, p. 136).

[23]*Op. cit.*, p. 521.

[24]It is just this distinction between actuality and existence,
and so between actual and existential dependence, that those who
express an exaggerated fear of "anthropomorphism" commonly fail
to recognize. When Paul Tillich argues, for instance, that "a God
who is not able to anticipate every possible future is dependent
on an absolute accident and cannot be the foundation of an ultimate
courage" (*Systematic Theology*, Vol. I, Chicago: The University
of Chicago Press, 1951, pp. 275 f.), he completely ignores this
distinction and so is forced to realize one legitimate theological
motive (the absoluteness of God's existence) only by sacrificing
another (the relativity of God's actuality). For a discussion of
the theological importance of the distinction as it is clarified
in Whitehead's philosophy, see Charles Hartshorne, *Reality as
Social Process: Studies in Metaphysics and Religion*, Glencoe, Ill.:
The Free Press, 1953, pp. 204-7.

[25]Cf. Rudolf Bultmann, *Glauben und Verstehen*, Vol. I, Tübingen:
J. C. B. Mohr, 2d ed., 1954, pp. 222 f.

[26]In the remainder of the discussion, I am particularly mindful
of the criticism directed to me in different ways in the reviews
of *Christ Without Myth* by Rudolf Bultmann (*Journal of Religion*,

July, 1962, pp. 225 ff.) and James M. Robinson (*Christian Advocate,* February 1, 1962, pp. 11 f., and *Union Seminary Quarterly Review,* May, 1962, pp. 359-62). I trust the following argument makes clear that, although, like any other Christian theologian, I naturally affirm Jesus Christ to be the decisive act of God, I understand this affirmation in a sufficiently different sense from Bultmann and Robinson to avoid any inconsistency with thoroughgoing demythologizing and existentialist interpretation.

[27] See *Systematic Theology,* Vol I., pp. 132-37.

[28] Theodore G. Tappert (ed.), *The Book of Concord,* Philadelphia: Muhlenberg Press, 1959, p. 365.

[29] *Ibid.*

[30] *Ibid.,* p. 366.

[31] This conviction is illuminated and supported by the results of the so-called "new quest of the historical Jesus." See James M. Robinson, *A New Quest of the Historical Jesus,* London: SCM Press Ltd., 1959; also my essay, "Bultmann and the 'New Quest,'" *Journal of Bible and Religion,* July, 1962, pp. 209-18.

[32] Cf. Gerhard Ebeling, *Wort und Glaube,* Tübingen: J. C. B. Mohr, 1960, p. 343 (English translation by J. W. Leitch in Gerhard Ebeling, *Word and Faith,* Philadelphia: Fortress Press, 1963, p. 327): "That man fails in the right use of the word in relation to his fellow man, and thus also in relation to God, makes the question of the word a burning question. What is the true, necessary, healing, justifying, and therefore unambiguous and crystal clear word, which, because it accords with man's destiny, corresponds to God? What is the word through which one man can impart God to another, so that God comes to man and man to God? That salvation is to be expected from God alone and that it is to be expected from the word alone, and that therefore it is both wholly of God and wholly of man--these statements are not paradoxes or oddities" (my translation).

7. NATURAL CAUSALITY AND DIVINE ACTION*

John B. Cobb, Jr.

The idea of God's action in history was prominent in the
Biblical theology of the past generation. This theology was generally opposed to philosophic explication of its doctrine of God, and
consequently it is difficult to say just what it meant by divine
action. In any case, that movement faded and, with it, talk of
God's acts.

However, the idea that God is active in a way that affects the
course of human affairs is too basic to the Biblical-Christian
tradition to be set aside with the demise of one theological movement. A God who in no sense acts in or on history would be a very
different God from that of Western religion and philosophy. God
must be some kind of a cause of events or else there is no point
in speaking of him at all.

To show that God is a cause of some kind, however, is a difficult task both because of the current confusion about theism and
because of the equal confusion about causality. Since a short paper
cannot deal adequately with either topic, I shall simplify, and
hence partly distort, by employing the scheme of the Aristotelian
four causes. My chief interest, like that of most of modernity,
centers on efficient causality, but the categories of formal, material, and final cause are also relevant for contemporary views
of God as cause.

In Section I, I argue that since the collapse of attempts to
see God as an efficient cause of and in the Newtonian world, theologians have turned increasingly to other ways of conceiving God's
relation to the world. This relation can be viewed as that of
formal, material, or final cause. Few if any theologians consistently and exclusively limit God's causality to one of these modes,
but strong tendencies in each direction can be found. Henry Nelson
Wieman, Paul Tillich, and Wolfhart Pannenberg respectively embody
tendencies to treat God as formal, material, and final cause.

* An earlier version of this paper was read at the meeting of
The Metaphysical Society of America in Toronto, Ontario, on
March 19, 1971.

From *Idealistic Studies* 3(1973): 207-22. Reprinted with permission.

However, none succeeds in developing a satisfactory position without including elements of efficient causality as well.

In Section II, I offer a brief analysis of the recent discussion of efficient causality and propose that the positive elements in this perplexing notion can be found in two related but distinct ideas: (1) grounds for prediction and (2) actual influence. In Section III, I show that the second of these provides the most appropriate basis for conceiving of God's causality. This allows for a demythologized but richly meaningful interpretation of divine action. God's major action consists in rendering effective an appropriate and creative final causation.

My whole discussion is heavily indebted to Whitehead's account of causal efficacy and its relation to creativity, possibility, and God. However, I have avoided use of his terminology and appeal to his authority.

I

Newtonian science directed attention increasingly to efficient causes, and the fate of the idea of cause has been deeply shaped by that fact. Further, Biblical language about God strongly suggests this kind of agency on his part. Hence Christian theology and modern philosophy alike have dealt chiefly with God's action in terms of efficient causation. In the dominant Newtonian model of natural causality, what is caused is changed, and change is ultimately explicable in terms of locomotion. Change in place (or change in speed or direction) is attributable to the impact of other masses. The change as effect is necessitated by the cause.

The primary way in which God as efficient cause could be viewed in relation to the natural world was as its maker. He created masses and set them in motion. Further he was the author of the laws that governed the motions. And finally he might be seen as occasionally altering the motions for special purposes.

Philosophical criticism dissolved the Newtonian idea of efficient causality. This idea entailed the necessitation of the effect by the cause. But Hume showed that such necessitation cannot be publicly observed. We observe more or less regular successions, but we do not observe any *necessity* in this relation.

The Newtonian idea of efficient cause allows the movement of thought from observed effects to inferred causes. Arguments to God from the world as a whole or from particular features of it were meaningful, if not conclusive. But if efficient causality refers only to observed regularity of succession, only observable

states of affairs can be inferred from effects. Inferential arguments to God are excluded in principle. Indeed, in this context,
any affirmation of divine efficient causation is meaningless. If
one continues to speak of God as creator of the world or as acting
in history, either his language is meaningless, or its meaning must
be explained in terms that do not entail efficient causation. Such
explanation is not easy, but it has been seriously attempted in
several ways. These will here be schematized under the headings
formal cause, material cause, and final cause.

If God is not viewed as efficient cause, one alternative is
to see him as a formal cause. The formal cause of the world as a
whole is constantly changing, and it so mixes evil with good that
few would be inclined to name it God. But if attention is focused
on creative and redemptive processes alone, then the formal cause
of these processes may be thought of as God.

For example, some define God as love. They do not mean, presumably, that every individual instance of love in its full concreteness *is* God. That would leave us with billions of gods, almost all dead. They mean rather that love as such, love as an essence or form, is God. Every loving act and thought participates
in love and hence in God. God is present in every such occurrence.
But God remains one and eternal.

The position of Henry Nelson Wieman can be interpreted as a
much more significant presentation of God as formal cause. For
him God is that process in which human good grows. That is the
process of creative interchange in which all participants are
transformed in unforeseeable ways. Wieman describes this process
with insight and skill.

It is possible to read Wieman as meaning that such processes
in their full concreteness are God, but that would mean unnumerable
gods or else launch us into speculation about the unity of all such
processes. Wieman opposes such speculation. The alternative is to
understand God as the common form of all such processes, that is,
as their formal cause.

Wieman's position has the great advantage of rendering God's
reality and his effective presence in the world indisputable.
There *are* processes in which human good grows, and Wieman has shown
that it is possible to describe what these processes have in common. Instead of arguing about the nature of God and speculating
in his mode of operation in the world, men can proceed to commit
themselves to the process of creative interchange and to further
its effectiveness.

However, problems remain. If God is the formal cause of
creative interchange and that only, his status is that of an abstraction. But for Wieman it is the actual process and not its
abstract form that is the suitable object of commitment. Much of
the persuasiveness of Wieman's work depends on images of God as
actual and acting that can apply only to the particular processes.
In other words, the apparent continuity of this conception of God
with historic Western meanings depends on a language that attributes to the common form an efficient causality characteristic
rather of its individual embodiments.

A second possibility is to view God as the ultimate in the
order of material causes. That would mean today that we analyze
the composition of entities or events guided by modern scientific
knowledge. We would, for example, view living bodies as composed
of cells; cells, of molecules; molecules, of atoms; atoms, of electrons, protons, neutrons, etc.; and these, perhaps, of quarks.
But assuming the analysis of quarks cannot be into some subquarkic
entities, we would have to say that the material cause of quarks
is prime matter in Aristotle's sense, i.e., that which exists only
in definite entities but which constitutes their matter. Today
we would do better to call it energy-as-such, or activity-as-such,
or in Whitehead's terms, creativity, rather than "matter," but it
functions for modern scientific vision as prime matter functions
for Aristotle's. Energy-as-such is certainly real, it gives
reality to everything else, but it does not exist in itself. It
is not a being, but it is that by virtue of which all beings are.

Can energy as such become the focus of devotion or commitment,
i.e., God? Something like this appears to occur in that philosophical Hindu tradition where Brahman can be interpreted in these
terms. Brahman is ultimate reality, that by virtue of which all
things are, and that into which all things return. He is not a
being, but the being of all beings. No concept applies to him for
he is beyond all forms. The forms of things come and go, but
Brahman is unaffected by this flux. He is indeed the dynamic and
eternal ultimate material cause of all things.

In the orthodox Western tradition the identification of God
with Being and the accompanying emphasis on the *via negativa* suggests a similar vision. However, for the most part Being has meant
the necessary being and the act by which beings exist rather than
being-as-such. The relation of the necessary being to contingent
beings has been understood as that act in which contingent beings
receive their being rather than as the being they embody. The

relation has thus been one of efficient causality rather than of
material causality. But recently, partly under the influence of
Heidegger's renewal of the question of being, a profound shift has
occurred. God is now widely understood as being-as-such rather
than as *a* being, even *the* necessary being. Paul Tillich is the
most influential exponent of this move.

Although Tillich does not understand his position as idenfi-
fying God with the ultimate material cause, the implications of
his move are definitely in this direction. Whatever else can and
should be said about Tillich's theology, God does function for him
as the ground of all beings in a way analogous to Aristotle's
prime matter and Whitehead's creativity.

If "ultimacy" and "ontological transcendence" are the keys
to the understanding of God, and if ultimacy can no longer be
sought in the chain of efficient causes, then the shift to seeing
God as material cause is strongly indicated. That there is an ultimate in the series of material causes is hard to dispute, whereas
ultimacy in any other direction is today problematic. Further,
the ultimate material cause must be ontologically different from
every other material cause in a fully radical way. It is eternal,
immutable, and transcendent of all categories of thought. Understood as energy or activity, it is readily symbolized in dynamic
categories and as creative act. Since it seems to be present and
effective to a higher degree in higher entities, it can be understood as more fully manifest in them, and it is easy to speak as
if it had a teleological thrust toward such manifestation.

It is understandable, therefore, that Tillich's language about
Being-itself employs symbols of directionality and even purposive-
ness. In this way he assimilates Being to the Western understanding of God. But he knows that he cannot attribute such character-
istics to being in any straightforward sense. Hence a doctrine
of symbolic use of language is important to him. He strives to
justify the symbolic attribution to God of modes of activity that
are strictly incompatible with Being as ultimate material cause.
The reader is left with the strong impression that God functions
also as in some respects final and efficient cause even though no
conceptual clarification is given as to how this is possible.

Tillich has pointed us to one solution of the current difficulty in conceiving God and his action. "God" can be identified
with "ultimate reality," and "ultimate reality" can legitimately
be explained as the ultimate material cause of all things. It
may be called energy, activity, or Being. Its reality and

importance cannot be intelligently denied once they are understood.

On the other hand, the difference between the ultimate material cause of all things and God as generally conceived in the
Western tradition is greater than it is made to appear. The
reader who interprets "Being" strictly as material cause, and who
distinguishes sharply between material causality on the one hand
and efficient and final causality on the other, will find strained
much of the conventional Western and Christian language Tillich
employs. Most important, the ultimate material cause cannot favor
good or evil. It is impartial with respect to all moral distinctions. Brahmanism has more consistently drawn out the religious
implications of worshiping ultimate reality in this sense than has
Tillich. Either some sense must be made of divine final and efficient causation or belief in God in the Western sense must be
abandoned.

The doctrine that God is final cause is deeply rooted in Greek
philosophy and generally congenial to the Biblical-Christian tradition. God is the good which inspires and moves all things. But
this has generally meant that God is conceived as an extant supernatural reality who can be known as the supreme and supremely attractive good. In the Christian tradition his goodness consists
especially in his gifts of creation and redemption which entail
efficient causality.

The modern mind does not allow for a supernatural sphere in
which such a God is now extant. The requisite spatial images of
transcendence have lost all credibility. If there is a supreme
final cause, it is not conceived as existing alongside the world
but rather as that toward which the world moves. Transcendence
is conceived temporally rather than spatially. God is man's future.

In the contemporary theologies of hope, man is viewed as open
to the future and as shaped by that future. For Pannenberg, who
is the most conceptually rigorous and consistent of these thinkers,
the fundamental category for understanding man is anticipation.
This is not simply one factor among others constituting his being
but that which grounds the will to live and structures and directs
the whole.

Anticipation is not imaginative entertainment of attractive
possibilities. It is rather the actual efficacy in the present
of the future. The way in which anticipation functions in the
present indicates that the future that elicits it is one of

consummation or fulfillment. All men exist by the power of the
future. The power of the future is God.

This view of Pannenberg, and comparable doctrines of Teilhard
de Chardin and Jürgen Moltmann envisage the End, which is not yet
extant, as potently effective in the present. This dynamic is
difficult to understand. There is little problem in seeing how
awareness of possibilities may affect action. But Pannenberg does
not think of the future in this way. It is not mere possibility.
But of course it is also not now actual. It is the not-yet which
will-be. That, too, could be understood if its future realization
were settled by past and present processes, but Pannenberg insists
that the causal relation is reversed. It is the power of the future that has shaped the past and now shapes the present.

There is a sense in which anticipation can be explained by
what is anticipated. This is the sense in which what is anticipated
is the final cause of anticipation. A final cause "acts" only in
the sense that it attracts. But Pannenberg's language about "the
power of the future" suggests another dimension to divine action.
He wants to make sense of Biblical and traditional notions of God's
agency. Hence God is not merely the future as it will be but also
the effective power of that future in every present. That power
raised Jesus from the dead! It seems, therefore, to include efficient as well as final causality.

The point here is not to criticize Pannenberg or other advocates of a theology of hope who associate God primarily with the
future. Our question is only whether by viewing God's action under
the category of final causality alone the problem of attributing
efficient causality to God can be avoided. The conclusion is that
this could be done only by an extreme truncation of what the theologians of hope are saying.

II

Although most contemporary philosophical and scientific discussion of cause deals with efficient cause, the theory of efficient cause is in a state of chaos. Arthur Pap writes of "the
vagueness of the principle of causality."[1] Ernst Nagel notes that
"the word 'cause' is highly ambiguous."[2] And Israel Scheffler asserts that modern writers have generally despaired "of the term
'cause' as a precise theoretical notion."[3] Although there are almost as many specific views of cause as there are writers seriously
addressing themselves to the problem, they may be conveniently
grouped as Humean and non-Humean.

The Humean view sees cause and effect in terms of regular succession of observable states of affairs. The regular succession can be formulated in laws, and law takes priority over cause. That is, "cause" is defined in terms of a law. The law has as its standard form: If A, B, and C, then X, where X is an aspect of an event. Such laws are sometimes called causal. However, A, B, or C may be laws, and there is general reluctance to regard laws as causes of events. Also the formalized law makes no reference to time, and most Humeans view temporal priority as essential to a cause. Carl Hempel represents the majority viewpoint when he specifies that A, B, or C is a cause only if it is an aspect of an event and temporally precedes X.

However, the temporal problem is complex. It is doubtful that physics can define time without reference to efficient causation, so the inclusion of temporal considerations in the definition of causality is circular. Some Humeans allow simultaneity of cause and effect. Some give up the time requirement altogether. Some insist that the cause is not only prior but also contiguous with the effect. Hempel seems to assume this. Nagel requires contiguity but admits "that no precise criteria exist for deciding when events are contiguous."[4] Pap regards the question as to whether all causes are contiguous to their effects as an empirical one. Russell denies that strict contiguity of cause to effect is possible.

With any of these Humean definitions, many things count as causes that are not regarded as such in ordinary language. For example, night is, by most of these definitions, a cause of day. Even the crowing of the rooster may count as a cause of dawn! Russell accepted these consequences, but most Humeans are embarrassed by them. They have attempted, thus far unsuccessfully, to devise definitions that would exclude such examples without excluding what they want to retain.

One response to this situation is to call for abandonment of the notion of cause in philosophy. This was the burden of Russell's famous essay on "The Notion of Cause." He noted correctly that the notion of cause is progressively extruded as sciences advance, and he contended that the common sense usage is hopelessly vague and confused. Meanwhile Michael Oakeshott urged the extrusion of the idea of cause from reflection on history. He argued that the explanation of an historical event is the total history that precedes it, but that it is meaningless to call such a nonrepeatable totality a cause.

Nagel recognizes the problem but notes that *some* notion of causality is still required. He writes: "It is beyond serious doubt that the term 'cause' rarely if ever appears in the research papers or treatises currently published in the natural sciences, and the odds are heavily against any mention in a book on theoretical physics. Nevertheless, though the *term* may be absent, the *idea* for which it stands continues to have wide currency. It not only crops up in everyday speech, and in investigations into human affairs by economists, social psychologists, and historians, it is also pervasive in the accounts natural scientists give of their laboratory procedures, as well as in the interpretations offered by many theoretical physicists of their mathematical formalism. Descriptions of laboratory procedures refer to changes produced by the operations of various instruments, as well as by human agents, and are unavoidably couched in causal language."[5]

Nagel is surely correct here. But it is interesting to see that when he illustrates his point, he introduces a non-Humean notion of cause. He notes that when a distinguished physicist explains the orbit of an electron, he uses such expressions as "hits," "knocks out," and "destroys the object." Nagel rightly recognizes that these are causal terms, but clearly their causal force does not arise from prior knowledge of general laws.

Michael Scriven has performed a similar analysis of historical writing. He finds rare the use of historical laws, and hence cause in the Humean sense is of minor importance to historians. However, their writings are full of causal language. He finds such expressions as "checked, furthered, resulted partly from, led to, stimulated, increased under the pressure of, enhanced by, entailed, made possibly by, forced, brought on, averted, pauperized, added to, gave a sharp stimulus to."[6] Scriven sees that this language witnesses to a primitive and ineradicable notion of causation that is not derived from knowledge of laws. Thus Nagel and Scriven both point to a notion of causality quite different from the Humean one. This notion has to do with the actual effect or real influence of A on B.

The real influence of one entity on another can be observed only in subjective experience. It is often pointed out that much of our ordinary notion of causality derives from immediate personal experience. Usually this is in the context of depreciating this ordinary notion. However, since prediction presupposes some kind of real effect of the present on the future, since that effect falls outside the sphere of perceived objects, and since such a relation of precedent affecting subsequent is immediately experienced, there is some *prima facie* wisdom in examining it where it can be examined.

Those who have considered immediate experience as a basis for our notion of causality have usually concentrated on our experience of acting. We seem to experience ourselves as agents causing events in our bodies and beyond to take place. A better starting point is ourselves as patients experiencing the causal efficacy of the past upon us. The direct experience of the cause-effect relation is in the effect rather than the cause.

The experience of which I speak can be approached phenomenologically, but a careful analysis of this kind is beyond the scope of this paper. I shall instead point out some indubitable convictions by which we all live. Since these convictions cannot reasonably be understood as inferences from observation of the world, they are strong testimony to the presence of causal feelings in immediate experience.

For example, I am convinced that as I finish saying a word the fact that I previously began that word is functioning as an important influence. That does not mean that I always finish every word I begin. But I do finish my words to a degree far in excess of the frequency of chance associations of the sounds involved.

I am also convinced that aspects of my experience are shaped by antecedent events in my body, especially my sense organs. I know, of course, that sometimes I am deceived with respect to particular instances. Visual experiences for which I think I am indebted to my eyes may be produced by electrical stimulation of my brain. But this is still derivation of experience from the body. That my subjective sensory experience largely derives from events in my body is a conviction I can neither prove nor doubt.

I am also convinced that some events precede others, that the present moment is not the first moment in all reality, and that the past can be distinguished from the future. That is, I have a certainty that some things have already happened, that the past is real. I know that my recall of past events is faulty, but I cannot doubt that the notion of the past is founded in reality. That too is unintelligible unless the past is somehow affecting the present experience.

These convictions witness that a primal aspect of human experience is derivation from the past or being influenced by antecedent events. This aspect of experience is so wholly pervasive that it is difficult to bring it into clear consciousness. We can do so best by imagining what an experience would be like that owed nothing to any prior event and then contrasting it with our actual experience. Indebtedness to the past turns out to be an exceedingly important part of all experience.

The reality of cause in this non-Humean sense appears so obvious that one must pause to consider why Humean theory remains
dominant in spite of its paradoxes and its acknowledged inadequa-
cies. The basic reason is the widespread commitment among philosophers to associate the notion of causality with scientific thought.
The experience of derivation from the past stands outside specific
scientific attention even if it is in fact everywhere assumed.

The tendency among Humeans is to subordinate the notion of
causation to that of explanation. Causation has ontological conno-
tations, whereas explanation belongs to the more comfortable sphere
of language and logic. The logic of explanation turns out to be
identical with the logic of prediction. An event is explained only
to the extent that facts and laws are provided on the basis of
which it could have been predicted. In the end the significance
of a cause is that it is a fact which together with other facts
and laws warranted prediction of an outcome. This is a quite different meaning of cause from "real influence." However, it too is
useful.

The word "cause" thus turns out to have two useful and appropriate references. Neither includes the notion of necessitation
essential to the Newtonian doctrine. The Humean view refers cause
to facts on the basis of which, taken together with laws, predictions can be made. In the non-Humean analysis cause refers to real
influence. The logical possibility of prediction depends ultimately on the ontological reality of actual influence, but the two
kinds of cause are quite different. One may predict the dawn from
the crowing of the rooster without supposing that the rooster influences the coming of dawn. One may know that a particular attitude will influence a man's decision without being able to predict
what the decision will be.

III

In Section I we saw that Hume's critique undercut the Newtonian idea of cause and with it the possibility of seeing God as
that kind of cause of or in the world. We saw also that Hume's
doctrine of efficient cause excluded the possibility of applying
his notion of causality to God's relation to the world. However,
we have now distinguished a third notion of causation which accepts the Humean rejection of necessitation but affirms the real
influence of past entities and events at least in human experience.
The reasons for excluding divine causality of the Newtonian and
Humean sort do not apply when efficient causality is understood as

influence. Hence the possibility of understanding God as an efficient cause in this sense requires fresh discussion.

Whether actual influence should be called "action" depends
on what is meant by "action." Often the language of divine action
has suggested the analogy of a man's bodily acting on his environment. That analogy leads to the refuted Newtonian notion of causality or the inapplicable Humean one. It is also theologically unacceptable. The appropriate analogy must be found in the influence
of one experience on another rather than in that of the body.

Consider a case in which I respond with anger to a condescend-
ing comment. In one moment I feel the condescension angrily. Does
the angry feeling have any consequences? Of course it does. In
the first place it tends to renew itself in subsequent experiences.
These repetitions are effects of the initial anger. In the second
place it affects the functioning of the organs of my body. Phys-
iologists can describe in detail the changes in heart beat, muscular
tone, adrenalin, and so forth. These, too, are effects of the angry feeling as efficient cause.

Mediated through these bodily changes there may be overt, sensible, observable actions upon the environment. But the experience
that constitutes itself as characterized by anger does not engage
in overt, sensible, observable actions upon those events it more
directly affects. Instead its self-constitution *is* the action by
virtue of which it influences subsequent events.

Similarly, if God acts or functions as an efficient cause, it
is not through overt, sensible, observable actions. He acts by
constituting himself in such a way that other events, such as human
experiences, take account of him. By constituting himself in a
particular way God affects the way in which he is taken account of
by others. In some instances this leads indirectly to overt, sensible, observable actions.

In Section I we noted that in the Western tradition God's action is closely bound up with final causation, but that it could
not be understood as final causation alone. From the perspective
now gained we can consider how efficient causality as real influence is related to human aims and purposes. How does one event or
experience affect the aim or purpose of another?

Consider a moment in which I make a resolve as to how to act
in subsequent moments. That resolve is felt in those later moments as an inherited aim or purpose. There is a tendency for that
purpose to be continued or reenacted in those moments. Thus the
way an experience constitutes itself affects the purposes operative

in succeeding experiences. Similarly God can be conceived as so
constituting himself as to influence the aims and purposes operative
in human experiences.

The argument has been that when efficient cause is understood
as real influence rather than as grounds for prediction, God *can*
be conceived as an efficient cause. Intelligible analogies for the
mode of such divine causation can be found. But the question remains whether this possible and intelligible divine causality is
actual.

Although proof in any strict sense is out of the question,
human experience can be so described as to highlight God's influence within it. Each experience not only selectively takes account
of its data, but it does so to some end. This end is not a distant
one common to all action of an abstract end like achieving good in
general. Rather, the way elements from the data are selectively
unified is purposeful. In each experience there is an aim to
achieve some quite particular immediate value. Furthermore, there
is in human experience an *eros* toward the realization of greater
rather than lesser values and toward the broader extension of value
in the future.

To be effective this *eros* must be resident in experience.
Hence it may be considered wholly immanent. But that could be
said also of the way the past functions. It too must be immanent
in the present in order to be effective there. Yet it is immanent
in the present *as the past*.

Similarly the *eros* toward the realization of value is best
understood as immanent in the present as something *given*--given
from beyond itself. It is given to the individual experience by
the universal *Eros* that is God himself. This interpretation is
supported by the strong tendency of religions which focus on the
increase of value rather than its transcendence to recognize the
movement toward the good as grounded outside the self in the good
itself or God.

Phenomenologically it is harder to identify God's influence
in human experience than that of the past. Yet it can be brought
to light by a similar thought experiment. Imagine an experience
composed exhaustively of ingredients from the past. Imagine
that any aim or purpose present in the experience is also exhaustively derived from the past. Imagine this continued throughout
life. Compare this with actual experience. This comparison can
highlight the great contribution made to actual experience by the
lure toward new, unforseen, and uncontrollable experiences, by

growth of concern and compassion, and by what is often called
openness to the future. The insightful philosophy of Ernst Bloch,
although understood by its creator as atheist, gives detailed witness to this power of the "Novum" in shaping human life.

One problem with understanding God as efficient cause of events
has been that it seemed to posit an interruption of the functioning
both of natural efficient causality and of human freedom. Theologians avoided the problem in part by a distinction of primary and
secondary causation. Thus natural efficient causation and freedom
functioned at the secondary level while God's primary causation explained the same events as *also* the direct effects of God's will.
In some instances, they supposed, the secondary causality was interrupted, but this was sufficiently rare to be irrelevant to the discovery of scientific laws. At the level of secondary causation,
efficient cause and human freedom were related negatively. What
was causally explained could not be free. Freedom was generally
affirmed of mind, and necessity of matter. The problems of such a
scheme are well-known.

When efficient causality is understood in terms of prediction,
God does not enter the picture, but some of the tension between
causal explanation and freedom remains. Whatever can be exactly
predicted appears to lack freedom. However, for two reasons, cause
as grounds of prediction leaves room for freedom. First, most predictions are statistical rather than deterministic. Second, both
statistical and deterministic predictions are of types of events
or aspects of events, never of events in their concrete actuality.

In principle, therefore, causality as basis for prediction
can never exclude freedom. Even so, to whatever extent causality
is conceived in terms of this model, its relation to human freedom
is negative. The greater the precision and detail of prediction
the less the scope of freedom. Furthermore, chance rather than
freedom is the appropriate word for this sphere of discourse.
Hence, insofar as divine action is confusedly associated with this
type of causality, it remains restrictive of human freedom. The
humanistic revolt against God is justified.

When efficient causality is understood as actual influence,
the relation of divine action to natural causality is quite different. Natural causation is the influence of the given world
upon a new event or experience. This actual influence is the ontological ground of the possibility of predicting certain aspects
of the future on the basis of known facts about the past and present. That God also influences events and experiences does not

detract from the influence of the world or the possibility of prediction. Divine influence does not restrict that of the world; it
supplements it.

The relation of natural causality to human freedom is also
quite different when viewed in these terms. The influence of the
natural world including my own past upon my present establishes the
context for each new experience. I cannot now be as if that past
had not occurred. In that sense it limits me. But that there are
now significant possibilities for me at all also depends on the
given world and on my past experience. The actual influence of my
past on my present is more basically to enlarge my range of freedom than to narrow it. If I have just begun a word, I am restricted
in that I cannot now be as if I had not begun a word or had begun
some other word. But I do not have to finish it. Having begun
the word gives me now the possibility of finishing it if I choose,
a possibility I would not now have if I had not begun it. A man
who keeps postponing decisions in order to keep his options open
has in the long run fewer options than the decisive man.

Finally, the relation of God's action to human freedom is
also different. For God to exercise real influence upon me does
restrict me in the sense that I must take account of that influence. But it does not determine *how* I take account of it. Instead, it provides a context of decision in which my range of
choices are extended and made more significant.

In conclusion I summarize my claims as follows. (1) Unless
God is understood as a cause of events in the world, we have no
reason to speak of him at all. (2) Newtonian and Humean notions
of efficient causality cannot illumine such a relation. (3) Attempts to understand divine causality as only formal, material, or
final are unsatisfactory. (4) Real influence is a fruitful notion
of efficient causality. (5) This notion can apply to God's relation to the world. (6) There is evidence for the actuality of this
influence. (7) This mode of causality supports rather than
threatens freedom.

NOTES

[1] Arthur Pap, *An Introduction to the Philosophy of Science*
(Glencoe, Illinois: The Free Press, 1962), p. 308.

[2] Ernst Nagel, "Types of Causal Explanation," in Daniel Lerner,
ed., *Cause and Effect* (New York: The Free Press; London: Collier
Macmillan Limited, 1965), p. 17.

[3]Israel Scheffler, *The Anatomy of Inquiry* (New York: Alfred A. Knopf, 1963), p. 25.

[4]Nagel, *op. cit.*, pp. 19-20.

[5]*Ibid.*, p. 12.

[6]Michael Scriven, "Causes, Connections and Conditions in History," in William Dray, ed., *Philosophical Analysis and History* (New York: Harper & Row, 1966), pp. 238-39.

8. RELATIVISM, DIVINE CAUSATION, AND
BIBLICAL THEOLOGY

David R. Griffin

The most influential way among Christian theologians of understanding the relation between divine and nondivine causation has been that based upon the schema of primary and secondary causation. I believe that this schema (besides being unintelligible, and resulting in an insuperable problem of evil for philosophical theology)[1] has unfortunate implications for understanding the relation between the work of the biblical scholar, on the one hand, and Christian faith and systematic theology, on the other. In particular, this primary-secondary schema of causation leads to a relativism which renders arbitrary both Christian faith and the practice of devoting special attention to the texts of the biblical tradition. Furthermore, the difficulties inherent in this schema have been instrumental, I believe, in leading many theologians to omit the category of divine causation altogether.

In the first part of this paper I will discuss the relativistic implications of the schema of primary and secondary causation. In the second part I will discuss an alternative understanding of the relation of divine and nondivine causation suggested by the process philosophy of Alfred North Whitehead. In the third part I will suggest some implications of this process view for conceiving the task of "biblical theology."

I *The Schema of Primary and Secondary Causation*

According to the schema of primary and secondary causation, divine and nondivine causation are on two different "levels." God is not in any sense "one cause among others"; rather, his causation is on a totally different *level* from that of all the worldly causes. While these worldly causes may be called "natural," they include all the distinctively human, and therefore "historical," influences as well as those of nonhuman nature. All of these worldly or natural causes are termed "secondary" causes, while God is considered the "primary" cause of every event. God's

---

From *Encounter* 36 (1975): 342-60. Reprinted with permission.

causation is termed "primary" not only out of deference, but also
because the "secondary" causes are instrumentalities of the divine
will.

In terms of this distinction, it is obvious that a "miracle"
could not be simply defined as an "act of God," since God is the
(primary) cause of *every* event. Rather, a miracle differs from
non-miraculous events only in that, while God normally uses secondary causes to execute his will, in performing a miracle he brings
the event about directly, without using any mediating instruments.

This notion of two different *levels* implies that there are
different *perspectives* from which to regard any non-miraculous
event. On the one hand, one can regard it in relation to God.
When so considered, it must be regarded as totally determined by
God. The divine causation is the sufficient cause for its existence
and total actuality, down to the most minute detail. Accordingly,
reference to the divine causation constitutes a sufficient explanation for the event in question. Reference to conditioning nondivine causes is not necessary, since these "causes" were themselves totally caused by God, and hence exercise no autonomous
(from God) causation, but are mere instruments of his purpose.

On the other hand, one can regard the non-miraculous event in
relation to its nondivine antecedent causes. Regarded from this
perspective, no reference to God's causation is needed. A sufficient explanation for the event can in principle be found within
the realm of "secondary" causation. There are various ways that
one can understand nondivine sufficient causation. If one is a
radical determinist, the antecedent secondary causes will be regarded as constituting the sufficient cause for any event. If one
is a dualist, the antecedent events will be regarded as constituting
sufficient causes for certain types of events (e.g., nonliving
ones for a vitalist, or nonhuman ones for a Cartesian dualist),
while the sufficient cause for other events (e.g., living, or human) may be regarded as consisting of the antecedent causes plus
the self-determination of the event in question. The nondualistic
nondeterminist may regard every event as requiring reference both
to antecedents and to self-causation for its sufficient explanation. But in any case, a sufficient explanation for any non-
miraculous event can in principle be found without any reference
to divine causation.

This understanding of the relation of divine to nondivine
causation has been widely accepted by "liberals" and "conservatives"
alike. Within the context of the primary-secondary schema,

liberals and conservatives differ only in regard to whether miracles
(as defined above) ever occur. Conservatives affirm the occurrence
of one or more such events, while liberals deny that they ever
occur.[2] At least they deny that there can ever be a sufficiently
good reason for affirming that an event has happened without any
"natural" (secondary) causes.

It is most important to see that this is where the issue lies
as long as the schema of primary and secondary causation is presupposed. The issue is not between "naturalistic" and "super-
naturalistic" explanations, since both groups affirm supernatural
causation. Nor is it between those who, while believing that all
events have natural causes, do and do not think that some or all
events require reference to God in order to have a "sufficient"
explanation. For, both groups hold that an *ultimate* explanation
for any event requires reference to its primary cause, God. And,
most importantly, both groups agree that God is not "one cause
among others," to be introduced as a supplementary factor within
the context of a discussion of natural causes. The term "divine
causation" can never refer to one cause among others; it is either
used to refer to the primary sufficient cause, which is on a different level from the natural causes, or it is not used at all.
Accordingly, the only real item for debate is whether God, who
usually employs secondary causes which provide sufficient explanations on their own level, *always* uses these.

This schema in its "liberal" form has understandably been
widely accepted, more or less self-consciously, by Christian biblical scholars. For it allowed them to retain as private citizens
faith in divine providence, and yet as public historians to accept
without qualification the almost universally accepted convention
that historians *qua* historians do not refer to divine influence as
an explanatory category. That is, while they could of course re-
port that, for example, Jones *believed* he was called by God to
perform a certain deed, the historian can never affirm that "Jones
performed this deed (partly) because he was actually *influenced
by God* to do so."

Since the idea of "divine causation" belongs to a different
level of discourse from that of "natural (including historical)
causation," this means that "faith" and "history" are separate
(but equal) perspectives, never to be merged into a higher synthesis of "faithful history." The liberal Christian who is a historian
need not and should not suppose that he is privy to an additional
causal factor (divine influence) unknown to his secular colleagues.

For, even though he believes in divine providence, he knows this
belief is irrelevant to the task of the historian, since God always
provides causes which are sufficient in terms of the level of explanation at which historians operate. Hence, he can be as fully
secular as his non-believing colleagues. For, unlike the conservative Christian historian, he can be fully secular even in regard
to the central events of the biblical records.

However, while this view has its advantages, it also has unfortunate consequences, both for Christian faith in general and
the role of the biblical scholar in particular. These consequences
can be seen by first looking at this view's implications for the
use of the terms "special act of God" and "revelation."

A. *"Special Acts of God" and "Revelation."* On the basis of some
views of the relation between divine and nondivine causation, there
would be a meaningful distinction between a "special act of God"
and a "revelation." For example, if one accepts some form of popular supernaturalism, according to which the world's processes
normally go along independently of God's action (except for perhaps
some sort of undifferentiated sustaining action), with God only
occasionally interrupting those processes by some special action,
these occasional interruptive actions could meaningfully be called
"special acts of God," whether or not any human beings recognized
them as such. In fact, they could have occurred long before any
humans appeared on the scene, e.g., the first creation of life
could be considered such an act of God. A conservative version
of the primary-secondary schema will have essentially the same import. God is equally the cause of all non-miraculous or ordinary
events, i.e., those with sufficient natural causes, so they are
all acts of God, while those events which cannot be explained in
natural categories, and must be referred immediately to the divine
causation, are extraordinary acts of God.

Hence, both the popular supernaturalist and the conservative
primary-secondary schematist can refer to certain events *in themselves* as "special (or extraordinary) acts of God." As such these
past events can be clearly distinguished from divine "revelations,"
since for an event to become a revelation it must be *received* as
such by someone. By definition, a revelation must be a revelation
to someone, whereas an act of God is what it is independently of
any person's recognition of it.

However, for the liberal primary-secondary schematist the
distinction between a special act of God and a revelation becomes
practically meaningless. There are no interruptions in the natural

causal nexus; hence there are no events which are acts of God in
an extraordinary sense apart from their being perceived as such.
Accordingly, special acts of God can only be defined as those events
which are *in fact received as revelatory*. And at first glance this
seems to preserve the distinction between a special act of God and
a revelation: the past event in itself is the special act of God,
the impact of this past event on the present existence of the believer is the revelation.

However, the distinction is not the same as it is for the popular supernaturalist and the conservative primary-secondary schematist. For them, an event was a special act of God prior to its
being received as a revelation, and as such was *appropriately* received as especially revelatory. Receiving the event as a revelation of God involved a correct evaluation of what the event already
was in itself, an event due to God's causation in an extraordinary
sense. But for the liberal primary-secondary schematist, the fact
that some past event is a special act of God is *totally* a function
of its being received as something special. There is nothing about
the event in itself, prior to its reception by the believer, that
distinguished it from all the events which were not found revelatory. Accordingly, *there is conceived to be nothing about the
event in itself which makes the believer's reception of it as a
revelation of God any more appropriate than his possible reception
of any other event*.

Accordingly, if the distinction between "act of God" and
"revelation" is virtually collapsed, so that the former is merely
a function of the latter, a complete relativism is difficult to
avoid. The reflective Christian can only confess that he or she
has *in fact* received certain events as the basic clue to the nature
and meaning of existence. But he or she cannot provide any conceptual basis for the *appropriateness* of this choice. And here
it matters not whether one speaks of choosing these events or being
chosen by them. In either case, descriptive statements are all
that can be made; there is no conceptual basis for any normative
statements as to which events people *should* receive as revelatory.

These relativistic implications follow whether one focuses
primarily upon the idea that (a) God is the sufficient cause of all
events, or that (b) all events can be adequately explained without
any reference to God at all. If the former is emphasized, then
all events are equally caused by God, so there is no basis for
distinguishing some of them as special acts of God. (Even if one
replies that it is intelligible to claim that, while God determines

all events equally, he determined the central events of the biblical tradition in such a way as to make them special mediators of
his self-revelation, one still has the problem discussed under
(B) below.) If the latter point is stressed, then all events are
equally *uncaused* by God, so there is again no basis for discrimina-
tion. This second line of thought leads easily to the notion that
"divine causality" is purely a "tertiary quality" as defined by
classical dualism, i.e., an attribute that is not at all in the
"objective" (to the perceiver) world, but is wholly in the mind of
the perceiver. Temporarily it may be held that, although one cannot
talk about divine causation on a past event, one can affirm that
God acts upon one here and now, causing one to perceive the past
event as a revelation. But this position can be undermined by a
couple of questions. First, why should God cause one to perceive
those specific events as revelational, if those events were not
already extraordinary in themselves? Second, if the world is a
nexus of natural causes and effects, closed to (extraordinary)
divine influence, why should one make an exception for one's present believing experience? (This second question will be forceful
to the extent that it is impossible to maintain some type of Kantian
dualism of perspectives.) On the basis of this kind of reflection,
doubt will increase as to whether the notion of divine causation
can be meaningful in any sense. This kind of reflection perhaps
accounts in part for the fact that the notion of "act of God,"
which was so central in Bultmann's theology, has been replaced
with other categories by his pupils. And these other categories
are ones which can provide no conceptual basis for avoiding complete
relativism.

I believe this development merely represents the logical conclusion, which could have been reached historically by any one of
several paths, of the combination of the primary-secondary schema
for relating divine and nondivine causation, and the liberal belief
that there are no events without nondivine causes. As long as
this liberal belief was not added, the primary-secondary schema
could seem meaningful. Although medieval theologians did have
their difficulties with it, these difficulties did not lead to
doubt about the very meaningfulness of the idea of divine causation.
For this idea had clear meaning, being definable both conceptually
and ostensively, in terms of the miraculous events. But once this
belief in miracles evaporated, it was only a matter of time until
the continued talk about divine causation would become intolerable
because unintelligible. For if "sufficient" really means

sufficient, then the idea of two sufficient causes for one event
is clearly self-contradictory.[3] Accordingly, if one holds to
divine causation, then pantheistic monism cannot be consistently
avoided. Or if one wishes to hold to the reality of world and the
genuine efficacy of its apparent causation, then the idea of some
supermundane causation upon the events becomes so superfluous as
to be meaningless. And the religious implications of this view
would be relativistic at best.

B. *Universal Love and Revelational Particularity*. The relativistic
implications of the schema of primary and secondary causation are
increased by reflection upon one other implication of the idea of
God as the sufficient cause of all events. If it is true that this
Sufficient Cause also loves all human beings equally, then why
would he have revealed his nature and purpose more to one set of
human beings than to another? Many Christians have been able to
accept the apparent contradiction between universal love and par-
ticularistic revelation, along with other apparent injustices.
But for those for whom the divine love is paramount, the tension
often becomes intolerable. As long as the idea is retained that
God totally determines the world's happenings, the only consistent
way to resolve the tension is to affirm that the various religions
are in fact equal paths to unity with God.

Such a position can take one of many forms. But in any case
the longstanding paradox between the *content* of the Christian
revelation (the universal love of God) and its *form* (its apparent
availability to only a limited portion of humanity) is overcome.
This resolution is certainly preferable to the more "orthodox" one
of denying in effect the equal love of God for all humanity. But
its relativistic consequences are problematic. Such a position
obviously would undercut any rational justification for giving
special attention to the Judeo-Christian tradition (a conclusion
which scholars of these traditions, especially non-tenured ones,
would surely like to avoid out of self-interest, if for no other
reason). But beyond this, the implications are paradoxical. If
the various religions are genuinely equal, they are presumably
equal in cognitive value. (Some advocates deny this, dinstinguish-
ing between truth and saving efficacy; but this only raises again
the question as to why God would give truth only to a limited portion of mankind.) If so, then there is no basis for maintaining
the doctrines about God's universal love and causation, and even
his self-revealing activity, since these are not affirmed by all
religions. In other words, the very doctrines that require a

revelational relativism are undercut by the relativism itself. Of
course, this is not surprising; it is only one more example of the
fact that every attempt to affirm an absolute relativism is self-
defeating. But it should make more pressing for us the need to
reconsider the basic doctrine (the schema of primary and secondary
causation) that leads to the dilemma of either denying God's universal love or affirming a self-defeating relativism.

II *A Process View of Divine and Nondivine Causation*

   The thesis of the second part of this paper is that the process
philosophy of Alfred North Whitehead provides a conceptuality in
terms of which the theologian can conceive the relation between
divine and nondivine causation in a way that avoids the aforemen-
tioned implications of the schema of primary and secondary causation,
i.e., complete relativism, and doubt as to the very meaningfulness of the notion of "divine causation in the world." In particular, on the basis of a Whiteheadian understanding, it is (A)
again possible to conceive of a "special act of God" in independence from a "revelation," and it is (B) not inconsistent to maintain that God loves all persons equally although the events through
which this love was decisively revealed were localized in time and
space. I will explicate these two parts of the thesis in this
order.

A. *"Special Act of God" and "Revelation."* The first part of the
paper suggested that, to avoid relativism, some way is needed to
conceive of some events as being "special acts of God" in themselves, i.e., prior to their reception as such, so that it is appropriate to receive them as especially revelatory of God. Also,
the liberal position is taken for granted here that this must be
done, if at all, without positing occasional interruptions of the
normal course of events. The affirmation of such interruptions is
increasingly incredible; it would violate one of the axioms of
modern historiography, and hence put the Christian historian outside the circle of recognized historians (which would be unfortunate if it is unnecessary); and, in application to Jesus, it would
imply a docetic rejection of his full humanity.

   Whitehead's philosophy provides a basis for at least three
ways in which events can be distinguished in regard to God's causation on them.[4] In the first place, *God's causation can be more
significant for higher types of events, especially distinctively
human events.* The world is made up of momentary processes, or

events. Each of these events is a partially self-determining synthesis of data received from all the events in its environment.
However, in low-grade events, such as electronic, atomic, and
molecular events, the self-determination is negligible. These
events are virtually determined by their antecedents.

God is in the environment of every nondivine event.[5] As such,
each event receives data from God as well as from nondivine causes.
Accordingly, to give a sufficient explanation of any event, reference must be made to God as well as to the influence of previous
nondivine events and to the self-determination of the event in
question.

The distinctive influence exerted by God is on the "aim" of
the event, the end toward which it determines itself. God provides
the event with an impulse, called an "initial (or ideal) aim," in
terms of which the event might respond to all the other influences
upon it and thereby determine itself. However, the event in its
self-determination may deviate more or less greatly from the initial aim. Because of this capacity for self-determination, even
vis-à-vis God, the event's own aim must be distinguished from the
initial aim received from God. The event's own aim is called its
"subjective aim." Hence, each event not only determines its responses to all nondivine causes in terms of its aim, but it also
determines its own aim. However, this double capacity for self-
determination is negligible in low-grade events. The options open
to them are so limited that there is very little possibility for
the event to exercise significant self-determination, and therefore
very little possibility for the divine initial aim to stimulate
the event to do something extraordinary.

Hence, even though God is one of the causes on each of the
world's events, his potential influence will be much more significant upon high-grade events, such as those constituting animal and
especially human psyches, in which there is considerable capacity
for self-determination. Reference to God *is* necessary in order to
account for some of the features of low-grade events, such as their
three-dimensionality, and the fact that they exemplify a significant form of order at all. But the divine influence upon these
events is so uniform that the features for which it accounts can
in most contexts simply be assumed. Although each of these events
is to some degree an "act of God," a reference to this fact generally does nothing to distinguish one such event from another, and
hence can in most contexts be omitted without loss. (Only in
those extremely rare events in which a new level of events emerged

in the evolutionary process would a reference to divine influence
be of significance for the uniqueness of the event.)

But in high-grade events, such as events of conscious human
choice, there is considerable capacity for self-determination. And,
whereas God, in relation to low-grade events, functions primarily
as the ground of order, he functions also as the ground of novelty
for high-grade events. Accordingly, if God presents an event with
an ideal aim toward a possibility that goes considerably beyond
what had been previously actualized in the tradition in which the
event occurs, and if that event actualizes that novel possibility,
then a reference to the divine influence will be essential in order
to account for the achievement of the event.

Incidentally, it should be stressed here that, in terms of
this conceptuality, there is no antithesis between divine influence
and creaturely self-determination. In fact, insofar as God is the
source of the lure towards novelty, it is precisely when an event
exercises the greatest degree of freedom beyond the weight of tradition that the divine causation should (sometimes) be considered
most effective. (The qualification "sometimes" is inserted paren-
thetically, since sometimes deviations from tradition are not
creative advances, but destructive aberrations, all things considered, and God's initial aims are always toward the creation of
greater value.)

To summarize this first point: what is needed is a way of con-
ceptualizing differences among events in terms of the extent to
which reference to the divine causation upon them serves to distinguish them from other events. The first way in which events differ
in this regard is the degree to which the divine causation, i.e.,
the initial aim, can *potentially* stimulate them to achieve something
distinctive in relation to the tradition in which they occur. This
potential is much greater in the higher-grade events, since they
have a much greater capacity for self-determination. Accordingly,
it is much more likely that events of the highest grade, i.e.,
human events, will be "special" acts of God. Hence, from now on
the discussion will be limited to human events.

A second basis for differentiation involves the *degree to
which events respond conformally to the initial aims received from
God.* Although two events may be equal in regard to the *potential*
influence of the divine causation upon them, they may differ considerably in the degree to which they are actually influenced by
God. That is, the subjective aim of the one event may conform almost exactly with the ideal aim received from God, while the

subjective aim of the other may diverge as far as possible from the ideal impulse it received from God. Accordingly, although there is some divine influence upon both events, it would not be meaningful to regard the latter one as an act of God to the same degree as the former one. Because of the self-determination of events *vis-à-vis* God,[6] they are acts of God to various degrees. And, in this respect the degree to which they are God's acts is decided not at all by God, but totally by them.[7]

There is a third way in which events can differ in regard to their relation to the divine causation that is relevant to the question at hand: This is the *extent to which the content of the conformal subjective aims of the events reflects God's own subjective aim*. God's eternal subjective aim is understood to be the increase of value in the world's events. It is in terms of this eternal subjective aim that he formulates initial aims for the world's events. Although God's subjective aim is unchanging, or rather because of this, the content of his initial aims for his creatures will vary greatly.

The reason for this can be explained in terms of the following notions: (1) God's initial aim for an event is always an aim towards the best possibility open to it, given its concrete context. (2) What is possible for an event is determined for it by its context. God can lure it to actualize a novel possibility, i.e., one that was not previously actualized by its antecedents in its tradition, but this possibility cannot be absolutely novel, but must be rather closely related to what went before.[8] (3) Accordingly, the best possibility open to a given event will be determined by its context, and therefore what God can even try to achieve in the present is limited by what has actually been achieved in the past. (4) Since different sets of possibilities have been achieved in the different human traditions, the content of the initial aims presented by God to members of these different traditions will necessarily vary.[9]

(Although this discussion is limited to human events, it is perhaps worth mentioning that the content of God's initial aims for subhuman events would differ greatly from the content for human events. Also, to explicate further the point made in the first part of this section, the content of God's aims for various electrons would be virtually identical; his aims for various cells would differ slightly more; and his aims for various chimpanzees, for example, would differ more; but it is only where there are greatly divergent psychic traditions within a species, and hence, as far

as we know, only among humans, that the divine aims will be greatly
different for different members of the same species.)

If it is conceivable that the initial aims for various events
will vary, it is also conceivable that some of them will reflect
the general aim of God more directly than others. We can conceive
this on the basis of an analogy with our own experience. In some
situations, the particular purposes we entertain and strive to
actualize are quite far removed from our basic life purpose. Someone who correctly understood our particular aims of the moment
would not understand very much about our general aim in life. But
in other situations, our momentary subjective aims rather directly
reflect our long-term aim, e.g., when the person whose general life
aim is to achieve security through fame strives for recognition in
a public gathering, or the person whose general aim is to be of
service to others performs a helpful deed. Someone who took those
particular acts as clues to the general aims of the persons would
be receiving a genuine "revelation." And these particular acts in
themselves, since they were based upon particular aims that directly
reflected the persons' general aims, would be "special acts" of
the persons in question.

By analogy, in some situations the best particular aims God
can present to particular events will be ones which do not very
directly reflect his general aim for his creation. For example,
although his general aim is always for what is best for the creaturely events, in some situation the best will not be very good.
In Whitehead's words: "The initial aim is the best for that *impasse*. But if the best be bad, then the ruthlessness of God can
be personified as *Atè*, the goddess of mischief. The chaff is
burnt." The subjective aims of the events which receive this type
of initial aim will not very directly express the general aim of
God, no matter how greatly the subjective aims conform to the
initial aims. Likewise, in regard to other events the best possibility will not be bad, and hence will not run directly counter to
God's general aim, but will be more or less neutral, and thereby
still will not significantly reflect the divine subjective aim.
But the context for some events will conceivably be such that the
particular aims proffered by God will quite directly reflect his
general aim. If these events then determine themselves such that
their subjective aims conform highly to the received initial aims,
these events can meaningfully be called *God's special acts*. In
this third criterion, the special character of the event is rooted
in something special about God's causation itself. Hence the

specialness of an event is not totally a function of the event itself, but is partially rooted in "prevenient grace."

Although these events in no way involve an interruption of the normal course of events, they can meaningfully in themselves be considered acts of God in an extra-ordinary sense, because they are events (1) in which the divine initial aims can, if actualized, account for a unique aspect of the events, (2) in which the initial aim is indeed actualized to a high degree and thereby allowed to be extraordinarily effective, and (3) in which the content of the initial aim, and therefore the subjective aim, reflects the general divine aim to an extraordinary degree.

Because these events are in themselves extraordinary acts of God in the above sense, it is therefore appropriate to receive them as special revelations of God. Of course, in the order of knowing, the revelation will come first, and reflection upon the nature of the mediating event will come second. But the reflection upon this past event will not, on the basis of the above ideas, necessarily lead to the conclusion that the specialness of the past event is only a function of the present perception of it, a conclusion whose relativistic implications would in time undermine the present perception itself. Rather, one can consistently conceive of the past event as having been extraordinary in itself, so that the response to it as a revelation of God involved a recognition of the extraordinary causation of God that went into it, and of its resulting extraordinary capacity to mediate a genuine revelation of God.

It perhaps should be added that this account does not mean a denial of the idea that a "revelation" involves a present action of God (as Holy Spirit) on the believer. Rather, this would be insisted upon. And in this account, the paradox of affirming a real influence of God on the present believer's experience to account for a dimension of that experience, while refusing to refer to divine influence to account for a dimension of the experience of a past figure, is overcome. According to the view proposed here, an event in which a "revelation" occurs may also be a special act of God, and might serve as the mediator or objective pole for another revelation in a later moment. That is, a certain human event (B) may receive a revelation through a previous event (A); hence, for B, event A is a "special act of God," and serves as the objective pole of the revelational experience. The subjective pole would be B's believing response, which would be directly influenced by God, as well as indirectly through A. This direct

influence of God may be such as to make B a special act. If so,
for a later event (C), event B might be the mediator of a revelational experience; hence, for C, event B, with both its objective
and subjective poles, would serve as the objective pole of the
event C. And so on. This account of revelation, like most modern
accounts, stresses the fact that a revelation by definition must
occur in the present, without, like many modern accounts, using
this insight as a justification for not ascribing any specialness
to the past (e.g., biblical) events in themselves.

B. *Universal Love and Revelational Particularity.* The notions
discussed above, to show the possibility of intelligibly conceiving
of some events as being in themselves special acts of God, also
suggest how the idea that God's universal love was revealed decisively in a particular tradition need not be an offense to liberals. For, the abstract possibility that certain human events
would actualize themselves in a way that would directly express
God's general purpose for his world could only become a *real* possibility after a long series of events had provided the requisite
conditions. As stated above, God can and sometimes does lure an
event to actualize a novel possibility previously unactualized by
the events in its tradition. But this novel possibility must be
such that it builds upon the particular possibilities that have
already been actualized in that tradition. In other words, there
is a certain inherent order among the abstract possibilities which
events can in principle actualize. Because of this order, certain
abstract possibilities are not real possibilities for certain
events, since these events do not stand in a tradition in which the
possibilities prior in the order have already been actualized, at
least with sufficient intensity and frequency to have become part
of the defining essence of that tradition.

Put in less abstract terms, Jesus would have not been possible
apart from Amos, Hosea, Jeremiah, and the Isaiahs. Someone similar
to Jesus would not have been possible without persons similar to
these prophets. Nor would these prophets have been possible without the Moses-tradition. Accordingly, it was simply not possible
for persons similar to the Hebrew prophets to appear in India
around the middle of the first millennium B.C. (Since some of the
ancient Chinese traditions were more analogous to the ancient Hebrew traditions than were the Indian traditions, it was possible
for there to be prophecy in China that was somewhat similar to
prophecy in Israel.)[10] All the more was it impossible for someone
like Jesus to appear in India, or for someone like Gautama to

appear in Israel (except insofar as there was historical influence
in one direction and/or the other).

Thus far the differences in the initial aims presented by God
have been explained in terms of the previous actualizations of the
various traditions. But can this be extended backwards *ad infin-
itum?* How can the differences among the various human traditions
be accounted for, if God always provides the best initial aims for
the events at hand? If human forms of life are thought to have
emerged independently in several places, there would be different
contexts presupposed by different groups of human beings from the
very beginning. But even if a single pair of "first humans" is
presupposed, the possibility of the vast differences among the
various human communities that were formed can be understood. For,
even if we assumed that at an early stage the content of the initial aims for all human beings were identical (*insofar as these
aims were relevant to ideas and images about reality*), the capacity
for self-determination in the first generation of human beings
(whenever this might be somewhat arbitrarily dated) provides the
ground for divergent initial aims in the second generation. Even
very slightly different responses by two groups of individuals to
identical initial aims (as qualified in the previous sentence) in
the first generation would mean that the second-generation members
of one group would have slightly different possibilities open to
them from those of the other group. Likewise, the nondivine environment of the two groups would differ more or less, and this
would likely influence them in divergent directions, and would
provide a further basis for divergent initial aims. Accordingly,
the two groups would differ more at the end than at the beginning
of the second generation, so that the initial aims for the third-
generation members of the two groups would differ even more.

On this basis, the great differences existing among the various
traditions by, say, the middle of the first millenium B.C., can
be accounted for, even if it is assumed that, once upon a time,
God presented identical initial aims (as qualified above) to all
human beings. Even slightly divergent forms of nonconformity to
the initial aims could, over several hundred generations, account
for the actual differences. Of course, I have spoken in very abstract terms about "groups" and "generations," whereas the initial
aims are for individual events. Hence, although there is a certain
justification for speaking of the changes as occurring in a generation as a whole and in a group as a whole, the actual course of
events is much more complicated, and provides even more opportunity

for the development of divergent traditions than my highly schematic sketch suggests.

In terms of these ideas, it is possible to maintain consistently that God loves all human beings equally, and yet that he revealed this love more decisively in one tradition than others. Accordingly, the Christian need not try to save his belief in God's equal love (and distributive justice) by accepting the relativistic conclusion that all religious and philosophic traditions are equal in regard to mediating the truth about deity. All that must be given up is the notion that God is (or could be) the sufficient cause of all the world's events, a notion which should never have been accepted in the first place, and whose rapid demise is desirable on other grounds as well. (Of course, the notion of God as omnipotent, i.e., as the sufficient cause of events, has been accepted for so long that it has become for many part of the defining essence of deity, so that it initially seems impossible for a being worthy of the name "God" not to be omnipotent in the traditional sense. But this is a topic for another place.)

III *Some Implications for Biblical Theology*

In this concluding section, I will briefly suggest some of the implications that acceptance of this process view of divine and nondivine causation might have for biblical theology. This form of biblical theology would be different, of course, not only from that which is based upon the traditional notion of divine causation, but also from the nontheistic forms which have resulted from the collapse of that traditional notion.

1. *No event would be conceived as simply or wholly an act of God.* For the theologian would think in terms of each event as having a multiplicity of antecedent causes upon it, and also of it as having some degree of self-determination, even in relation to God's initial aims.

2. *Every event would be conceived as being an act of God to some extent.* For God provides an initial aim to each event, and this aim will always have *some* influence; also, God's previous causation had more or less influence on the nondivine antecedent causes that more or less determine the event in question. Accordingly, the process biblical theologian would not speak as if any (let alone all) events could be "completely intelligible" apart from all reference to God. This would hold for so-called "natural" events as well as "historical" ones, since the difference between the two is only one of degree (although a great degree), not of kind.

3. However, one would assume that not all events were acts of God
to the same extent, so that *God's influence would only sometimes
be a significant enough factor to mention* in contexts in which one
is attempting to account for the distinctive features of the events
in question (as opposed to contexts in which one is discussing the
creaturehood of events, which they all have in common). Hence,
while most events would be described in terms of the same causal
determinants employed by most (nonpositivistic) historians, one
would be open to, and even alert to, the possibility that some
events could not be as adequately accounted for as most other
events without reference to divine influence.

4. "Faith" and "history" would not be thought of as two different
perspectives; rather *Christian (or Jewish) faith would be regarded
as the perspective in terms of which one could most adequately
understand the development of the biblical tradition* (and all other
historical developments, for that matter). This fourth point needs
further amplification.

The primary-secondary schema for understanding the relation
between divine and nondivine causation fitted nicely with the modern
idea that all events could be explained without the "God hypothesis," and with Kantian philosophy in particular, to support the
notion that (the science of) "history" could not talk of God. Accordingly, Jewish and Christian faith, according to which God is
believed to be (at least) an important determinant of the course
of events, was put in a different category from, e.g., Freudian
and Marxist faith, according to which sexual or economic factors
are believed to be (at least) important determinants of the course
of events. Hence, a Marxian, employing his "faith" in the supreme
causal efficacy of economic factors to reconstruct the course of
events, could in principle be a respectable historian. His non-
Marxian colleagues might criticize his results, but it would be
because they found his reconstruction unconvincing, perhaps because
of its onesidedness, and not because in employing his economic
perspective he was introducing an illegitimate causal factor and/or
not being "objective." For, most (nonpositivistic) historians
recognize that they favor certain types of causal explanation over
others, and that their "faith" in the special efficacy of certain
factors can only be justified by using their perspective to reconstruct history in an especially illuminating, convincing manner.

But the faith that God is an important causal factor in history
has not been treated in the same way. Anyone who would dare to
use divine influence as an explanatory category would, if not

simply ignored, be criticized for resorting to illegitimate (for
the historian) explanations, and for allowing his personal, subjective beliefs to intrude upon what should be an "objective" enterprise. And this attitude has been manifested by theistic as
well as nontheistic historians. The long dominance of the primary-
secondary schema, the heavy influence of Kantian modes of thought
upon many of the most creative biblical scholars, and the understandable anxiety to achieve respectability in a secular culture,
go far to explain this fact. (Also, certain theological themes,
such as justification by faith, the hiddenness of God, and the *pro
me* character of all genuine theological assertions, were interpreted so as to make a virtue of a necessity.)

    If the process understanding of God's causal influence upon
worldly events were adopted, this would mean a simultaneous rejection of the primary-secondary schema of causation, and of the
Kantian dualism between "scientific" or "objective" reason, which
necessarily constructs a closed causal nexus, and "practical" reason or "faith," which alone can think "God." Accordingly, the
philosophical grounds for excluding "divine causation" in principle
from historical reconstruction would be overcome. The historian
who is a process theist could use this category when the evidence
seemed to warrant it. The historical reconstruction would in intention be as fully "objective" as any, in that the intention
would be to reconstruct the course of events as accurately as possible, including the most important causal factors. Of course,
the reconstruction would not be "objective" in the sense of being
free from presuppositions about historical causation. But no reconstruction is objective in this sense, except perhaps for posi-
tivistic accounts which succeed in avoiding causal categories
altogether. Since every nonpositivistic historian uses his "subjective" faith-perspective in the belief that it, far from distorting
the "objective" facts, first allows them to be adequately reconstructed, the historian who is a process theist could use his
faith perspective with the knowledge that it is not formally different in kind from the perspectives presupposed (more or less
critically) by other historians.

5. However, although the acceptance of a process perspective would
remove the philosophical grounds for the historian's not using the
category of divine causation, strong *emotional* grounds would still
remain. The reference to "acts of God" has for so long implied
the interruption of natural causation, and hence has fallen into
such disrepute, that any mention of divine influence by a historian

qua historian would undoubtedly bring instant scorn. And he would
doubtless have difficulty getting his colleagues, theistic or
otherwise, to listen to a discourse on Whiteheadian philosophy that
would explain that his reference to God was really all right! Accordingly, it will probably be best for historians who are theists
to continue following the convention of not speaking of divine influence *qua* historians, at least until process philosophers (and
others with doctrines of divine influence that do not entail the
interruption of natural causes) succeed, in philosophical discussions about historiography, in making a good case for the legitimacy
of employing divine influence as one of the explanatory categories.

In light of the above considerations, I propose that *"biblical theology" could be understood as the discipline that attempts
to carry out the task* that the biblical historian who is a (process)
theist could in principle attempt, i.e., *of reconstructing the development of the biblical tradition employing "divine influence"
as one of the categories*. This would involve the incorporation of
philosophical and historical astuteness in one individual. For
example, this type of biblical theology would be engaged in attempting to understand the relation between the divine and human
agencies in Jesus, and hence would not be leaving "Christology
proper" to someone else to worry about. Likewise the biblical
theologian would not simply describe the position(s) of the book
of Job, but would be engaged in attempting to answer the question
as to why the good suffer, and the wicked seem to prosper.

In short, on the basis of replacing the primary-secondary
schema with the process view of the relation between divine and
nondivine causation, the notion of divine influence could be meaningfully retained, and the gulf between biblical scholars and
philosophical theologians could be overcome.

NOTES

1. Cf. my "Divine Causality, Evil, and Philosophical Theology:
A Critique of James Ross," *International Journal for Philosophy of
Religion*, 4, 3, (1973).

2. The thought of Rudolf Bultmann provides a good example of
the liberal interpretation of the primary-secondary schema. My
explication and critique are in *A Process Christology* (Westminster,
1973), pp. 90-108.

3. Cf. the article cited in note 1.

4. Whitehead uses the term "event" in a much broader sense
than I am employing it in this paper. I am using it here to refer

to a single "actual occasion," which in Whitehead's thought is the
limiting type of event; cf. *Process and Reality* (Macmillan Co.,
1929), pp. 113, 124. One moment of human experience provides an
example of an actual occasion. Accordingly, as "event" is being
used here, it does not refer to events that are observable through
sense-perception, such as battles, storms, sunsets, the falling of
a rock, and human bodily acts as observed from without. Any of
these would involve a whole nexus of events.

5. It is being presupposed here that God is a "living person,"
an everlasting series of occasions of experience. Therefore I
must use the qualifier "nondivine" to designate worldly events,
since there are divine events as well. The divine event is always
one of the events in the environment of any given nondivine event
by which it is influenced. Hence, since "efficient causation"
refers to the influence of one actuality upon another, God is one
of the efficient causes upon every nondivine event. But this does
not mean mechanistic causation, or complete determination; no event
(as used in this paper) can completely determine another event,
since there are always many efficient causes, and since the affected event has some capacity for self-determination.

6. It is because of an event's freedom even in relation to
God that Whitehead distinguishes between the event's own "subjective aim" and the "initial (or ideal) aim" (often called the "initial subjective aim"). This freedom is indicated by statements
such as the following: "an originality in the temporal world is
conditioned, though not determined, by an initial subjective aim
supplied by [God]"; *ibid.*, p. 164.

7. There are two distinct senses in which God's activity is
dependent upon the world's responses, and these are related to
two distinct meanings of "God's acts." In each moment God constitutes himself by responding to the previous worldly events in such
a way as to formulate initial aims for the next stage of the world.
This self-constituting response to the world's efficient causation
upon him is an act of "final causation" on God's part, since he
is determining himself at the moment in terms of his general purpose. After God has thus constituted his momentary state, replete
with initial aims for the succeeding stage of the world's advance,
the succeeding events of the world prehend that divine event in
terms of those initial aims. This is divine activity in the sense
of efficient causation. It is this second sense that is being
discussed in the present part of the text. God's effectiveness as
an efficient cause is dependent upon the responses to his initial
aims. In the discussion under (B) in the text below, the point is
that God's final causation, his act of self-determination in which
initial aims are formulated, is partially dependent upon how the
worldly events determined themselves in the previous moment of the
creative advance.

8. Whitehead constantly insists upon the fact that what can be
actualized in any actual occasion is determined by its past; cf.
ibid., pp. 101, 123, 127, 168, 202. The only reason any novelty
beyond the past is possible is that the actualities it receives
influence from include God, and that the possibilities received
from God include some that are closely related to, but different
from, the possibilities received from the nondivine actualities;
cf. *ibid.*, p. 377.

9. *Ibid.*, p. 373.

10. Cf. H. H. Rowley, *Prophecy and Religion in Ancient China
and Israel* (Harper, 1956).

9. ON THE MEANING OF "ACT OF GOD"*

Gordon D. Kaufman

> What we desperately need is a theological ontology that
> will put intelligible and credible meanings into our ana-
> logical categories of divine deeds and of divine self-
> manifestation through events. . . . Only an ontology of
> events specifying what God's relation to ordinary events
> is like, and thus what his relation to special events
> might be, could fill the now empty analogy of mighty
> acts, void since the denial of the miraculous.
>
> Langdon Gilkey[1]

The concept "act of God" is central to the biblical understanding of God and his relation to the world. Repeatedly we are
told of the great works performed by God in behalf of his people
and in execution of his own purposes in history. From the "song
of Moses," which celebrates the "glorious deeds" (Exod. 15:11)
through which Yahweh secured the release of the Israelites from
bondage in Egypt, to the letters of Paul, which proclaim God's
great act delivering us "from the dominion of darkness" (Col. 1:13)
and reconciling us with himself, we are confronted with a "God
who acts."[2] The "mighty acts" (Ps. 145:4), the "wondrous deeds"
(Ps. 40:5), the "wonderful works" (Ps. 107:21) of God are the fundamental subject matter of biblical history, and the object of
biblical faith is clearly the One who has acted repeatedly and with
power in the past and may be expected to do so in the future.

I

However hallowed by Bible and by traditional faith, this notion of a God who continuously performs deliberate acts in and
upon his world, and in and through man's history, has become very
problematical for most moderns. We have learned to conceive nature
as an impersonal order or structure. The rising of the sun, the
falling of the rain, the development of the solar system and the

---

*This paper was originally published in *Harvard Theological
Review*, 61:175-201 (1968).

evolution of life, catastrophes like earthquakes or hurricanes as
well as the wondrous adaptations and adjustments through which the
myriad species of life sustain and support each other, terrifying
plagues and diseases as well as powers of healing and restoration--
all are grasped by us as natural events and processes. All are
understood to proceed from natural causes and to lead to natural
effects; in no case is it necessary to invoke the special action of
God to account for such occurrences. Indeed, we have learned,
especially in the last three or four hundred years, that it is precisely by *excluding* reference to such a transcendent agent that we
gain genuine knowledge of the order that obtains in nature, are
enabled to predict in certain respects the natural course of events,
and thus gain a measure of control over it. The deliberate exclusion of reference to the action of God in the understanding of
nature does not, of course, involve a claim that nature has become
transparent to man, that there is no longer mystery in this world
before which we must stand in awe. But it does mean that a particular kind of mystery is excluded: it is not to an inscrutable but
personal will, apt in any moment to act in new and unpredictable
ways, that such features of our world are to be referred, but simply to the mystery and obscurity of the cosmic process itself,
whose infinite scope and impenetrable depths our limited minds cannot fathom.

It is precisely this question about the kind of mystery which
nature manifests that is at issue in the modern theological discussion of miracle. The proponents of a doctrine of miracle as interruption of natural order claim that any view holding that such deliberate acts of God do not (or cannot) occur reduces or obscures
the genuine mystery in our lives, hidden ultimately in God's inscrutable will; for it involves the claim that the basic (and in-
violable) order or structure of nature is in some real sense discernible by us. But those who deny the appropriateness of this
view can claim that it is precisely the doctrine of miracle that
refuses to face the mystery of existence, for it disposes too easily of the unusual or uncomprehended by referring them to that which
is supposedly known and can be trusted, the will of a God who loves
and redeems his creatures; thus, the proponents of a doctrine of
miracle erode the genuine mystery of our existence, seeking to
overcome their anxieties as personal beings in an impersonal world
by the postulation of a purposive and personal God as its Creator
and Lord. In this argument it is clearly the opponents of miracle
who have won the day. Few any longer are disposed to explain the

occurrence of particular events by referring them directly to God's
intervention in the natural order. Although many theologians still
wish to say such occurrences are possible "in principle" (for "with
God all things are possible," Matt. 19:26), it is clear that both
their practical decisions and actions and their theological theories
are controlled by the assumption of the fundamental autonomy of
natural order. In view of the fact that this is completely inconsistent with the supposedly authoritative biblical conception of
God as one who continuously *acts* in and upon nature as its Lord, it
is little wonder that contemporary talk about God sounds hollow and
abstract, and for many of us has become uncomfortable and difficult.

A frequently proposed way out of this dilemma is to concede
that nature, as we experience it and have learned to describe it
in science, is indeed autonomous and self-contained, but that God
acts in man's history, revealing himself, covenanting with man,
rescuing men from the various forms of bondage into which they have
fallen. Though nature may be ruled by impersonal iron necessity,
history is the realm of freedom and purpose in which values are
cherished and ends are pursued; though teleological conceptions
may well obstruct and even make impossible the work of the natural
scientist, without such categories as *purpose* and *act* the historian
could not even begin his work. Hence, if God is to be conceived
as one who acts, it is in terms of our experience of history that
we must understand him: he is one who acts through the events of
history as history's Lord. Although in our understanding of nature
we are instructed by modern secular science, in our interpretation
of history we can be believers.

The shallowness of this proposal--though it has often been
enunciated in the desperation of contemporary theology--should be
immediately apparent. In the first place, no one conceives of or
experiences "history" in this kind of sharp isolation from "nature."
All historical events take place within the context of natural
process and order and involve the movements and reordering of
physical bodies and material objects of many sorts. Moreover, many
natural events--one needs think only of rainfall and drought, earth-
quake and disease, birth and death--have significant historical
consequences. It is impossible to speak of history as though it
were a realm of freedom and decision entirely separate from nature.
Certainly the biblical perspective is not characterized by such
nonsense. It is a measure of the desperation of contemporary
theology and faith, in the face of the power of the modern scientific world view--a desperation already manifest in Kant's

metaphysical agnosticism[3] to which such theological views are
heavily indebted--that this way out was attempted at all. It will
not do to speak of God as the agent who made it possible for the
Israelites to escape from the Egyptians, if one regards it as simply a fortunate coincidence that a strong east wind was blowing at
just the right time to dry up the sea of reeds. The biblical
writer's view is coherent and compelling precisely because he is
able to say that "*the Lord* drove the sea back by a strong east
wind" (Exod. 14:21); that is, it was because, and only because,
God was Lord over nature, one who could bend natural events to his
will, that he was able to be effective Lord over history.

In the second place--even if the sharp bifurcation of nature
and history could be made intelligible--referring acts of God to
historical events really helps little to resolve the fundamental
problem. For the modern experience of and interpretation of history, just as surely as the modern view of nature, is entirely in
terms of intramundane powers and events. We may well agree that
history is a realm in which decision and action, pursuit of ends
and appreciation of value and meaning, have genuine reality and
effectiveness; we may be prepared to argue that some measure of
genuine freedom and creativity must be presupposed to account for
the creation and cumulation of culture, teleologically modifying
nature in such diverse ways. But this certainly does not incline
many of us to speak of *God's* free and creative activity in and
through the historical process. Indeed, the orientation of the
modern historian explicitly precludes such extraworldly reference:
his task is to explain and interpret the movement of man's history
entirely by reference to the interaction of human wills, the development of human institutions and traditions, and the effects
of natural events and processes, that is, exclusively in intramundane terms. Doubtless he may refer to historic decisions and
to creative ideas and imaginative visions, but these are always
the work of human political or military leader, artist or philosopher or dreamer. Never does he invoke a transcendent agent to
explain what has occurred, and never does he suppose it necessary,
or even intelligible, to refer to some injection into the human
historical process from beyond in order to understand even the most
radical historical reversals or the most creative beginnings: all
are to be understood by reference to human powers and actions in
the context of the natural world.

It is not out of some unbelieving perversity that the modern
historian thus thinks and writes; rather, since this is the way we

in fact experience history, this is the only way in which it is
intelligible to us. Nor is this an attempt to ignore or reduce
the mystery of the historical movement in which we are immersed by
disregarding its depths and obscurities; few would claim to understand "where history is going" or "the pattern of history." The
mystery remains. But it is the mystery and obscurity of human
creativity and willfulness, the mystery and incomprehensibility of
cosmic process, not the mystery and inscrutability of the purposes
and will of a personal and loving God who is moving the world toward a consummation known only to him.

Inasmuch as our modern experience and understanding of history
is quite as secular as our experience and understanding of nature,
the concept "act of God" can no more readily be interpreted by
reference to historical events than to natural. But since the root
metaphor that informs the Western notion of God and gives it its
special character is that of a supreme Actor or Agent, it is little
wonder that the notion of God has become empty for us, that "God
is dead."[4] An agent is experienced and known in and through his
acts; since we no longer grasp events as genuinely acts of the
transcendent God, the Agent himself has faded away for us into
little more than a word inherited from our past. In this situation
three alternatives confront us. The first, and probably most common, is to grant that "God is dead," that is, that life is to be
understood in humanistic and naturalistic terms; if the word "God"
is used at all, it will only be in perfunctory and conventional
ways, not out of the awareness and conviction of a genuine trans-
human agent. The second, followed, for example, by Paul Tillich,
is decisively to reinterpret the notion of God in such a manner
that the conception of agent is no longer implied; then the reality
of God will be sought in other dimensions of experience than
"acts." The third, which I shall attempt here, is to subject our
ordinary notion of "act" to a reexamination to see whether it is
possible to reinterpret the conception of "God's act(s)" in a sense
to some extent continuous with ordinary usage but nevertheless
theologically significant and philosophically intelligible.

If the conception of God's "act" can be developed as the fundamental metaphysical category for interpreting his relation to
finite beings, the theological task is much facilitated. God
himself can be viewed as *Agent*, one who has intentions and purposes that he realizes in and through creation; thus his creative,
providential, and redemptive activity can be rendered intelligible
in fairly straightforward terms, reasonably continuous with

biblical language. Such a defining image of God is not only ad-
vantageous when interpreting the heavily anthropomorphic terminology
about God's love, mercy, justice, and wisdom; it also provides a
way to interpret his transcendence,[5] thus preserving his radical
independence and aseity even while making possible an understanding
of his relation to the world. Furthermore, if it is possible to
understand God as an active being in this quasi-personal sense,
it is much easier to work out the complex metaphysical problems
having to do with his relation to other agents, men.[6] Conversely,
if "act"-language is abandoned in theology, or is subordinated to
the language of being or cause or process, it becomes difficult to
regard much of the traditional terminology as anything more than
poetic metaphor or outright equivocation.

II

An act (as we ordinarily think of it) is something done or
performed, a deed; it is a particular and generally a specific
event brought about by an agent. Acts may be of shorter or longer
duration, and although an act always has a certain unity governed
by the end or objective that is being pursued, it need not be completed in a single unbroken stretch of time, but may be interrupted
and then resumed (as with the act of building a house or writing
a book). But in all cases a particular act has a certain unity and
specificity; it is some particular thing achieved, a definite deed
done. It is not mere activity, but activity bound together and
given a distinct order and structure by the intention of an agent
to realize a goal.[7]

The goal seeking characteristic of an act must be distinguished
from the immanent teleology that Aristotle ascribed to living organisms. The latter simply follow patterns built into their very
structure and handed on from generation to generation: thus the
acorn becomes an oak which again produces more acorns. In the
case of an act, this ruling pattern does not exist; instead, the
agent deliberately posits the end he intends to realize--and it
may be something quite new, which had not existed before or which
he had not done before. Thus, an act involves an element of creativity not characteristic of lower forms of life than man. The
cumulation of such (creative) acts produces the *historical* order,
culture, a new order of being superimposed on the process of life
and not to be simply identified with it. To understand the teleological movements of living organisms, which involve the repetition
of unfolding patterns long since established--the acorn simply

becoming another oak--it is necessary only to postulate that the
same pattern somehow be transferred from generation to generation.
The purposive movement of an act, however, inasmuch as it is no
mere repetition of previous pattern but involves creative production
of the new, cannot be understood in this way. In this case there
must be an *agent* who performs the act, a reality in which is lodged
the teleological intention to be realized through it. Such an
agent must be capable both of formulating the intention to be realized in the future (he must have powers of imagining the presently
nonexistent) and of working through time in such ordered fashion
as to realize his goal. The successive moments of time here are
bound together not by a preestablished pattern implanted in the
organism but by the purposive activity of the agent. Thus, *act* and
purpose should not be reduced to Aristotle's notion of the teleology
at work in all organisms; our proper model here is human purposive
behavior.

Acts may be broken down into constituent acts (or subacts),
each of which makes its necessary contribution to the larger act.
Thus, my act of constructing a bench will include within it many
subacts, hammering, sawing, measuring, and so forth. Each of these,
involving as it does its own unification of activity toward a particular goal, can be considered an act in its own right. Fastening
one board to another is a particular act, but so is driving in each
of the nails used to secure that board; we may, if we choose, regard each blow on the head of a nail as itself a distinct act. But
there is a limit below which acts may not be further analyzed into
constituent acts. We would not, for example, regard the movement
of the hammer through each separate inch of the path toward the
head of the nail as a distinct act; such fractions of activity in
which no end, not even a subordinate one, is attained, though essential constituents of the act of hitting the nail, are not themselves acts. To be regarded as an act, the movement must realize
some posited objective, however slight or unimpressive, such as
striking the nail. The same sort of rule governs the upper limit
of the size and inclusiveness of an act as the lower: so long as
the subacts are bound together into a single overall teleological
unity, we may speak of them as one act. Thus, building a house is
a particular act, but it may be viewed as part of the larger act
(if done with this larger end in view) of establishing a village
or even founding a nation. Moreover, several individuals, or even
groups, can participate in the same act, if their activity is ordered toward a common end (cf. an "act of Congress"). We would

be hesitant, however, about describing the complicated and long
historical process of, for example, the rise of science as *an act*.
This is not because of its complexity per se, but because the many
constituent events of this development can hardly be conceived as
ordered toward and controlled by some definite end posited by some
particular individual or group: it is difficult to see this process
as *an act* performed by *an agent* (even a collective agent). Although
many acts doubtless contributed to this development, the peculiar
kind of unity to which the term "act" points does not characterize
the process as a whole.

An "act of God," now, in the literal meaning of the phrase,
would be a deed performed by God, an event that did not simply "happen," but that was what it was because God did it.[8] Certainly this
is the picture of the "mighty acts of God" found in scripture. Here
God does things just as do men: he enters into battle, he makes
covenants with his people, he builds and destroys cities and nations, he cares for the poor and helpless and brings to judgment
the wicked, he comforts the afflicted, he causes the sun to shine
and the rain to fall, he brings plagues and destruction but also
healing and well-being, he has created this very world in which we
find ourselves, and he will yet create new heavens and a new earth.
Each of these is a particular act done by God either simply on his
own initiative to further his ends or in response to something
done by men.

It may be supposed that the difficulty we moderns feel with
such talk of God's acts arises simply and entirely from our unwillingness or inability to think in terms of supernatural causes of
historical events. And thus, on the one hand, traditionalists may
declaim in the name of faith against what they regard as modern
unbelief, while, on the other, secularists will laugh at the naïveté
of those who suppose God really does something. These contrary
positions both arise from the common assumption that an act of God
is to be thought of as a particular miraculous event that God directly causes,[9] and as long as this conception is left undisturbed,
the impasse cannot be resolved. In order to do so, it will be
necessary both to analyze with more subtlety certain roots of the
modern difficulties with the notion of God's acts and also to
elaborate more fully some of the implications of the previous analysis of an act for the notion of God's act.

III

The modern difficulties here do not arise exclusively, as is
often supposed, from our unwillingness to believe in some transcendent *cause* of events; they arise quite as much from our inability to conceive *these events themselves*, in view of the way in
which we (necessarily?) conceive nature and history. In this paper
I shall confine myself largely to the second problem, leaving
questions about the mode of God's causal impingement on the world
for treatment elsewhere.[10]

According to the modern view, events are not conceived as individual atoms that are more or less independent of the natural
and historical context or web within which they fall. All events
are so interrelated and interconnected in many complex ways that
to think or to describe any particular event always involves us in
reference to those events which preceded it as necessary conditions
for its occurring, to those events which surround it and thus
specify it by both defining its boundaries or limits and providing
the context within which it falls and the background against which
it is perceived and known, and to those ever widening circles of
events which it will condition and shape in a variety of ways. One
of the greatest of Kant's achievements in the first *Critique* was
his demonstration that we not only think in terms of such an interconnected and unified web of events, but that such a unified
whole is a necessary condition for having experience at all; that
is, it would not even be possible to experience totally isolated
and unconnected particulars. The success of modern natural science
in describing, predicting, and in some measure controlling events
in the natural order is due precisely to the discovery of ways to
discern and formulate fundamental structural regularities obtaining
between events (laws of nature), but this growing success makes
it increasingly difficult even to conceive what an event occurring
somehow independently of this web might be.[11] A similar development has occurred in historical work. The great achievement of
modern history is its success in developing methods of analysis,
criticism, and evaluation of the "sources" with which the historian
works, methods that enable the historian to give a wholly satisfactory and convincing interpretation of the order and character
of the events with which he is dealing without reference to anything
beyond the historical process and its natural context. The pre-
supposition of modern historical understanding (as of scientific
knowledge) is that each new event emerges out of, and can and must
be understood in relationship to, the historical context in which

it appears. Though the event may qualify and transform the future
course of that history in significant ways, it never appears within
the historical process as an inexplicable bolt from the blue.
When a historian has to deal with remains so fragmentary that he
is unable to propose a hypothesis about their proper place in the
continuing movement of history, he never assumes this was because
of some supernatural origin, to do so would imply a conception of
breaks in the historical process that would vitiate even the possibility of knowledge of the past. His conclusion (rightly) is
that we simply do not have sufficient evidence to say what happened
here. But there is no question in his mind (or ours) that if we
did have the requisite evidence, we would be able to understand in
intrahistorical terms the events in question. Not only is secular
history written in terms of such assumptions, the whole enterprise
of modern biblical criticism and interpretation proceeds (quite
properly) on the same basis.[12] Without such assumptions about the
continuity of the historical process, the analogy of preceding
events and periods with our own (secular) experience, and the necessity of criticism of documents, it would not even be possible
to think what a historical event is, as Ernst Troeltsch long ago
clearly perceived.[13]

   It should not be supposed that this modern conception of
nature and history as a web of interrelated events that must be
understood as a self-contained whole is a somewhat arbitrary move,
that we could just as well, if we pleased, go back to earlier notions of a much looser weave in the nature of things such that occasionally events without finite cause might appear. The development toward the modern conception was a necessary and natural one
fostered by an increasing awareness of the conditions of knowledge
and experience, and the tremendous growth of modern scientific and
historical knowledge is both its consequence and confirmation. Nor
should it be supposed that the discovery of certain indeterminacies
on the microatomic level opens the door once again to the older
conception. I have not been arguing for a (quasi-mechanical)
determinism of all events by their antecedents, but rather that
the modern pursuit of knowledge presupposes the interrelation and
interconnection of all events in an unbroken web. That there may
be some measure of "play" or indeterminacy on the atomic level,
and that there is genuine creativity and self-determination on
the human level, I am quite prepared not only to admit but to argue.
But this indeterminacy and this freedom occur within and are continuous with contexts such that statistical descriptions can always

be made and are usually quite precise, and (in the case of human
actions) understanding in strictly human terms is demanded. My
point is that it is precisely the gradually developing awareness
of the interconnected web of events which has made possible the
high-level description and understanding characteristic of modern
science and history. Therefore, it is no longer possible for us
to think (when we think clearly and consistently) of individual
or particular events somehow by themselves: every event is defined
as a focal point in a web that reaches in all directions beyond it
indefinitely;[14] it is never grasped (in our modern experience) as
an independent substance that can exist and be thought by itself
alone.

    This being the case, we can see why we have great difficulty
with the traditional notion of "act of God." This phrase seems to
refer to events that have their source or cause directly or immediately in the divine will and action rather than in the context
of preceding and coincident finite events: indeed, the finite nexus
apparently need not be thought as conditioning the newly injected
event in any significant way, though a chain of consequences within
the finite order presumably ensues from it. Acts of God in this
sense, seen from man's side, are absolute beginning points for
chains of events that occur--not at the "beginning" of the world
and history--but *within* ongoing natural and historical processes.
It might be supposed this could be made intelligible by viewing
the movement through time of nature and history under the metaphor,
for example, of a flowing river, with new streams (acts of God)
from time to time emptying into the onward flow, thus becoming part
of the cumulating rush of waters; but here also, we must remember,
such streams can always be traced by a recursive movement to their
(finite) sources somewhere back in the hills, precisely what this
notion of God's acts renders impossible. I want to emphasize that
the problem we are considering does not arise in the first instance
out of difficulties connected with conceiving a transcendent agent;
it is rather the difficulty--even impossibility--of conceiving the
finite event itself which is here supposed to be God's act. That
is, the problem is not that such acts invoke a no longer believable
mythology of some being beyond this world (however serious that
problem may itself be); it is rather that what is said to happen
in this world, in our experience, is not intelligible. An "event"
without finite antecedents is no event at all and cannot be clearly
conceived; "experience" with tears and breaks destroying its continuity and unity could not even be experienced. It is incorrect

to suppose, then, that all that is required here is a reformulation
of our categories so as to make room for an occasional act of God;
the problem is that certain logical preconditions of connection,
continuity and unity must obtain if there is to be any experience
at all (Kant), and precisely these conditions are contradicted by
the notion of particular "acts of God" being performed from time
to time in history and nature. Or, to put the matter in a somewhat
different way: it is impossible to conceive such an act either as
a natural event or as a historical event, as occurring either within
nature or history; in short, it is impossible to conceive it as any
kind of event (in the finite order) at all. Our experience is of
a unified and orderly world; in such a world acts of God (in the
traditional sense) are not merely improbable or difficult to believe: they are literally inconceivable. It is not a question of
whether talk about such acts is true or false; it is, in the literal
sense, meaningless; one cannot make the concept hang together consistently.

IV

Having noted certain difficulties for the modern consciousness
with the notion that God performs particular more or less individual
acts in history, let us return to the earlier analysis of *act* to
see whether there are possibilities of reformulation. I will be
able to present here only in brief outline a way to conceive God's
act in analogy with human acts and yet consistently with the re-
quirements of modern scientific and historical work; many important
details, relating both to the (analogical) concept of God as Agent
and his mode of affecting finite processes, remain to be worked
out.[15] However, if the proposed reconstruction is successful, the
(analogical) concept of God's act can be utilized as the fundamental
metaphysical category for interpreting his relation to finite reality, that is, as the form of all his diverse relations to the
world, the schema that gives them intelligible unity. If we are
going to understand the fullness and diversity of creation in its
manifold relations to the one God, we must have a concept that is
at once general enough to cover the infinite complexity and many-
sidedness of those relations and still gives them a sufficiently
unified form to be intelligible. I suggest that the notion of
act, having the specificity of referring immediately to an agent
and yet the generality of comprehending all the relations into
which an agent can enter, can provide the basis for developing an
analogical concept appropriate to perform this function.

Two points particularly must be recalled from the earlier discussion. First, comprehensive or complex acts may be analyzed or
broken down into constituent elements and sub-elements, some of
which are themselves simpler acts, some biological or physical processes or motions; or, stated conversely, simple or particular acts
are often phases of overarching complex acts--we will call these
"master acts"--which unify and order various sorts of behavior and
otherwise disconnected stretches of time. Second, that which makes
an act an *act* is the deliberate ordering of behavior toward the
realization of a previously posited end. I want to argue now that
the customary interpretation of certain relatively restricted events
--the crossing of the Red Sea, the dispersing of the hosts of Sennacherib, the virgin birth or resurrection of Jesus--as particular
acts of God is too simple. For it overlooks the significance of
the relation of "simple acts" to "master acts."

It is the master act, rather than each simple act taken by
itself, that renders any given piece of activity intelligible.
Simple acts, being constituent phases of a complex act, are always
secondary and derivative, for they are not performed simply for the
sake of their own end but rather as a step toward the master end:
the nail is not hammered simply to get it into the board (that is
a subordinate objective) but in order to build the house. Doubtless
certain subordinate acts must be performed in order to complete
the complex act, but they have their purpose and gain their character from the latter, and we can be said to "understand" them only
when we see them in the light of the master end. Thus, we do not
find it particularly illuminating to say simply, "The carpenter is
driving nails," for that in itself is hardly meaningful activity;
rather, it is when we see that the carpenter is nailing together
boards in order to construct a house that we understand what he is
doing.

If we are to understand properly the phrase "act of God," then,
we should use it first of all to designate the *master act* in which
God is engaged, not the particular and relatively limited events
that might first attract our attention. The latter must be regarded
as secondary and derivative, to be grasped and interpreted in the
light of God's master end, not in their own terms. This means for
a monotheistic theology that it is *the whole course of history*,
from its initiation in God's creative activity to its consummation
when God ultimately achieves his purposes, that should be conceived
as God's act in the primary sense. In the biblical documents God
is not portrayed as one who performs relatively disconnected and

unrelated acts that lead in no particular direction or toward no
definite goal; he is one who planned "the end from the beginning"
(Isa. 46:10), and his activity throughout history is ordered toward
his ultimate goal, the final establishment of that "kingdom which
has been destined for [his creatures] from the creation of the
world" (Matt. 25:34 Goodspeed). Even the appearance of Jesus Christ
far down the course of history "was destined before the foundation
of the world" (1 Pet. 1:20), and what he brought into history is to
be understood as but a foretaste of the final glorious consummation.
The movement of history as portrayed in the Bible is no mere succession of events--not even a succession of "acts of God"--leading
to no clear goal or end: from its beginning and throughout, it is
given shape and direction by the ultimate objective that God is
bringing to pass. Since, as we observed previously, activity proceeding from a single agent and ordered toward a single end, no
matter how complex, is properly to be regarded as *one act*, this
whole complicated and intricate teleological movement of all nature
and history should be regarded as a single all-encompassing act of
God, providing the context and meaning of all that occurs. It is,
of course, an act that has not yet run its course, an act that will
not be finished until the eschaton.

This conception of God's master act does not encounter the
same difficulties with the modern presuppositions about the unity
and structure of nature and history as did the notion of various
relatively independent act-events. For here God's act is not a
new event that suddenly and without adequate prior conditions rips
inexplicably into the fabric of experience, a notion consistent
neither with itself nor with the regularity and order that experience must have if it is to be cognizable. Rather, here God's act
is viewed as the source of precisely that overarching order itself:
it is God's master act that gives the world the structure it has
and gives natural and historical processes their direction.
Speaking of God's act in this sense in no way threatens the unity
and order of the world as a whole.[16]

It is meaningful to regard the fundamental structures of nature and history as grounded in an *act* (of God), however, only if
we are able to think of them as developing in time. An act is
intrinsically temporal: it is the ordering of a succession of
events toward an end. If we could not think of the universe as
somehow developing in unidirectional fashion in and through temporal processes, it would be mere poetry to speak of God's act.
For this reason, prior to the late nineteenth and early twentieth

centuries, while a static-structural view of nature prevailed, it
was very difficult to think of nature as ordered by God's act in
any further sense than being created (and sustained) by him. But
a scientific revolution occurred in the nineteenth and twentieth
centuries: geologists began to see the earth not as a more or less
static given, but as having a history through which it developed
during many ages to its present form; biologists came to see life
not merely as a structure of species, but as a unitary evolutionary
process in continuous development from lower forms to highly complex ones; and astronomers even discovered that the supposedly
eternally stable heavens actually manifested a continuously expanding movement through billions of years, seeming to go back to some
primeval originating "explosion." In short, scientists came to
think of nature, in all her levels and forms, as in historical process, as moving and developing and evolving in time. Thus, to
conceive the whole cosmic movement as comprehended within a single
"act" through which God is achieving some ultimate purpose is consistent with the modern understanding of nature as in process of
evolutionary development.[17]

It will be objected immediately that science finds no evidence
of teleological or purposed order in this movement, that the most
one can observe is simply a kind of natural evolution. With this
I will not quibble: I am not claiming that the cosmic process provides *evidence* for believing in a God active through it; I am
claiming merely that the evolutionary picture of nature and life
currently painted in our scientific knowledge is not inconsistent
with such belief. The purpose that informs an act is an interior
connection between the various phases of events known to the agent
who is performing it, and it is seldom directly visible to external observers, especially to those who can see only a tiny fraction
of the total act in question. If God is acting through the process
of nature's development over billions of years to accomplish some
ultimate objective, this would hardly be apparent in the observations of lowly men, with a life-span of a mere three score years
and ten and careful scientific observations and records going back
at most only a few hundred years. To use a geometrical figure: one
could hardly expect man to discern the teleological curvature of
the movement of world history as a whole when he has accessible
to his direct inspection scarcely more than an infinitesimal arc
of that curve. Such teleological activity by a cosmic agent could
be known only if he should in some way choose to reveal it to his
creatures.[18]

Thus, to conceive the entire movement of nature and history as the expression of one overarching act of God is consistent both with the meaning of the term "act" and with the modern understanding of the cosmos as in evolutionary development. True, no evidence has been offered here to sustain such a view of an ultimate teleology working in nature, and I do not propose in this paper to offer any. That would involve us in an examination of the psychological, historical, and logical grounds for belief in God, and it would require sketching out doctrines of God and of revelation.[19] In short, it would lead far beyond the scope of the present inquiry. We are concerned here with the very restricted objective of clarifying and reinterpreting the notion of God's act in such a way that it will be intelligible in the light of current scientific and historical assumptions about the interconnectedness of all events. Unless this can be done, all speech about God as "Lord" of the world, as providentially guiding history, as loving and merciful father of mankind, as active agent in any significant sense at all-- speech that is essential for Christian and Jewish faith--is hollow and empty, whatever be one's grounds for believing in God. Both the present sort of analysis (dealing with God's relation to the world) and exploration of the wider question of the grounds for speaking of God at all will be required if the highly problematic status that all such talk presently has is to be overcome.

V

Having proposed an interpretation of "act of God" in its primary and widest meaning, as designating the overall movement of nature and history toward God's ultimate goal, I must return in conclusion to the more customary understanding of the phrase as referring to particular events in which God does something "unusual" or "special" in history. Is this ordinary meaning of the phrase to be ignored or dispensed with entirely? Is it not such *particular acts* in which faith believes and for which prayer cries rather than a cosmological overview? Have we not so transformed--and, some might say, "watered down"--the meaning of God's activity as to render it religiously irrelevant or empty?

To these questions two remarks may be addressed. (1) The question whether the phrase "act of God" can have any referential meaning at all is primarily intellectual or theoretical. In saying this I do not mean to ignore or disparage religious or existential aspects of this problem, for they are also there, but the principal difficulty here is that our understanding of the world, of experience, of history, has become such that there seems no way to conceive or imagine cosmic purposive activity working in events. That is, it is the *theory* informing all our experience and thought that appears radically inconsistent with that older personalistic (or anthropomorphic) theory of the world, which everywhere informs the biblical literature and our most fundamental theological conceptions. Unless this problem of theory, of conceptualization, of the basic categories of experience can be resolved, we are condemned either to live in an intolerable tension between our religious language and life and the rest of experience—a tension always threatening to disintegrate and destroy both the self and its faith—or to give up Christian faith and talk as outmoded and no longer relevant to the actual structures of our lives and world. It is a problem in theory, then, that we must address here, and it should not be surprising if the treatment of that problem will be, in the first instance, theoretical. We must find some way to *think* about the world once again with the categories of act and purpose if we wish to continue using these categories to speak of God and his relations to men. I freely admit, therefore, that I am proposing here a rather theoretical understanding of the notion of God's act.

The principal point I have tried to emphasize in this paper is that it is no longer possible for us to view the events in nature and history as relatively independent occurrences, each to be perceived and interpreted more or less in its own terms; for us the world has become a unified whole such that particular events are always experienced and understood in terms of their structural connections with the rest of experience, as described and clarified by scientist and historian. The order or structure of the whole thus has a kind of precedence, with us, over any particular happening, and we are inclined to discount even our own immediate experience—for example, to regard it as hallucinatory—if it cannot be understood in terms of that underlying and omnipresent order. In the more loosely textured world of earlier generations particular "acts of God" could be experienced and accepted more or less in their own terms, no matter how extraordinary they might appear, for who could say what character a new event might have? In our tightly structured world it is necessary to find place for God's activity in the fundamental order of things before it is even possible to speak meaningfully of his acting in particular events, for the conception of the latter and the very criteria with the aid of which we perceive and interpret them is derivative from and dependent upon our understanding of the basic order. Hence, if we are to

speak of particular acts of God at all, we must first learn to speak
of his act in and through the structure and movement of the whole.
It is precisely a way of conceiving that act which is proposed in
this paper.

(2) This proposal of theory, however, opens up once again a
way to understand the notion of particular acts of God of more limited scope. These are not to be regarded (as in the traditional
mythology) as more or less impulsive decisions in which God does
something in history in quite unexpected and inexplicable fashion:
they should be understood (quite consistently with the eschatological
orientation of much biblical, and all New Testament, thought) as
functions of and subordinate steps toward God's ultimate goal. The
master act of God (which he has not yet completed) is the temporal
movement of all nature and history toward the realization of his
original intention in creation. This complex act comprises many
events and processes of all sorts as its constituent phases and
elements. Some of these, themselves teleologically ordered toward
certain subordinate ends or goals which are necessary steps toward
the master end, may quite properly be regarded as (subordinate)
acts or subacts performed by God as he works out his purpose.

Assuming (on the basis of Christian claims) that God has revealed something of his purposes for man and the world, one finds
it possible to discern, with the help of modern knowledge of nature
and history, some of the stages (subacts) through which the created
order has moved as God has gradually been performing his master
act.[20] The creation of the solar system, the emergence of life on
earth, the evolution of higher forms of life and finally man--each
of these (as well as many other natural processes and events) represents an indispensable step toward the realization of God's ultimate objectives for creation. Furthermore, the crucial phases of
the actual movement of human history, and the emergence of *Heilsgeschichte* within that history, can be regarded as further subordinate acts of God: the beginnings of agriculture and later of civil-
ization, the development of increasingly complex and interdependent
modes of social, political, and economic organization making possible differentiation and specialization in socio-cultural life,
the emergence of primitive religious cultus and conceptions (especially in the Near East) providing a background against which faith
in Yahweh could appear. Specific events of quite limited scope
such as the remarkable escape of a few Hebrew tribes from Egyptian
slavery, the creation of the Israelite kingdom under Saul and David,
and the later exile and return of the inhabitants of Judah are acts

through which God moved human history and consciousness toward a fuller awareness of who he is and what his purposes for creation are. Within this sequence, the ministry and death of Jesus Christ can quite properly be understood as the supreme act through which God at once made himself known to man and began a radical transformation of man according to his ultimate purposes for man. Events in other cultural histories and the more recent events in Western history may all be seen in this way as governed or guided by the activity through which God is moving the whole of creation toward the eschaton, as subordinate acts within God's master act.[21] Thus, the whole course of history (including the history of nature and the evolution of life) can be apprehended once again as under God's providential control.

This does not mean, of course, that every natural or histori-cal event need be or should be regarded as a distinct subact of God; only those events which move the creation forward a further step toward the realization of God's purposes could properly be so designated. There are many natural processes, for example, which, though originally set in motion by God's creative activity, now function as fundamental rhythms or orders that support and sustain the more complex processes of the teleological movement, thus giving the world a certain constancy and structure. It would hardly be appropriate to regard the continuing steady functioning of such processes as new "acts of God"; they are, rather, the product of his earlier (creative) work, still sustained by him no doubt, but now serving as the (relatively completed) foundation on which he can build as yet unrealized superstructures. Furthermore, when certain finite processes evolved through the various stages of life to the level of conscious and free behavior, the purposive activity of finite agents began to appear within the historical process. Inas-much as these acts in and of themselves, even though teleological in form, had (and have) their sources and goals within the finite order itself, they are not necessarily to be considered as direct subacts of God. Indeed, they could and often did (and do) go counter to God's purposes and acts, as with man's falling into cumulating patterns of sin. On the Christian view, perhaps only once in his-tory--the march of Jesus to the cross--has there been a direct one-to-one correspondence and coincidence of human activity with divine. Only those natural and historical events which directly advance God's ultimate purposes--those which are essential constituent phases or steps of God's master act--may properly be regarded as (subordi-nate) acts of God within nature and history.[22]

This understanding of God's subordinate acts does not in any
way undermine or threaten the unified and structural character of
experience, or the methods or conclusions of science and history.
For between particular events and overarching structures and con-
tinuities, the same formal relationship obtains in the theological
interpretation as in that of modern history or science: in all these
cases the particular is seen in the context of, or as a phase of, a
more comprehensive whole. Of course, the theological view posits a
teleological movement in that whole which is not discernible to the
naked scientific eye, but this eschatological goal in which faith
believes does not itself disclose to faith the complex of particular
historical steps through which God must move to achieve his end;
man becomes aware of these only a posteriori, as creation gradually
moves onward through its historical course and man learns to discern
the several phases of that movement in his science and history.
There is here, then, place both for the most rigorous application of
scientific and historical methods to the analysis and interpretation
of (past) experience and also for faith that the temporal movement
of the whole, including the particular developments of our individual
lives, is under God's providential care.

It must be admitted that the doctrine of providence here entailed is more austere than the pietistic views often found in Christian circles. God's subordinate acts here are governed largely by
his overarching purposes and ultimate objectives, not simply by the
immediate needs or the prayerful pleas of his children. This is
no God who "walks with me and talks with me" in close interpersonal
communion, giving his full attention to my complaints, miraculously
extracting me from difficulties into which I have gotten myself by
invading nature and history with *ad hoc* rescue operations from on
high. This is the Lord of heaven and earth, whose purposes we cannot fully fathom and whose ways are past finding out (Rom. 11:33).
"It is he who sits above the circle of the earth, and its inhabitants
are like grasshoppers" (Isa. 40:22). His thoughts are not ours, and
our ways are not his (Isa. 55:8). He has brought this world into
being for his own reasons, he is moving it through a history in accordance with his own objectives, and he shall accomplish his purposes when the eschaton comes. Doubtless we men, both as species
and individuals, have place within those purposes, and certain of
his subacts are responsive to our acts; in this we can rejoice, finding meaning for our lives and comfort for our souls. But the place
we have is his to determine and assign, not ours; at the very most
our lives are but almost infinitesimal constituents in his

all-comprehending act, and his responsiveness to the particular-
ities of our activity must be understood as a function and phase
of his master act ordering all human and cosmic history. Though
faith grounded on the conviction that in Christ God has disclosed
his true will and nature may trust confidently until the end that
he will deal with us justly and with love, we should hardly expect
that he can or will bend his cosmic activity much to meet our private and peculiar needs or wishes. Indeed, it is precisely this
steadfastness in his own purposes that makes him the faithful God:
who could entrust himself to one who changed course with every turn
in the breeze?

Christian piety has too long been nurtured largely on those
psalms and other biblical materials which portray God as a kind of
genie who will extricate the faithful from the difficulties into
which they fall; it is this erratic and fickle God who cannot be
reconciled with the modern understanding of the order in nature and
history. Far better would it be to nourish our piety on the paradigmatic Christian story: a man praying that this cup might pass
from him, but submitting his will to God's, no matter what the consequences; that prayer answered not with legions of angels to rescue
him but with lonely suffering on a cross, culminating in a cry of
despair before the moment of death--and then a resurrection of new
life, new faith, new hope, new love, in a new community born after
his death. The God who works in this fashion to turn the darkest
despairs and defeats into further steps toward the realization of
his beneficent ultimate objectives, without violently ripping into
the fabric of history or arbitrarily upsetting the momentum of its
powers, is one who can also be conceived as working within and
through the closely textured natural and historical processes of
our modern experience: he is a God who acts, a living God, the
adequate object for a profound faith, and his action is not completely unintelligible to a mind instructed and informed by modern
science and history.

NOTES

[1]"Cosmology, Ontology, and the Travail of Biblical Language,"
Journal of Religion, 41:203, 200 (1961).

[2]See the well-known book of that title by G. Ernest Wright
(London: SCM Press, 1952).

[3]It should be recalled here that according to his own testimony
in the first *Critique* Kant had "found it necessary to deny

knowledge, in order to make room for *faith*" (B xxx [Kemp Smith
trans.] (New York: Macmillan, 1929); cf. B xxivff.).

[4]There are, of course, many other contributing factors to
contemporary unbelief, such as the experience of massive evil in
our time. But the problems with which we are concerned in this
paper have a certain logical, if not existential, priority over
such difficulties.

[5]See my two papers, "Two Models of Transcendence," in *The
Heritage of Christian Thought*, ed. R. E. Cushman and E. Grislis
(New York: Harper and Row, 1965), and "Transcendence without
Mythology," *Harvard Theological Review* 59: 105-32 (1966). [Re-
printed as Chapters 4 and 3, respectively, in this volume.]

[6]When "act"-language is used in this way to interpret ultimate
reality, freedom and creativity are given significant place on the
metaphysical ground floor, in contrast with cosmologies that make
either causal or teleological order (or some form of chance or
indeterminism) fundamental. Thus, such a position can provide a
metaphysical grounding for human freedom and creativity which is
simply unavailable to other cosmological or theological positions.

[7][The notion of an *act* is really much more complex than can
here be described. (See A. R. White, "Introduction," in *The Philosophy of Action* [London: Oxford University Press, 1968], for an
outline of this complexity. Other essays in this volume, as well
as those cited in Chapter 8, note 8, should also be consulted.)
I have attempted here only to point to dimensions that may help to
clarify the notion of "act of God."]

[8]We can still sense something of this meaning even in the
conventional or legal usage of the phrase to designate a terrible
catastrophe--such as being struck by lightning or destroyed by
storm--although such events are now understood to be due entirely
to impersonal natural causes; their unexpectedness, man's power-
lessness before them, their terrifying impact on human affairs may
still evoke some sense of a powerful and inscrutable will working
its way through the events of nature.

[9]It may be observed here that though Aquinas worked out an
elaborate doctrine of "second causes" which he held were the usual
media of God's work, he maintained that God could and sometimes
did work directly and immediately, and this possibility was regarded
by him as theologically indispensable (*Summa Theologica*, I, Q 105),
as indeed it is if one works with a theory of second causes like
that of Thomas. But it is precisely this way of conceiving God's
direct and immediate action in particular events that is no longer
plausible or intelligible.

[10]Though I would not be inclined simply to adopt A. N. Whitehead's or Charles Hartshorne's organismic models for rendering intelligible God's impingement on the world, certainly much is to
be learned from their careful and detailed treatments of this matter. The principal difficulty with them, it seems to me, is that
God's effective initiative and autonomous agency are rendered highly
problematical, and I am concerned to keep these at the very center.
[As suggested on pp. 158-159 below, I am now quite doubtful that
it is logically consistent with the meaning of "God" to speculate
on the means or modes of his direct impingement on the world.]

[11]For example, is it even possible, any more, to think clearly
what is meant by the "virgin birth"? It might be supposed that

this idea is clear enough: it involves conception without the activity of a male partner. But how are we to think of such conception? Are we to suppose that at some point a male sperm appeared within Mary's womb, there fertilizing an egg? If so, how are we to think of this? Were the requisite number of atoms and molecules created instantaneously and out of nothing within Mary's body and somehow infused with life? How is it possible to conceive this in view of the assumptions (indispensable to science) about the conservation of mass-energy, and of the slow evolution of life? If we do not suppose a male sperm was somehow created in Mary's womb, do we think of this conception as without benefit of fertilization at all? Or did the egg fertilize itself? I am far from contending that any or all of these questions can be or need be answered; my point is that the way we have come to think of conception and birth under the tutelage of modern biology makes it inevitable that such questions will arise. For we cannot clearly think (though we can, perhaps, *imagine*) what an event without prior finite causes and conditions would be (and in many cases, as in conception, we know much about what these essential conditions are), and so, no matter at what point in the process of conception and birth we begin, we inevitably and necessarily inquire about the antecedent conditions. *The very definition or concept of event implies for us such connection with indispensable antecedent (finite) conditions,* and it is no longer possible for us to think an "event" as simply supernaturally caused. That is, for us all chains of events, such as the growth of the boy Jesus, presuppose preceding chains of events, such as the development of Mary's pregnancy, and these in turn presuppose other chains; and this continuous recursive movement may not be halted simply arbitrarily. The question, then, is whether it is even possible to conceive clearly the idea of a supernaturally caused event, or (what is the same thing) the occurrence of a finite event without adequate finite causes, or whether such a notion is not quite as self-contradictory as the notion of a square-circle. Cf. Schleiermacher: "every absolute miracle would destroy the whole system of nature. . . . Since . . . that which would have happened by reason of the totality of finite causes in accordance with the natural order does not happen, an effect has been hindered from happening, and certainly not through the influence of other normally counteracting finite causes given in the natural order, but in spite of the fact that all active causes are combining to produce that very effect. Everything, therefore, which had ever contributed to this will, to a certain degree, be annihilated, and instead of introducing a single supernatural power into the system of nature as we intended, we must completely abrogate the conception of nature" (*The Christian Faith* [Edinburgh: T. and T. Clark, 1928], §47, 2).

[12]A good recent analysis that shows clearly why this must be the case, as well as how theologians and biblical historians have often sought to evade the full implications of this matter, will be found in Van A. Harvey, *The Historian and the Believer* (New York: Macmillan, 1966).

[13]See the essay, "Über historische und dogmatische Methode in der Theologie," *Gesammelte Schriften* (4 vols., Tübingen: Mohr, 1912-1925, II, 729-53.

[14]It is, of course, A. N. Whitehead who has worked out most fully both the necessity of conceiving events in this way and also the full cosmological implications of such a conception. (See, e.g., *Science and the Modern World* [New York: Macmillan, 1925], esp. Chap. 7; and the doctrine of "actual occasions" in *Process and Reality* [New York: Macmillan, 1929].) One may learn much from

Whitehead's ontological and cosmological analysis and construction even though one does not wish to commit oneself to his theology.

[15]For some suggestion of my way of treating some, though by no means all of the problems connected with conceiving God as Agent, see my two papers on personalistic conception of divine transcendence ("Two Models of Transcendence," and "Transcendence without Mythology") [and also Chapters 7 and 8 of the present volume]. Much remains to be done, however, especially on the problem of conceiving God as *effecting* his purposes within and for history. Resolution of this issue will depend in part on the success with which one is able to conceive how a human agent effects purposes, and then drawing out the analogy to interpret the divine activity. [See addition to note 10, above.]

[16]John Macmurray even argues that the "only way" in which we can conceive the world as a unified whole is by thinking it as "one action" (*The Self as Agent* [London: Faber and Faber, 1957], p. 204). For if the overarching unity of the world were conceived simply in terms, for example, of the category *process*, it would be "a world in which nothing is ever done; in which everything simply happens; a world, then, in which everything is matter of fact and nothing is ever intended. We should have to assert, in that case, that there are no actions; that what seem such are really events" (p. 219). That is, the concept of process cannot comprise the unity of the entire world because it cannot contain our own actions as part of that overall unity.

[17]It is not consistent, of course, with the assumption that nature is not grounded in anything beyond herself, but that is a different point from the one I am making in this paper, one deserving full discussion in its own right, though it cannot be pursued here.

[18]I cannot here go into the complicated question of whether God has revealed himself, and, if so, how this is to be understood. [See Chapter 7, below.] Suffice it to recall that precisely this is the Christian claim: the knowledge of God and of his purposive activity in and for the world is not attained primarily through observation of nature but rather through his self-disclosure. "For he has made known to us in all wisdom and insight the mystery of his will, according to his purpose which he set forth in Christ as a plan for the fullness of time, to unite all things in him, things in heaven and things on earth" (Eph. 1:9-10).

[19][See Chapters 5, 7, and 10.]

[20][A much fuller treatment of this history of God's activity will be found in my *Systematic Theology* (New York: Scribner's, 1968), Pts. II and III. Further elaboration of certain features of it also appears in the present volume, Chapters 7 and 8.]

[21]It will be evident from this description that God's act must be conceived under only one image of activity, such as the carpenter making a table or the farmer cultivating a field or the parent educating his child. Within the schema of God's act we are including: first, his creation and maintenance of the material orders of nature, and also his ordering them in such a way that life can emerge from them; second, his creation of life and his ordering it through an evolutionary process in which higher and more complex forms gradually emerge from lower and simpler forms, ultimately producing self-conscious life; and third, his creation of the culture-producing being, man, his guidance of man's

historical development so as to make possible the emergence of a
genuinely free and responsible being, and his dealing with free
(and sinful) man in such a way as to redeem him from his self-
imposed bondage and enable him to become what had been originally
intended. Obviously the forms of "act" appropriate to all the
diverse forms of finite being here represented--ranging from bare
matter to free spirits--and appropriate to the objectives God is
seeking to accomplish with each will be quite various, and it would
be a gross error in our theological construction if we attempted to
assimilate them all to one form of (human) act, for example, that
of man the maker. It is essential that we develop our analogies
from the full range of human activities if we are going to render
God's relation to his world intelligible by means of the basic
schema, *act*.

[22][It might be objected by some that this interpretation of
God's act as including subacts actually performed by human agents
requires us to think in terms of two agents for the same act, and
this is at least paradoxical and quite possibly unintelligible
(see Michael McLain, "On Theological Models," *Harvard Theological
Review*, 62: 183 [1969]). I would point out, however, that whatever the difficulties confronting full philosophical conception
of such a notion, it is clearly in accord with our ordinary speech
about actions and deeds. For example, when we say, "Hitler
killed six million Jews" (or "Christopher Wren built St. Paul's
Cathedral" or "Columbus discovered America"), we do not mean he
personally performed every murder; indeed, he may not have pulled
the trigger on a single person. Nevertheless, we regard a large
measure of the responsibility for this horrendous crime as his,
and we clearly think of it as his *deed*, however much the acts and
responsibility of other agents of lower rank were also involved.]

10. UNDERSTANDING AN ACT OF GOD

Frank G. Kirkpatrick

A Methodological Catch-22

There is a certain catch-22 element in any discussion of the nature of an act of God. The discussion necessarily involves two distinct concepts, that of an act and that of God. If the notion of *an act* becomes the focus of discussion and the notion of God remains relatively unexplored, traditional assumptions about God's ubiquity, transcendence, ontological otherness, etc. normally obstruct our willingness to admit that God can perform an act in anything like the way human agents perform acts. If the notion of *God* becomes the focus of discussion and the notion of an act remains relatively unexplored, traditional assumptions about acts being subject to causal explanation normally obstruct our willingness to admit that *any* agent's act (including God's) can be explained without violating the canons of causal law.

The only way to cut through the catch-22 dimension of the problem is to suggest at the outset that the two concepts (an act, God) are so related to each other that only by understanding what is involved in the explanation of *any* act by *any* agent can a case be made for conceiving God as an agent--and that only by conceiving God as an agent can any case be made for modifying some of the traditional attributes ascribed to Him, such as His absolute transcendence of the ontological structures of the world within which human agents act, without sacrificing His divinity.

In other words, to avoid the charge that a picture of God as an agent is not a literal picture of what God *really* is, since agents are too limited and finite, one must first show that what being an agent entails is sufficiently expansive to permit God to be both an agent *and* worthy of worship. The real trick is developing a notion of agency which entails for *any* agent the kind of power, supremacy and freedom from significant restrictions upon his scope of action that God, as agent, must have if He is to be 'really' God. It is not possible to develop a notion of agency such that God can be *both* an agent *and* many of the things traditionally claimed for Him, such as not being a singular entity, not

capable of performing distinct acts which are peculiarly His, im-
passible, beyond all human conceptualization, and exempt from the
basic metaphysical principles of reality.

What I would like to suggest, and then to argue, is that we
entertain the thought-experiment that God is an agent, a singular
being, existing as a distinct entity alongside other entities and
sharing, at least in part, a common world with them (i.e., existing
in time and having some locus from which his action proceeds). It
is then possible, through an investigation of what an act is and
what being an agent entails, to make a case that being an agent
imposes no significant limitations on God's ultimacy and worshipfulness.

One basic stranglehold on the concept of God as an agent is
the assumption that all acts are exhaustively accounted for by
causal explanation. Any act, including a divine act, would therefore have to be regarded as unfree, hence, not the kind of thing
to be attributed to God in an unrestricted manner. If it can be
shown that acts, by their very nature, are occurrences not completely subject to causal law, then the case can be made that to
explain an act is not to capture it without remainder in a net of
scientific, causal law. If the agent and his act are free, at
least in significant respects, from that kind of net, then a divine
agent, with no meaningful limitations upon his scope and efficacy
of action, is necessarily free from the kind of restraints implied
by causal law. Part of what it means to be worthy of worship is
to possess the kind of power, and the freedom to use it in such a
way, as to affect decisively the fulfillment of others. As agent,
God would possess both and hence be worthy of worship (provided,
of course, that His use of power was benevolent).[*]

God as Singular

In order to get the analysis under way, the thought-experiment
requires only that we accept the intelligibility of the notion of
God as a single being, subject to the same metaphysical principles

---

*To be worthy of worship a being must possess two kinds of things:
power to effect its decisions without restraint and the use of that
power in ways that enhance the worshipper. It is possible to imagine a most powerful being who uses his power to degrade beings dependent on him. It is also possible to imagine a most loving,
morally righteous being who does not have enough power to accomplish
his loving purposes. Neither being would be worthy of worship.
In this essay, however, I am concerned primarily with the first
requirement: the capacity to act in such ways and with such power
as to effect decisions without significant restraint. Only if
that requirement is met is it possible to ask whether the power and
action are employed for benevolent purposes.

of explanation as other single beings. We can invoke Whitehead's
famous claim that God is not an exception to metaphysical principles, invoked to save their collapse, but their chief exemplification.

In support of our claim that it is intelligible to understand
God as an agent, 'alongside' other agents, we can also call upon
Edward Pols's claims that "The most fundamental and concrete sense
of power accessible to our intelligence is power in the sense of
agency," and that power in the sense of agency necessarily means
"the power of an agent regarded as an entity."[1] Therefore, if
ultimacy has to do with power, then only *a* being can have the
requisite ultimacy because only an agent-being can exercise power.

Clearly, the full explication of what is entailed by the notion
of God as a singular being is not possible here. All that is necessary as a basis for the remaining discussion of God's acts is
a commitment to the *possibility* that divine uniqueness and transcendence need not be so radically construed as to deny that God is
a singular entity. That commitment will be strengthened, I believe,
by seeing in the following discussion just what is entailed by the
notion of an agent in relation to his acts and to other agents.
As William Power has recently pointed out, transcendence as a
concept "can best be articulated in terms of identifying and describing an unsurpassable concrete or enduring individual in the
context of a metaphysical theory."[2]

Such a concept of transcendence might have two essential component meanings: 1) that any being is other than (over-against or
alongside) other beings. The notion of being 'alongside' other
entities is simply another way of saying that God is an individual.
As a singular, distinct, unique entity God can be 'picked out' from
among other beings and things as 'this' particular being. To say
that He is alongside other beings merely means that there *are* other
beings, (no matter how dependent they might be upon God's decision
to sustain them in existence) with some degree of ontological independence from God; 2) that any free being with the power to act
is transcendent of the limits of his past in the sense that he can
create a future which is not yet. In this sense, transcendence
would be relative to the power and freedom of the agent. With
this second meaning of 'transcendence,' one could affirm God as
the transcendent being (the superlatively powerful and free being)
while recognizing relative degrees of the same kind of transcendence
in other beings. But both meanings of transcendence presuppose
and build upon the concept of singular beings ontologically alongside each other.

The Gordian knot which holds captive any further discussion
of God's acts as straightforwardly intelligible is the assumption
that God cannot be an agent like other agents. Once the intelligibility of God's nature as agent is established, as it can be only
by the principle that He is a singular being (since agents must
be singular beings), then it becomes possible to show how the categories of action apply to His acts just as they do to the acts of
other agents.

God's Relation to the World

If we are willing to entertain the idea of God as a singular
being, we can now move to the second major issue in understanding
an act of God: God's relation to the world. We will bypass, for
the moment, the full justification of using the agent/act category
for God, since that will be the subject of the next phase of the
discussion. In this phase, we are concerned primarily with how
that category best explicates God's relation to the field of His
action. The three possibilities which have been offered are: 1) the
world is to God as the body is to a human agent; 2) the world is
not directly the recipient of God's act but is affected only
through His use of intermediaries; and 3) God is one agent among
many, acting within a common world. Since I have already indicated
my sympathy for the third possibility, I will discuss why I find
the first two possibilities unattractive.

Working backwards, option 2 relies too heavily upon agnosticism
regarding our knowledge of God's real being. As a result it quali-
fies unnecessarily, I believe, the model of agent/act, thereby
putting God at too great a distance from any acts He might perform.
The notion of intermediation presupposes that the agent works his
will upon one thing (the world) by means of some other thing (his
body) in the first instance. If one assumes that God's essential
being is beyond conceptual grasp because it ontologically transcends
the world, then clearly the vehicle of mediation (God's body) will
also be unknowable, and a form of *double* mediation will be required.
Gordon Kaufman seems to accept this position when he says that "the
instrumentalities through which God *qua* His transcendence acts are
by definition completely inaccessible to us . . . we have no access
to God's "body"; we cannot directly observe His "behavior."[3] The
obvious difficulty with this position (which follows from the assumption that God is unknowable in Himself) is that it makes problematic the intelligibility of God's action, which is the very thing
the model of God as agent is supposed to provide. Unless in some
sense, we can directly observe God's behavior (or vehicle of

mediation) as we observe the behavior of other agents (their bodies:
no matter how unobservable their 'inner life' might be), we will
have no significant conception of how God relates to the world.

The virtue of the first model (the world *as* God's body) is
that it promises to obviate the difficulties Kaufman runs into in
understanding how we can link God to his observable acts in the
world. The problem with intermediaries is really the problem of
the relation between a non-observable intention and its observable
effect. In our relation to our own bodies, any link between intention and effect (I intend to raise my arm and it rises) is relatively non-problematic.* Such an act is usually called *basic*,[4]
requiring no intermediate vehicle (except the use of the natural
processes of my body which permit the intention to be carried out).
In this instance, such as winking at someone, I do not need to
employ some other 'body' to get my intention enacted. If I wish
to open the door, however, I must use my body as the intermediate
vehicle to enable me to pull the door open. When someone sees the
'bodily me' pulling open the door, he can reasonably infer that
the opening is my act. But in the case of God, according to Kaufman, we do not see his body 'in' the act, and therefore we are in
ignorance as to what kind of body he has by means of which he carries out his intention. But David Griffin suggests that all God's
acts are like the raising of my arm, requiring no intervening body
between the intention and its effect. Therefore, he concludes that
the most adequate model for understanding God's relation to his
basic acts is that of an agent to his own body, in this case the
world.[5]

What Griffin does not consider, however, is whether it is possible for an agent to act without using the vehicle of his own body
in order to affect some object which is not his body. It is at
least conceivable that an agent could move an object other than
himself simply by willing it without using a physical mediator.
Speculation has called such an act 'telekinetic' or 'psychokinetic.'
It is not known whether such acts do occur but conceptually they are
not incoherent. They would involve an agent willing that something
happen, not necessarily to his own body or by means of his own
body, and simply as a result of the willing, it happens. As John
S. Morreall has said, "while most of us have not had the experience

---

*In the sense that the difficulty of understanding how arms rise
upon the instigation of an intention is not resolved by an appeal
to supernatural or transcendent forces. It is certainly problematic
in the sense that it has given rise to a vast amount of philosophical
literature and argument.

of psychokinesis we have a pretty good *concept* of moving objects
outside ourselves just by willing them to move."[6]

If Griffin's concern is that a non-mediated form of action be
found for God's relation to the world, then the possibility of a
telekinetic kind of act, (or basic action at a distance) in which
God simply wills something to happen and it happens, would permit
His non-mediated relation to the world. But it would not require,
as Griffin's own position does, the notion of the world as God's
body since God would not *need* a body, in the physical sense, to
effect His intention.

This alternative to Griffin's view, while not logically required, does have the virtue of permitting us to understand God as
an independent entity alongside other agents. If the world is
God's body, then we, as parts of the world, would have relatively
little independence from God since we would be merely parts of His
body. But if we exist alongside God, each acting upon the world
in ways appropriate to our nature, God simply by willing, we by a
combination of basic acts and employment of our bodies, then the
relative ontological independence from God we seem to need if we
are to enter into genuine personal relationship with Him and intelligibility of His action and ours would be provided for.

The Model of Agency and Its Application to God

The fundamental strength of the model of God as an agent
alongside other agents, however, is its ability to make the fit between the understanding of agent/act developed by recent philosophical analysis and our understanding of God as agent as tight as
possible. If God can be thought of as a singular being, acting
within and upon a shared ontological structure alongside other
agents, then in principle there should be no serious qualifications
on our application of the principles of agency to His action. The
greatest fear of making the fit a literal one is that God's action
then will become too restricted to be truly ultimate. But what
are the necessary limitations inherent in the notion of the agent
acting? It is my belief that the kind of limitations in question
are not seriously damaging to God's supremacy and worshipfulness;
that, in fact, the virtue of the model of agent is that it provides
not just a metaphor or remote analogy useful for preserving the
uniqueness of God but that it provides the very meaning of that
uniqueness. This meaning requires, however, that God be *an* agent,
a singular being in relation to other beings who have their own
ontological individuality.

One aspect of the agent model which has appealed to recent commentators is that which Gordon Kaufman calls the element of "interpersonal transcendence."[7] The virtue of this concept, according to Kaufman, is that it preserves God's mysterious unknowability while at the same time linking His acts with our knowledge. We assume, argues Kaufman, that in any act there is an irreducible distinction between the 'real' agent hidden behind the act and the observable, public face of the act by which the agent reveals himself. What we observe is the effect of the act and/or its vehicle of mediation, i.e., the body of the agent. What we cannot observe is the essential agent, i.e., the agent in himself.

While it is important to maintain that the agent is not his act and that in some sense the agent always transcends his act, it is dangerous both to press too hard the distinction between the mysterious 'real' agent and the observable act by which he reveals himself, and to maintain, as Kaufman does, that God's form of transcendence must be somehow categorically different from the interpersonal transcendence common to human agents.

On the first point Michael McLain has argued forcefully that the exclusive use of the interpersonal model "implies a 'residually Cartesian' understanding of the self"[8] which bifurcates our modes of knowledge in a way that "is not adequate to the facts at hand."[9] McLain wants to substitute a model in which the agent's relation to his act carries the primary meaning of transcendence. The agent, by means of his intention, is able to transcend his immediate experience and to carry out his intention through multi-faceted agency or modes of activity. This agent/act model, as McLain calls it, takes more seriously than does Kaufman's interpersonal model both the embodiedness of the agent who reveals himself as well as the observable side of his action. The agent remains embodied, not dualistically haunted by a mysterious inner self, but the intentions he entertains remain transcendent of their empirical manifestation.

McLain does not suggest that God's body is visible in his acts. The stress in McLain's argument lies more upon the need for a *locus* from which the agent issues forth his intentions and actions. The *kind* of body which would constitute this locus may be difficult to conceive but the thrust of McLain's argument is that some kind of locus is necessary to the full notion of an agent. If, additionally, we accept the possibility of basic action at a distance then God's actual body need not be present or observable in the act itself. To suggest God's embodiedness in this context

is not to suggest or even argue for its necessity. What we need
is some notion of singularity *from which* intentions and the power
to effect them proceed. If that can occur out of a disembodied
agent, well and good. Particularly if embodiedness suggests the
decay intrinsic to a *material* body, it would not be appropriate to
God.

I believe McLain is much closer to an adequate view of the
agent than is Kaufman because of his insistence that the agent not
be dualistically conceived. At the same time, his model has the
virtue of employing Kaufman's interpersonal model without sub-
scribing to its defects.

> The agent/act model provides the fundamental framework
> within which the meaning of a transcendent reality is
> meaningfully described. . . . The use of the second model,
> the one rooted in our interpersonal experience, prescribes
> the limits within which the qualifications of the first
> model may take place.[10]

The difficulty with McLain's final position is not that he has
failed to elaborate the virtues of the synthesis of the agent/act
model and the interpersonal model but that he fails to see how the
models can be applied literally to God, even though thanks to his
own analysis, he has given a full and adequate meaning to the concept of transcendence. McLain is rightly concerned that God not
be unnecessarily limited in His action, and that, therefore,

> the use of the agent/act model to render meaningful the
> concept of 'transcendence' involves the qualification of
> human agency in the direction of an agency not beset by
> limitations.[11]

The removal of these limitations leads to the notion of

> an agent whose will is not that 'of a determinate being,
> operating within a certain charter of function or scope
> of effect', but is rather 'a fully creative agent, one
> who is defined only by his unrestricted freedom . . . the
> notion of an agency unrestrictedly free. . . . It is the
> notion of a radically transcendent reality, one who es-
> capes the limitations of finite existence.'[12]

McLain does not, unfortunately, spell out in detail what these
unacceptable limitations of finite existence are, except to suggest
that 'unrestricted freedom' means that no obstacle exists to the
full and complete realization of one's intention. He assumes that
being finite, or, as in the quote from Farrer, being 'a determinate
being,' entails encountering some resistance in the field of one's
action. But why this should be a significant limitation on God is
not clear, especially if, as a determinate agent, he has the
requisite power to overcome (with due regard, perhaps, for the

freedom and integrity of the others) any *ultimate* obstacles to
his goals. There is a two-fold sense of restriction here, one of
which is significant, the other of which is not. The unimportant
restriction is that of being an entity alongside other entities.
The important restriction, which in the case of God would not be
empirically actualized, would be one in which the other beings
ultimately thwarted or frustrated his intention.

Each entity has some others with whom it has to deal in
carrying out its intentions. Unless, contrary to the spirit of
the Biblical tradition, one wanted to make God completely unrelated,
then he necessarily will act in relation to others. It is not the
fact of dealing with others that should constitute an important
restriction on God, but the *nature* of the relationship. As long
as God retains power sufficient to override recalcitrant counter-
intentions and forces, his being-in-relation would constitute no
meaningful restriction whatsoever.

McLain's reluctance to press the literal application of his
own improved model of transcendence shows itself most tellingly,
I think, with respect to the central issue toward which this
discussion is leading. That is the issue of whether God can perform
single, discrete acts which are exclusively his. All of the commentators on the topic seem to agree, notwithstanding their different starting points and models, that God cannot be the sole
agent of particular acts. For an analysis of that issue, we need
to develop one remaining aspect of the concept of action: the conceptual distinction between acts and events. While noted often in
passing, this distinction has not, to my mind, been sufficiently
utilized in treating an act of God. If it is utilized properly, I
believe it can enable us to talk of particular acts of God without
compromising God's transcendence. Failure to use the distinction
between acts and events has considerably weakened the work of most
interpreters of God's acts because they have not been able to see
how God could remain transcendently free *and* perform specific acts
within a closed causal nexus.

Acts and Events

Perhaps the greatest contribution of the linguistic analytic
approach to the concept of action has been its distinction between
acts and events.[13] In our own experience we know without inference
the difference between performing an act and having an occurrence
(event) merely happen. This difference is crucial to our understanding of ourselves as personal agents since it is only in acts
freely initiated that we manifest that quality of personhood or

agency which distinguishes us from the less-than-personal world.
When we act intentionally, it is truly *we* who are acting. When a
biological event occurs within our bodies we do not normally say
that *we* are doing it.

The most important consequences of the act/event distinction
are that 1) the acts of human agents cannot be exhaustively explained in categories which reduce them to causally necessary happenings, and 2) if God is also a free agent, his acts, likewise,
cannot be fully explained by categories of causal necessity.

It is crucial to observe, however, that the explanation of
an act is more *inclusive* than the explanation of an event and
therefore *does not conflict with it*. As John Macmurray says:

> now when no reason can be assigned for an observed change,
> and it is therefore not an act, we call it an 'event'
> and refer it to a 'cause'. What then do we mean by a
> 'cause'? We mean the source of an occurrence which stands
> to an event as an agent stands to his act, but which is
> not an agent . . . a cause is a source of occurrences
> which is a non-agent; an existent which is other than
> an agent.[14]

As something other than an agent, Macmurray contends, a cause is
not self-explanatory. The very notion of cause entails that behind it there is a further cause and behind it a still further one
and so on. On the other hand, if we discover a freely determined
intention as the source of an occurrence, we cannot get back behind it (without annihilating the distinction between intention
and cause) to find *its* cause. When we reach an intention we reach
the end of our search for the final explanation of why that particular act occurred.

For example, if my arm rising was brought about by my intention to signal my wife, it can be described accurately, though only
partially and incompletely, by reference to causal mechanisms. As
my arm rises these mechanisms make it possible for the elbow to
bend, the muscles to tighten, the nerves to relax, etc. None of
these biological events occurs without causation. And I clearly
do not intend in any direct way the organic processes taking place
in my muscles. But the rising of my arm still occurs and still is
explainable ultimately only by reference to my intention to raise
it, regardless of the fact that in raising it I make use of natural
organic forces. If we could, for the moment, forget about the
origin of the arm rising, i.e., my intention, and concentrate just
upon the movement itself we could describe it in purely causal
terms. At no point in the rising (after its initiation) do we see
the intervention of intention. Everything that takes place as the

arm rises proceeds naturally and according to causal law. But
when we reintroduce the intention which initiated the rising we
add a factor which is not adequately accounted for in causal terms
since it is not a cause in the narrow sense.

The difficulty in accepting this distinction between an intention which initiates an act and the causes which control the
events which carry the act to completion is our belief that the
distinction leads inevitably to an incoherence in understanding
the world. We have come to believe that there are 'laws of nature'
so tightly woven within the world that any occurrence which is
partially explained by something which is not subject to these laws
is unintelligible or absurd. A free act is seen as something
which violates or upsets these laws of nature.

The way around this difficulty, as Macmurray reminds us, is
by remembering that a law of nature essentially is a *description*
of what happens in the world *provided that no agent interferes*.
The laws of nature are descriptions of a world without agents:
a world of occurrences in which intentions play no role. As long
as there are no intentions or free acts then the laws of nature
will completely and without remainder account for all the happenings
within the world.

But if there are agents and if their acts are freely initiated,
then the laws of nature cannot account for or *exhaustively* explain
them. However, there need be no conflict between the initiation
of an act and the processes by which it is carried out. An intention need not violate the laws of nature inasmuch as the intention
initiates the act and the laws of nature account for its realization
subsequent to its initiation. There is a sense in which an agent
always interferes in nature because he must interrupt what otherwise would be the natural, causal flow of events (e.g., until and
unless I decide to lift my arm it will remain hanging at my side).
Assuming that the decision is freely made, not predictable in the
same way that completely causal events are, then causal laws are
not sufficient to account for it. In this case, the full explanation of the act will have to include reference to a non-causal intention as well as to the causal events 'within' its enactment.
The interference of the agent with the causal region of nature is
not, therefore, a violation of causal law but its employment by a
dimension of reality which 'goes beyond' causal law. As G. H.
Von Wright has said:

> The idea that causal connections are necessary connections
> in nature is rooted in the idea that there are agents who
> can interfere with the natural course of events. The

> concept of causation . . . is therefore secondary to the
> concept of a human action. . . . The determinations of
> action . . . are of a totally different kind from causes
> and effects among events in nature.[15]

Edward Pols has called the realm of caused events the 'infrastructure' of the act. Insisting that an act has an 'ontological
authenticity,' Pols argues that the act "embraces, makes use of,
even in some measure dominates the realities of the infrastructure,
but neither act nor infrastructure cancels the authenticity of the
other."[16]

As long as there is such a thing as a free act, and as long
as the initiation of such an act does not contradict or exclude
the occurrence of events which are not in themselves freely initiated but which can be employed in the realization of an act,
there need be no metaphysical problem in accepting the reality of
a coherent relationship between acts and events. Thus the existence
of causal laws, or laws of nature, need be no barrier to our acceptance of intentional acts. The peaceful co-existence of acts
and causal law requires only that the latter recognize the limits
of its application.

Particular Acts of God

To come now to the heart of the debate over God's acts, I
believe that it is the failure to use the distinction between act
and event to its fullest that has weakened what is generally said
about God's ability to perform specific acts and which has made
claims about God's acts go on the defensive in the face of what is
mistakenly taken to be the imperial sweep of scientific explanation.
It has for the most part been assumed, from Bultmann to Kaufman,
that there is an unbroken causal nexus into which every occurrence
must fit and in relation to which any divine act becomes absurd.
Gilkey has said that "a vast panoply" of divine deeds is now no
longer regarded as having actually happened because of "the liberal
insistence on the causal continuum of space-time experience."[17]
Bultmann has maintained that:

> In mythological thinking the act of God . . . is under-
> stood as an action which intervenes between the natural,
> or historical, or psychological course of events; it breaks
> and links them at the same time. The divine causality is
> inserted as a link in the chain of the events which follow
> one another according to the causal nexus. . . . The thought
> of the action of God as an unworldly and transcendent action
> can be protected from misunderstanding only if it is not
> thought of as an action which happens between the worldly
> actions or events, but as happening within them. . . . The
> action of God is hidden from every eye except the eye of
> faith.[18]

McLain, in agreement with Kaufman, says, regarding specific acts of God, "we cannot view these actions for which God is the sole agent, since this would involve introducing unintelligible surds into an ordered world."[19]

Frank Dilley likewise sees the problem as reducing to only two alternatives: "Either a conservative tradition affirming miraculous acts of God, whether spectacular or 'hidden,' or a God who acts solely through the general orders and processes of nature and history."[20] In other words, if specific acts of God are to be defended it can only be through option one, which is equivalent, for Dilley, to affirming miraculous violations of the natural order. Schubert Ogden also accepts the conclusion that "God's action . . . cannot be simply identified with any particular historical event or events."[21] Ogden goes on to qualify this somewhat by insisting that in some sense "man's action actually *is* God's action. . . ."[22] Ogden does not deny that in some events "the ultimate truth about our existence before God is normatively represented or revealed."[23] But as David Griffin has pointed out Ogden's understanding of the revelatory aspect of God's act

> does not do justice to the objective intention implied in saying that a certain action is peculiarly someone's, in a sense that other of his actions are not. For, objectively speaking according to his explanation, a special act does not *express* the person's inner being any more than his other actions do; it does *reveal* his inner being more than other actions do, but this is due to its being received in a certain way by others.[24]

Griffin, who represents the process view more adequately than anyone else on this topic, goes on to assert the importance of affirming acts of God which are 'peculiarly' his. Such acts would be ones

> a) for which God's aim was such that, if the aim were actualized, the event would optimally express God's being, and b) which did in fact actualize God's aim or will for it to an optimal degree.[25]

The most fully elaborated denial that God can perform specific, exclusive acts has been made by Gordon Kaufmann. He explicitly affirms the necessity of thinking of a tight causal web as the locus for any occurrence whatsoever. "Every event is defined as a focal point in a web that reaches in all directions beyond it indefinitely."[26] Kaufman seems to be so concerned that nothing tear or break into the continuity and unity of this web, that he does not pay sufficient attention to the distinction between caused events (which are the essential components of the web) and intended acts (which, if the earlier distinction is valid, cannot

be completely contained by the web). Because he is wedded to the
notion of "nature and history as a web of interrelated events that
must be understood as a self-contained whole," it is impossible
for him to conceive of any event having its source "in the divine
will and action rather than in the context of preceding and coincident finite events."[27] We would be forced to think of God's
acts as

> absolute beginning points for chains of events which occur--
> not at the 'beginning' of the world and history--but
> *within* ongoing natural and historical processes. . . . Our
> experience is of a unified and orderly world; in such a
> world acts of God (in the traditional sense) are not merely
> improbable or difficult to believe: they are literally in-
> conceivable.[28]

The crux of the problem which Kaufman poses is that on the
basis of the reasons he uses to rule out specific divine acts, he
must also, and for the same reasons, rule out human acts. This,
presumably, he does not want to do. But by invoking the relation
of acts employing events in their realization it is possible to
restore the agent's freedom, maintain the integrity (but limited
scope) of causal law, and create room for divine acts without re-
sort to mystery or absurdity.

The knot which has traditionally held divine acts captive in
a closed causal network can be cut by distinguishing between descriptions of events and explanations of actions. This is one of
the primary virtues of the agent/act model for understanding acts
of God. As long as we can 'make room' for human acts within the
otherwise 'closed' nexus of events, there would be no reason why
divine acts could not have the same room, assuming that God is at
least as much of an agent as we are. In this sense, *all* acts are
"absolute beginning points . . . within ongoing natural and historical processes" (the very characteristic Kaufman feared would
make God's acts "literally inconceivable").

Although we have indicated in a general way how acts can be
related to the natural laws which hold for events, we also need to
establish, in a way not applicable to human agents, how God can be
held responsible *both* for his specific acts *and* for the natural
laws into which they are inserted. For God must have a degree of
control over natural laws which no human agent can possibly have.
They must be in some sense peculiarly His, but in a way that does
not obviate the distinction between His relation to them and His
relation to specific acts within them.

The only assumption we would need to make in this regard is
that God is an agent with sufficient power to be able to use the

forces of nature for His purposes. This degree of power is no
different in kind from the power we use when we use the forces of
nature to carry out our intentions. The difference between God and
us would be one of degree, God having no effective limitations on
His utilization of the laws of nature. He could even be assumed
without incoherence to have created and to sustain the laws of
nature (an ongoing act) as well as to perform specific acts within
and through them.

God's Act at the Red Sea

Our analysis of the relation between act and event was intended
to raise an objection to the acceptance of the assumption that all
occurrences are exhaustively subsumable under causal law. When we
apply the results of our argument to a particular act of God,
therefore, it is natural to expect a very different interpretation
than one based on that assumption. Kaufman, for example, claims
that

> it will not do to speak of God as the agent who made it
> possible for the Israelites to escape from the Egyptians,
> if one regards it as simply a fortunate coincidence that
> a strong east wind was blowing at just the right time
> to dry up the sea of reeds. The Biblical writer's view
> is coherent and compelling precisely because he is able
> to say that "*the* Lord drove the sea back by a strong east
> wind" (Ex. 14:21), i.e., it was because, and only be-
> cause, God was Lord over nature, one who could bend
> natural events to His will, that He was able to be ef-
> fective Lord over history.[29]

Kaufman of course, cannot make an intelligible explanation of this
purported act of God because it suggests a divine interruption of
the natural flow of unbroken finite events, which on his initial
assumption is absurd. But if there is a categorical difference
between the explanation of an act and the description of an event,
then there should be nothing more, nor less, mysterious about explaining an act (willed by God) which intervenes in the natural
order than there is about an act willed by a human agent.

Let us look at how this distinction might be applied to the
specific case Kaufman has raised. It is irrelevant for this purpose to decide whether there ever was such an 'occurrence,' let
alone whether it was 'truly' an act of God. Let us assume, as a
thought-experiment, that there was a parting of the waters at the
Red Sea. Let us say that what is to be explained is a sudden drying
up of the sea by a strong wind. According to those who claim it is
an act of God, the wind dried up the sea as a result of having been
moved by God for that purpose. To understand this as an act of
God we need to invoke exactly the same principles by which we

understand a human act. If the agent's intention had not intervened in the otherwise natural flow of events, what would have happened would have been completely predictable and explainable in
causal terms. Just as a human agent does not violate natural law
by deciding to raise his arm, so God does not violate natural law
by deciding to move the wind in order to dry up the sea. In both
cases the agents employ natural forces in order to carry out their
intentions and in neither case is violence done to the notion of
causal law inasmuch as their intentional intervention occurs only
at the limits of causal law. Neither act can be completely explained by causal law but neither act transgresses causal law.

If we add the assumption that God has sufficient power to
control the wind, then the alleged act of drying up the waters of
the Red Sea is neither more nor less intelligible, in principle,
than any human act. God's decision to part the waters was a decision to intervene, as any agent must do when he acts, into the
otherwise regular, predictable nexus of natural events. Like any
agent, God's decision is free, transcendent of causal law but not
in conflict with it, and is revelatory of his personality. But
his act is also his in a particular, distinctive way, and, most
importantly, it is intelligible to our human understanding.

If we are willing to entertain the possibility that God is an
individual agent, then it is possible to understand his action
without reducing it to causal terms but also without requiring a
sacrifice of intelligibility. Whether he has acted, even whether
he exists, are questions not touched on here. But if he does exist
and has acted, then understanding an act of God becomes a coherent
conceptual task unlocking the methodological catch-22, and thereby
preserving the freedom and power which makes God God.

NOTES

1. Edward Pols, "Power and Agency," *International Philosophical
   Quarterly*, XI, #3 (September 1971), pp. 295-96.

2. William L. Power, "The Notion of Transcendence and the Problem
   of Discourse About God", *Journal of the American Academy of
   Religion*, XLIII, #3 (September 1975), p. 531. I am aware of
   the possible ambiguity of the notion of 'endurance,' especially since the new meaning given it by process thought.
   I am taking the term here in a non-process way, but I do
   not want to foreclose discussion on the merits of the process
   position.

3. Gordon Kaufman, "Revelation and Cultural History," *God the
   Problem* (Cambridge: Harvard University Press, 1972), pp. 158-59.

4. See, for example, Arthur C. Danto, "Basic Actions," in Alan R. White, ed. *The Philosophy of Action* (Oxford: Oxford University Press, 1968), pp. 43-58.

5. David R. Griffin, "Gordon Kaufman's Theology: Some Questions," *Journal of the American Academy of Religion*, XLI, #4 (December 1973) pp. 554-72.

6. John S. Morreall, *Analogy and Talking About God: A Critique of the Thomistic Approach* (Washington: University Press of America, 1979), p. 39.

7. Gordon Kaufman, "Two Models of Transcendence," *God the Problem*, pp. 72-81.

8. F. Michael McLain, "On Theological Models," *Harvard Theological Review*, 62 (1960) pp. 162-63.

9. Ibid., p. 166.

10. Ibid., p. 180.

11. Ibid., p. 179.

12. Ibid., p. 171. The internal quote is from Austin Farrer's *Faith and Speculation*.

13. See, for example, Richard Taylor, *Action and Purpose* (1966): G. H. Von Wright, *Explanation and Understanding* (1971); A. I. Melden, *Free Action* (1961), among a host of others.

14. Macmurray, *The Self as Agent*, (London: Faber and Faber, 1957), especially the chapter "Causality and the Continuant," p. 152. Macmurray carefully limits the meaning of the terms 'cause' and 'reason.' This can be confusing inasmuch as 'cause' is often used very broadly in the current literature on action. A 'cause' for Macmurray is what brings about an event and is, therefore, non-intentional. A 'reason' is what initiates an act and is quintessentially intentional.

15. G. H. Von Wright, *Causality and Determinism*, (New York: Columbia University Press, 1974), p. 1-2. The philosophical understanding of action rehearsed here should not be taken to be the only position accepted by most philosophers of action today. Action is still at one level a mystery and its relation to causality for many philosophers does not admit of simple explanation (thus the enormous literature already devoted to the issue). Nevertheless, it is testimony to the cogency of the view presented here that so many philosophers tacitly admit that there is a *prima facie* case to be made for a metaphysical distinction between acts and events.

16. Edward Pols, "The Ontology of the Rational Agent," *Review of Metaphysics*, V. XXXIII, #4, June 1980, pp. 691-92.

17. Langdon Gilkey, "Cosmology, Ontology, and the Travail of Biblical Language," *Journal of Religion*, 41 (1961), p. 195.

18. Rudolf Bultmann, *Jesus Christ and Mythology* (New York: Charles Scribner's & Sons, 1958), pp. 61-62.

19. McLain, op. cit., p. 183.

20. Frank Dilley, "Does the 'God Who Acts' Really Act?," *Anglican Theological Review*, XLVII (1965), p. 80.

21. Schubert M. Ogden, "What Sense Does It Make to Say, 'God Acts in History'?" in *The Reality of God* (New York: Harper & Row), 1966, p. 179.

22. Ibid., p. 181.

23. Ibid., p. 184.

24. Griffin, "Schubert Ogden's Christology and the Possibilities of Process Philosophy," in *Process Philosophy and Christian Thought*, ed. by Delwin Brown, Ralph James, Jr., and Gene Reeves (Indianapolis: Bobbs-Merrill Co., Inc., 1971), p. 353.

25. Ibid., p. 358.

26. Kaufman, "On the Meaning of 'Act of God,'" *God the Problem*, p. 133.

27. Ibid.

28. Ibid., pp. 134-35.

29. Ibid., pp. 122-23.

11. RELIGIOUS AUTHORITY AND DIVINE ACTION

Maurice Wiles

'Begin at the beginning, and go on till you come to the end:
and then stop.' The King of Hearts' advice is not as easy to follow as might seem on first hearing. It is not simply that I want
to speak about the interrelation between two major subjects and
there is a certain arbitrariness in choosing with which of the two
to start. The problem is far more fundamental than that. Where
for the theologian is 'the beginning'? At whatever point he does
begin he is always uneasily aware that way back behind the point
that he has chosen there probably lie a number of unquestioned
assumptions which have largely prejudged the kind of answer he will
give to the very question he is setting out to investigate. This
difficulty is not, of course, peculiar to the theologian. None of
us, whatever the subject of our investigation, can ever really
'begin at the beginning'. But if this is a difficulty which the
Christian theologian shares with other scholars it is none the less
real for that. One obvious and important feature of the tradition
in which the Christian theologian stands is that it gives some kind
of special authority to the Bible, to the church and above all--
though it is sometimes a little bit elusive to know exactly what
is meant by saying this--to Christ himself.

Now, if we agree that the acceptance of some authority of this
kind, even in the most general sense, is a part of the tradition
within which a Christian theologian works, we shall have to acknowledge that when we take up the question if divine action, of what
we can properly mean by speaking of God acting, we appear to be
deeply committed already on the subject of our investigation--and
that in a twofold manner.

In the first place, we are committed in what I would call a
formal way by the bare fact that we do accept certain books or
certain people as having special authority for us; there is, that
is to say, an element of prejudgment in relation to our theme implicit in the mere fact of such an acceptance in itself quite apart
from what the particular books or people in question may actually

Reprinted from "Religious Authority and Divine Action," *Religious
Studies* 7 (1971): 1-12, by Maurice Wiles by permission of Cambridge
University Press.

say. For whatever may be our precise conception of the inspiration
of the prophets or biblical writers, whatever may be our precise
understanding of the guidance by which church councils or the
Magisterium reach their decisions, it has normally been understood
to involve some kind of special divine action, action of a distinctive kind, in relation to those people or those occasions.

   But we are also committed in a second way, in what I would
call a substantial way, by the content of what those authorities
do in fact say to us. This is very much more than a matter of the
Bible being a book which includes a number of miracle stories.
The idea of divine providential action seen in a series of specific
historical events runs right through the Bible, so that a well-
known book of biblical theology can very properly be entitled 'God
who acts'.

   Thus form and content serve to reinforce one another. Unless
God acts in a special way in special events it is difficult to see
how we could have religious authorities from within history with
the degree of specialness which Christians do in fact ascribe to
their authorities. And those very authorities in fact do speak of
a God who acts in precisely that kind of way. A Christian, therefore, it is widely felt, must accept a conception of God's acting
in the world of this kind--or else, everything collapses; nothing
would remain that could merit the title of being specifically
Christian.

   Now it seems to me that there are obvious difficulties in
affirming this view of special divine actions in the world. A
good many people, I would suggest, do feel misgivings about it but
continue to affirm it nevertheless because they do not believe that
it is possible to affirm a recognizably Christian faith on any
other terms. The situation is similar to that by which many people
have maintained--and indeed still do maintain--a near fundamentalist
understanding of Scripture, despite being well aware of the grave
difficulties inherent in that position, because they do not believe
it is possible to affirm the Bible to be divine revelation in any
serious sense on any other terms. It seems important therefore
to ask whether this conception of divine action is as necessary to
a recognizably Christian faith as on the face of it it appears to
be.

   The kind of misgiving to which I refer is I think clear enough
but it can perhaps be made clearer by a comparison with the realm
of science and the concept of God's action in the natural world.
In the Newtonian system, as is well known, nature functioned for

the most part as a self-regulating system, but certain special
actions on the part of God were required to correct, for example,
the irregularities caused by the mutual attraction of the planets.
As further advances in knowledge made possible normal scientific
explanations of these phenomena, so this 'God of the gaps' was
edged further and further out of the world. This process has not
meant, however, that it has become impossible to speak in any way
at all of God in relation to the natural world. Rather, I would
want to say, it has made possible the reaffirmation of a more profound concept of God as the transcendent ground of there being a
world at all. Is there then any parallel in the historical field?
Do traditional accounts of the Christian faith really involve a
God of the historical gaps? And if so, would modification of that
conception lead to the impossibility of affirming a recognizably
Christian faith at all or might it lead to the possibility of re-
affirming it in a more profound and more satisfactory form?

No one has been more acutely aware of this problem in our own
time than Rudolf Bultmann. It is an essential part of that fundamental concern which gave rise to his programme of demythologiza-
tion. Yet Bultmann insists most emphatically that the concept of
God's decisive act in Jesus Christ must be maintained, for it is
in his judgment the very heart of the Christian gospel. For this
he has been vigorously attacked by many of his critics who have
claimed, in the words of one of them, that 'these two words (act
of God) set up a whole mythical universe'.[1] The criticism has been
levelled from both sides. Some have seen in his insistence on the
necessity to retain the idea of an 'act of God' a welcome victory
of his Christian heart over his demythologizing head; they have
regarded it as an arbitrary limit to his demythologizing programme
imposed upon him by his Christian convictions but thereby calling
in question the necessity and the validity of the earlier stages
of his demythologizing. Others, from the more radical side, have
seen in it a regrettable failure of nerve, an unjustifiable refusal
to press through with his programme of demythologizing to its
logical and desirable conclusion. Bultmann has defended himself
by claiming that the concept of an act of God as he understands it
is not mythological at all but analogical. Whether or not that is
a satisfactory terminological distinction is not a matter of great
importance for us here; but the substantive content of the distinction he is trying to establish is of central importance to my
present concern. This is how Bultmann himself makes the point in
answering his critics:

> Mythological thinking represents the divine action
> . . . as an action that breaks into and disrupts the con-
> tinuum of natural, historical, or psychical events--in
> short, as a 'miracle'. In so doing it objectifies the
> divine action and projects it on to the plane of worldly
> occurrences. In truth, however, . . . an act of God is
> not visible to the objectifying eye and cannot be demon-
> strated in the manner of worldly events. The idea of un-
> worldliness and transcendence of the divine action is only
> preserved when such action is represented not as something
> that takes place *between* worldly occurrences, but rather
> as something that takes place in them, so that the closed
> continuum of worldly events that presents itself to the
> objectifying eye remains untouched. God's act is hidden
> to every eye but that of faith. The only thing generally
> visible and demonstrable is the 'natural' occurrence. It
> is in it that God's hidden action takes place.
>
> In faith the closed weft (of cause and effect) pre-
> sented or produced by objective observation is transcended,
> though not as in mythological thought. For mythology
> imagines it to be torn asunder, whereas faith transcends
> it as a whole when it speaks of the activity of God.[2]

Now there are certainly many serious difficulties in what
Bultmann is trying to say here, but I do not think it is difficult
to see the nature of the fundamental distinction he wants to make
by which an 'act of God' is not a mythological concept in his
sense. It is closely parallel to the familiar avoidance of a
'God of the gaps' approach to the natural world. Divine acts do
not take place 'between worldly occurrences'--i.e. in the gaps left
by natural events, but in them in a hidden manner which does not
affect in any way the closed weft of cause and effect. Moreover
this does not involve, for Bultmann, a weakening of the religious
significance of the conception of God's activity in history; rather
it makes possible its fully transcendent character.

If something of this kind is a fair account of what Bultmann
intends when he speaks of an 'act of God', a number of important
questions have to be faced. Is it a possible conception? or is it
a muddled attempt to hold on to the old religious language while
abandoning the religious reality which that language was designed
to express? If it is a possible conception, are there grounds for
affirming it to be true or at least worthy of belief? And, even
if there are, can we claim that it does justice to the main traditional affirmations of the Christian faith?

It is easy to put the challenge that Bultmann's notion of an
act of God is vacuous in a down to earth no-nonsense manner. In
an article entitled 'Does the "God who acts" really act'?[3] an
American writer, F. B. Dilley, argues that the biblical theologian
must choose between acknowledging the reality of the miraculous or
else admitting that the concept of a 'God who acts' has no proper

content. The challenge is a healthy one but at least as Dilley
puts it it seems to be posed in too stark a form. In the course
of the article he quotes a part of the passage from Bultmann which
I have already cited and comments: 'Unfortunately it does not take
much reflection to perceive that although this theory may be very
attractive, it is impossible to make it really work.'[4] That Bultmann's conception is a difficult one, that ultimately we may have
to admit that it does not really work, I do not want to deny. But
I think it does require rather more reflection than Dilley claims.
He does not seem to me to pay sufficient attention in his criticisms
to the logical oddity of religious language. Has the concept of a
'God who creates man in his own image' no proper content if a
wholly evolutionary account of man's origin is accepted? Most of
us would say that the evolutionary account is in no way incompatible
with the concept of a creator God, whose creating is not identical
with but analogous to human creating. It does not seem to me to
be any more impossible in principle to speak of an active God whose
action is to be seen 'in' rather than 'between' worldly occurrences.
Of course the possibility of saying something does not prove its
truth. In both cases, creation and divine action in history, it
is not enough to argue that the concept is a possible one; we must
go on and give grounds to show that it is reasonable to make the
particular affirmations concerned.

     In the case of creation it is man's experiencing of the world
as contingent, as in some fundamental sense given, as not self-
explanatory, which has given rise--in my judgment rightly given
rise--to the affirmation of God as creator. What then are the
grounds which have led men to speak of a God who acts in history?
I want to suggest that the conviction is very largely rooted in
the fact that so much of the most profound personal experience has
about it a quality of response; men have found a meaning and a sense
of purpose, bigger than their own comparatively narrow concerns,
being elicited as it were by the events of history--sometimes events
of an obviously impressive kind, sometimes events of an outwardly
insignificant character. What I am trying to describe is not a
matter of conscious inference, not a worked out way of explaining
experiences to oneself; rather, to use a phrase that John Hick
has made familiar in relation to the natural world, it is a matter of 'experiencing-as,' of experiencing what happens to us and
what we achieve as being in response to an overall purpose at
work in the world. It is in the attempt to articulate this way
of experiencing life that men have spoken of God as acting in
history--a phrase vividly expressing the experience of receptivity

which it is intended to express but which can also be dangerously
misleading if taken too literally. There is no question of course
of this being a kind of deductive proof any more than the cosmological argument can properly be regarded as such; it needs to be
seen as one part of that total response to the world in which
theism is grounded. All I want to claim here is that there is a
fundamental aspect of human experiencing which can suggest a possible line of justification for the kind of talk about divine action
which I am trying to explore.

But I have still to face my third question. Even if such a
view of divine action is both possible and reasonable, does it do
justice to the main traditional affirmations of the Christian
faith? This question can be spelt out in a number of different
ways. I intend to break it up into two separate questions: (i) can
it account for the particularity of the divine action of which
Christianity speaks? (ii) is its description of divine-human relationships true to the personal character of God in his dealings with
men, as Christian faith understands them, or, to put essentially
the same point in a slightly different form, is its account of
divine action one in which the word 'action' is being given a
proper sense and is something more than a piece of linguistic
legerdemain?

(i) First then, the problem of particularity which is so
prominent in any Christian account of God's activity in history. I
begin once again with a parallel with the doctrine of creation.
The natural world, like human history, is an ambiguous mixture of
natural evils and natural beauty. Even if we rightly reject any
form of Gnostic dualism which seeks to free God from all responsibility for the former, we seem bound to speak of some aspects of
the natural world as giving rise more directly to the apprehension
of God's creative role than others. I do not think that we can
properly speak of God being more creative in one place than in
another; the transcendent creator-creature relationship does not
permit of being graded in terms of less and more. Nevertheless I
think we may speak of certain aspects of the created order as
particularly potent vehicles for human awareness of divine
creativity.

With this analogy in mind let us turn to the far more acute
problem of particularity in historical experience. Not all events
elicit equally the sense of response to purposive activity of which
I have been speaking. For the Christian the life of Christ, and
certain other events also within what is commonly referred to as

'salvation history', have an outstanding potency of this kind and
are seen as special divine actions. No one stresses the particularity of the divine action in Jesus Christ more than Bultmann.
Since I have used him as my exemplar of a conception of divine
action which is sure to appear to some to be seriously 'reductionist' in character, I must in fairness emphasize that he cannot
possibly be accused of being 'reductionist' in any sense with regard to the specialness of the divine action in Christ. For him
authentic existence (or, in my language, a sense of life as purposive in response to the prior purposive activity of God towards
man) can only be realized on the basis of the particular historical
event of Jesus Christ. I can only align myself with those who have
criticized Bultmann for the absolute and exclusive nature of the
claim that he makes here. As Schubert Ogden puts it:

> The New Testament claim "only in Jesus Christ" must
> be interpreted to mean not that God acts to redeem only in
> the event of Jesus and in no other event, but that the only
> God who acts to redeem any event--*although in fact he re-*
> *deems every event*--is the God whose redemptive action is
> decisively revealed in the word which Jesus speaks and is.[5]

But this, or course, does not remove, it only restates, our
problem. How can God's action be 'decisively revealed' in certain
events and not in others? Can we give any proper meaning to this
less exclusive form of affirmation about the special nature of
God's action in Christ without falling back into all the difficulties of an action of God which is different in kind from his activity elsewhere, an action which is to be seen 'between' rather than
'in' the worldly occurrences concerned? If we cannot, then whatever the possibility and the reasonableness of conceiving divine
action in the way that I am suggesting, we would have to admit that
it failed to do justice to the basic affirmations of a distinctively
Christian faith. I want to argue--though tentatively and in a
way that certainly admits that there may be counter-arguments
which will cause me to change my mind--that it is possible, that
my proposed conception of divine action is *not* incompatible with
speaking of God's redemptive action as 'decisively revealed in the
word which Jesus speaks and is'.

I have claimed that it is in the experiencing of life as
having the quality of response that the reality of divine action
is known. This is in line with Bultmann's oft-repeated warnings
against a false objectification of God. It does not mean that the
whole concept of God or of divine action is purely subjective in
the pejorative sense of that elusive term, which would imply that

they were simply ways of describing certain human feelings. It
does mean however that the idea of divine action cannot be ex-
tracted from its context of being experienced and then considered
in isolation from all forms of human response. In some words of
Daniel Williams: 'Every "act of God" is presented to us in, through
and with the complex of nature and life in which we are. When we
say God elected Israel or that he sends his rain on the just and
the unjust, we must not ignore the complex analysis of assignable
causes and factors in Israel's history or in the cosmic record of
rainfall. We have no way of extricating the acts of God from their
involvement in the activities of the world.'[6]
     Now it is an inevitable feature of the variety to be found
within human history that some people by virtue of their personality
and of their situation are more fully responsive to the divine
action than others. Their words and actions in turn will provide a
particularly important focus for calling out such responses from
others who follow them. And since that quality of life in them to
which those others will respond was itself grounded in responsiveness to the divine action, we may rightly speak of the events of
their lives as acts of God in a special sense towards those of us
who are influenced by them. In calling them special acts of God
we would not be implying that there was any fundamental difference
in the relation of the divine action to the particular worldly
occurrences of their situation; we would be referring to the depth
of response and the creative potential for eliciting further response from others embodied in those particular lives or those
particular events.
     It would be a natural, but I believe ultimately mistaken, fear
to imagine that by describing divine action in this way we are
giving a purely humanistic account in which the reality of the divine is ultimately obliterated. Rather what we are doing is
avoiding the error of thinking that we can ever describe divine
action in any other context than that of its experienced response.
This approach finds clear and direct expression in some words from
Peter Baelz's book, *Prayer and Providence*, where he discusses the
problem of how we can speak of more and less in the activity of
God. He writes:

> God's providential activity is to be discerned in the
> way in which he meets and overcomes that which stands out
> against and resists his creative will. Here we see more
> of him than in any other situation. His activity meets
> with the creaturely response which it seeks and towards which
> it is directed. It is fulfilled in the response which it
> evokes. It penetrates and enables the relatively independent

activity of the creature. It supernaturalizes the natural.
In such providential and redemptive activity we come to
discern a deeper aspect of God's being. There is a 'more'
of God to be apprehended here than elsewhere. His word
speaks more clearly, his work is more complete. Christians claim to discern such distinctive activity of God
in the life and work of Jesus. Thus on the cross, as he
makes his final, life-giving act of self-surrender to his
Father, Jesus exclaims, 'It is finished,' and Christians
ascribe in response to this a completion and finality to
the divine work. Creator and creature are here at one.
The divine love has conquered. God remains eternally the
same God; but in and through the obedient response of
Jesus his activity is more fully discerned, because more
fully expressed. And since it is more fully expressed,
there is a very proper sense in which we may speak of God's
special activity.[7]

Clearly there is both room and need for continuing discussion
how far this approach which I have tried to exemplify from that
rather lengthy quotation from Peter Baelz can provide an adequate
understanding of the saving events of Christian history. For the
moment I want simply to claim that it is not in principle incapable
of doing justice to the idea of certain events being divine acts
of a specially decisive kind--and, as I am suggesting all along,
if it is capable of doing so at all it may be expected to do the
job in a way which will be free of many of the difficulties that
are attendant on more traditional statements of the unique character
of certain events in Christian history.

(ii) I must turn to the second charge which might be brought
against the approach I am advocating, the charge that it cannot do
justice to a properly Christian conception of God's action because
it does not conceive that activity in a sufficiently personal way.
The charge might reasonably be developed along some such lines as
these. You, it might be said, have drawn analogies at various
points between the view of God's relation to the natural world and
that of his relation to history. But, it might be claimed, Christians have been able to accept an account of God's creative relationship to the world which is of a general rather than a varying
kind without imperilling the sense of a fully personal religion
just because that more variable and personal approach of God to man
is to be found in his activity within history. To argue therefore
from an analogy with God's creative relationship will not do. That
relationship by itself is not adequately personal to sustain the
needs and convictions of the religious life. If God's relationship
to men were all of the more generalized kind which is implied in
our understanding of him as creator, the religious realities to
which Christian faith testifies would evaporate. The kind of

understanding of God as creator to which we are being led in this
modern age is tolerable precisely because it is *not* the measure of
all his relationships towards us.

My primary answer to objections of this kind would be that
they seem to me to operate with too simplified a conception of God
as personal being. The traditional distinction between an I-thou
and an I-it relationship has too many values in theology but if applied in too straightforward a manner to divine-human relationships
it can lead to an excessively anthropomorphic picture. God's relationship to man must never be understood in sub-personal terms but
the test of where this is happening is more reliably to be found
in what the relationship as conceived implies for human life than
in what picture of God appears to be involved. We cannot, I have
argued, speak significantly of God or of his acting in an objecti-
fied way, wholly separated from the human response, and it is
therefore the total relationship which must be assessed in determining whether our understanding is true to a properly personal
conception of God. Now the position which I am tentatively advocating is one in which divine action is throughout most closely
correlated with human responsiveness. Thus the total relationship,
it would seem to me, is being understood in a personal way in every
sense in which that can properly be applied to a theological discussion of divine-human relationships.

But the objection may also be met along somewhat different
lines. I suggested as an alternative formulation of the objection
that it might be questioned whether the kind of divine action envisaged could properly be regarded as action in any real sense.
This way of putting the problem draws attention to a difficulty
which is attendant upon any attempt to bring together the convictions of biblical religion and a wholehearted insistence on divine
transcendence. It is a recurrent theme at the heart of the issues
with which the Fathers wrestled in the course of that confluence of
Greek philosophy and biblical faith which marks the first centuries
of the Christian era. The classical solutions to that problem, as
seen for example in the writings of Aquinas, have always had to
qualify the notion of divine action in a somewhat embarrassed and
equivocating manner. Since God is complete in himself, eternal
and changeless being, any talk of his acting in the world at all--
let alone in the specific and particular ways of which the Christian tradition speaks--must be very carefully qualified. In
Aquinas' own language, 'being related to God is a reality in
creatures but being related to creatures is not reality in God'.[8]

Now of course behind all such language lies an extremely subtle and
complex philosophical position. Nevertheless I think the point
still stands that within the main Christian tradition the 'reality'
of God's acting has had to be severely qualified. Schubert Ogden,
whose work I have already quoted, speaks of 'the timeless Absolute
of classical metaphysics, who may be said to act only in some Pickwickian sense that bears no real analogy to anything we know as
action.'[9] He goes on in the same essay, which is entitled 'What
sense does it make to say "God acts in history,"' to make use of
the insights of process philosophy, as outlined by Whitehead and
Hartshorne, to develop a conception of divine action similar to
that which I am advocating here. Dilley ends his article of challenge to the biblical theologian by looking in the same direction.
Its last words are: 'Perhaps someone with one eye on Whitehead and
the other on the Bible will bring in the next era in theology.'
Ogden's claim is that by working along these lines he is enabled to
put forward a view in which the divine actions can be seen as acts
of God in a much more real, though of course still analogical,
sense than when seen in terms of the classical metaphysical tradition. His account has certainly its own difficulties which I cannot investigate now. But I think he has at least made out a strong
case on the basis of which it is not unreasonable to claim that the
account of divine action which I have been adumbrating not only
gives a sufficiently 'real' sense to the notion of God acting but
one that may even have positive advantages on that score over more
traditional accounts.

I must come back now and try to relate the conception of divine
action which I have been sketching to the notion of religious authority, and in particular to the authority of the Bible. Unless we
give some kind of special place to the Bible, I do not see how there
could be a distinctively Christian theology at all. If therefore
the existence of the Bible as an authority or its essential contents
should prove to be incompatible with the account that I have given,
the argument which I have been trying to develop would fall apart.
The question must therefore be put: does the Bible as a religious
authority conflict with what I have been saying in either the formal or the substantial way which I distinguished at the beginning?

The former need not, I think, detain us very long. In effect
I have already answered it in my attempt to show that my view is
compatible with speaking of God's redemptive activity as 'decisively
revealed in the word which Jesus speaks and is.' If certain events
can be given such special importance without implying a different

kind of activity on God's part in relation to the worldly occurrences concerned, then clearly the records which partly record and
partly constitute such events can properly be regarded as having
religious authority without that fact implying any special inter-
ventionist activity as responsible either for their composition or
for their recognition as authoritative.

Such an approach also opens the way to ascribing some measure
of religious authority to the Scriptures of other faiths without
necessarily destroying the idea of something distinctive or decisive about the Christian Scriptures in doing so. In the present
situation in which Christian theology has to learn to do its task
in a way which takes seriously other expressions of religion in
the world, this seems to me to be a positive advantage. Just as
the Christian understanding of God contains within itself the
seeds of criticism which have led to the modification or abandonment
of, for example, certain ideas of hell, despite the formal attesta-
tion of those ideas within the Christian tradition itself, so I
believe the same understanding of God is ultimately incompatible
with certain exclusivist conceptions of religious authority despite
their substantial presence within the historical tradition of the
faith. Modifications of the idea of religious authority along these
lines are not simply something that is imposed from without; they
arise also from within.

But the second issue--the issue of the compatibility of the
biblical contents--is more difficult. In so far as those contents
are defined as giving special attention to particular events no
new difficulty arises, which I have not already discussed. But
the Bible does more than that. It does not merely witness to
events, it interprets them; it understands them in a particular way
and that way is undoubtedly very different from the way in which
I am proposing that they should be understood. There are exceptions
but I would judge that almost overwhelmingly the Bible's way of
understanding those special events to which it bears witness is one
in which the activity of God in relation to the worldly occurrences
concerned is conceived to be of a different kind from that which is
operative in the general run of worldly occurrences. Is it consistent then to regard the Bible as a religious authority, which as I
have said seems to be an inescapable necessity for a Christian
theology, and at the same time to transform as drastically as my
account would involve its own understanding of those events to
which it bears witness?

This issue came to the fore in an extreme form in the recent
'Death of God' controversy. William Hamilton asks the question:
'if Jesus' demonology, cosmology and eschatology (are) taken as
first century views, appropriate then, not so now, needing reinterpretation and understanding, but no literal assent, what is
inherently different about Jesus' theology?'[10] In other words,
once we cease to take over and accept for ourselves the biblical
understanding of the world in its totality (if indeed there is or
ever was such a thing) by what criterion do we decide what it is
proper to accept and what to reject? The question is a fair one,
and can be met in two ways. In the first place we may ask whether
Jesus' belief in God is not more central to what he stands for than
his belief in eschatology and demons, so that if that goes Jesus'
person and teaching simply cease to be really interesting. I think
a distinction of that kind can be drawn, though it would be grossly
misleading to suggest that either the eschatology or demonology
were so peripheral that no serious issue at all arose in their case.
But secondly and more significantly we need to ask whether there
may not be other supporting grounds, in the field of natural theology for example, for continuing to affirm the theology of Jesus
in a way which it might not be reasonable to do in the cases of
eschatology and demonology.

In trying to apply these two tests to our present case, I would
claim that it is the specialness of the events rather than the
special way in which the divine action was understood to be operative in them that is most fundamental. I admit that this is not
an easy distinction to make but I think that it can be made. And
secondly I would claim on the basis of my earlier discussion to
have shown (admittedly in very bare outline) that there may be
good reason in our total understanding of the world today for continuing to affirm the former and not continuing to affirm the latter. Thus, while I have no desire to disguise or to minimize in
any way the extent of the difference between the way that I am
proposing for understanding the special divine activity of which
the Bible speaks and the Bible's own understanding of it, I do
want to argue that this very considerable difference does not pre-
vent me from continuing to regard the Bible as a religious authority
of the utmost importance.

'Begin at the beginning, and go on until you come to the end:
and then stop.' But the end-point is as hard to identify as the
beginning. In stopping at this point, I do not wish to suggest for
a moment that I believe myself to have solved the problems which I
have been discussing. My hope is rather that I have said enough to

provides a sufficiently coherent account of a possible approach to these puzzling questions for others to develop or, more probably, to expose the flaws and shortcomings in what has been said.

NOTES

[1] Otto Kuster cited by H. Zahrnt, *The Question of God*, p. 246.

[2] Cf. ed. H. W. Bartsch, *Kerygma and Myth*, Vol. 1, pp. 197, 198-9.

[3] *Anglican Theological Review*, Vol. 47 (January, 1965), pp. 66-80. Cf. also L. B. Gilkey, 'Cosmology, Ontology and the Travail of Biblical Language'. *Journal of Religion*, Vol. 41 (July 1961), pp. 194-205.

[4] art. cit., p. 78.

[5] ed. C. W. Kegley, *The Theology of Rudolf Bultmann*, p. 122.

[6] D. D. Williams, "How does God act?" an essay in Whitehead's metaphysics' in edd. W. L. Reese and E. Freeman, *Process and Divinity*, pp. 179-80.

[7] P. Baelz, *Prayer and Providence*, pp. 81-2.

[8] Aquinas, *Summa Theologica* 1 a, 13, 7.

[9] *The Reality of God*, p. 180.

[10] Edd. J. L. Ice and J. J. Carey, *The Death of God Debate*, p. 223.

12. GRACE AND FREEWILL

Austin Farrer

. . . The mere assertion of something existent or actual in
our environment is of metaphysical interest only; it finds its
place, for example, in an argument against Berkeleianism. Physical
assertion begins to be of common interest when it tells us where
a certain energy or a certain resistance is to be met, and what it
can be expected to do. So equally with asserting the existence of
God. The bare assertion belongs to a dispute against metaphysical
atheism. Practical assertions concern God's particular action.
Not but that the action-reference may be indirect. We may seem to
be saying something of vast importance when we assert the divine
attributes; and if the assertion of the attributes is felt to be
implicit already in the assertion of the existence, the practical
importance will inhere in that assertion too. But the practical
significance of the attributes lies in the particular actions they
imply. God's power, wisdom and goodness are taken to bear manifold
fruit in his creation; they mean that he will everywhere do effectively and wisely what is best. General active tendencies are
of no significance where there is no particular action; least of
all as attributed to God, whose activity cannot be supposed ever
to be out of exercise.

When we were speaking of empirical verification in relation
to God's action we said that it could be called no more than general; but this was not to say that the action verified is general;
the notion is really meaningless. We can talk about the general
action of a law, either civil or natural; but this is to speak by
metaphor. A law does not act; a multitude of agents, whether physical agents or *agents de police*, act in conformity with it. Or
again, a real action may have a general effect, as when I scatter
water from a watering-can. But the action is particular.

If God acts in this world, he acts particularly; and if I had
no conception of the particular lines along which his purpose works,
and were not ready to experiment with my guesses, I could not associate my action with the divine and the whole scheme of religion

as we have set it out falls to the ground. And anyhow it is plain
that Christians attribute many particular actions and many particular purposes to the divine will; and hold that they would be
shown many more, had they but the perceptiveness to see them.

The question, how we make out or identify the line of the
divine action, is a question of detail, of practice, and of day-to-
day religion. A more obviously general and philosophic problem is
how to conceive the relation between the divine action and the
activities of created agents. Reflection on the relation goes back
to the classic age of Israelite prophecy, if it goes no further.
Isaiah was convinced that the Assyrian invasions were the scourge
of God, a Father's correction of his sons' rebellion. But he knew
that the Assyrians were not somnambulists under a divine hypno-
tism. The Assyrian was a rod in the hand of God's indignation,
but he had no notion of being anything of the kind. His motives
were acquisitive or political. If we can make out a prophetic
theory about the mechanism of the divine control, it lies in the
openness of men's thoughts to pressures of which they are unaware.
The Assyrian feels the force of the reasons for harsh action
against Judaea; but the reasons might not have occurred to him, or
an alternative use of his troops might have seemed more rewarding.
The hearts of kings are in God's rule and governance; he turns
them as it seems best to his godly wisdom.

To take the matter a stage further--how did the prophet suppose that the divine influence came to bear? Perhaps it is unjust
to treat pictorial language as philosophical theory; but one can
only say that the Hebrews were ready to talk about the Breath of
the Lord as though it were a finite force, an agent among agents,
moving the cogitations of the heart as the wind sways the trees.
It needs no words to show that such an idea is impossible to us
as anything but poetry.

We may say of the Hebrews, that they commonly saw divine effects as having creaturely agents, but found it needless to enquire
how the divine hand wielded its instruments; they were content to
use the simplest pictures. And the modern Christian is really in
no worse or better case. He begins with the assumption that certain
events, within himself or without, are divine effects. He does
not doubt that they are the immediate act of natural agents, for
if they were not, how would they be in this world of ours at all?
If he speculates on the way in which the divine control takes effect, he probably goes no further than to tell himself that there
is room for it to act; for the grid of causal uniformity does not

(to any evidence) fit so tight upon natural processes as to bar
the influence of an over-riding divine persuasion. If asked what
on earth he can mean by 'persuasion' or 'influence' in such a connexion, he may simply refuse the challenge. What sense is there in
demanding an exact account of an action which, by hypothesis, is
outside our knowledge?

If he is up in traditional philosophy he can elaborate his
refusal by an appeal to the doctrine of analogy. According to
this doctrine, we *believe* that God's way of acting is the infin-
itely higher analogue of our way, but we cannot *conceive* it otherwise than in terms of our own. God's agency must actually be such
as to work omnipotently on, in, or through creaturely agencies
without either forcing them or competing with them. But as soon
as we try to conceive it in action, we degrade it to the creaturely
level and place it in the field of interacting causalities. The
result can only be (if we take it literally) monstrosity and confusion.

The argument is painfully negative and prompts the retort:
'You have shown me why the idea of a First Cause cannot be expected
to work. I should have thought this to be a good reason for dis-
carding it. What can you do with a First Cause which stands in
no workable relation to second causes? You are blocked at the first
move you have to make.' There may be several counters to this objection; heaven knows there are few finalities in metaphysical
dispute. But the best counter is surely the practical one. It
can be shown that the direct relating of finite causal agency to
divine action is a task which, in our living concern with the
divine, we never attempt, and have no means of placing in a practical light.

The first point to be observed is that God's agency does not
strike us in the springing-point of causes but in the finished
effect. Isaiah does not begin from a speculation into the mystery
of Assyrian motives, but from the divine act of scourging Israel's
back with an Assyrian rod. His reference of the effect to its
divine cause does not go by way of the Assyrian's choices even
though he turns aside to muse upon them. The religious mind goes
direct from the divine handiwork to the divine maker; it is like
the amateur's identification of a work of art. This, he says, is
surely a Rembrandt; in style, merit and feeling it is his. He
knows nothing of Rembrandt's methods. Let us suppose that the
picture is an ideal composition. Did the artist paint out of his
head, or did he set the scene with models dressed and posed, and

the light carefully arranged? How many basic pigments did he use,
and how did he lay his brush-strokes? Did he follow set precepts
or recipes in the grouping of shapes and colours? Here are questions which the art-historian can very likely answer, but in which
the amateur may be utterly at sea; and yet he may be talking good
sense when he says 'This is a Rembrandt'.

If we ask how the amateur knows, we realise at once that he
cannot compare the painter's art or mind with his picture, so as
to judge the second worthy of the first. The painter's artistry
is not an experienceable object. Our amateur can but judge from
authentic pictures already studied. Yet to say this is not to say
that Rembrandt and his artistry are superfluous terms, interrupting
a comparative study of actual pictures. For what one judges is
not simply that the newly-met picture is formally like its brothers.
One judges that the likenesses and unlikenesses too are such that
a man who had painted the acknowledged canvases might have painted
this one also. And when we so judge we draw on our understanding
of human inventiveness and of human purpose; we know how creative
minds in any field like to vary their inventions; we have judged
from his acknowledged canvases how Rembrandt liked to vary his.
It is true enough that the amateur works from the pictures he
knows; yet he uses them as evidence for answering the question what
Rembrandt might paint, and whether he painted this; referring to
Rembrandt's artistry the completed product, not the steps traversed
in producing it; for of these we are supposing our amateur to be
ignorant.

The application of the parable scarcely needs drawing out.
A Christian has his accepted works of the divine hand, which give
him his types of Providence in action. In view of these he appre-
ciates the ever-new works of God. And his appreciation is of
achievement, not technique; in the terms of our parable, he is in-
escapably amateur.

He is so, for no accidental reason. The artistic amateur
could become an art-historian and pry into technique; the religious
mind cannot do anything of the sort. The practical relation of
his action to God's is one which does not allow the technical
question to arise.

Let us consider the religious predicament. We are faced with
the work of God. Speculatively we shall hold that it embraces
whatever happens. Practically we are concerned with a drift of
divine action both manifest to us and involving our own. There is
no escaping in this connexion the analogy offered by our neighbour's

conduct and our need to interpret it. That our neighbour does act,
there is no question; we see the signs of it in the movements of
his body. The question is, what he is at, and how it concerns us.
For the purpose of the comparison we are making, the whole world
of events must be said to compose the bodily motions of the divine
will. Measured by the mighty mass, the divine purpose (we must
confess) is sparingly signified to us.

My neighbour's conduct bears upon me as a finite system of
action, basically physical, with which I have to engage the similar
system of my own. It is so, whether my concern is to fit into his
plans or to fit him into mine. Merely to establish communication
with him I must work my throat, and make impressions on his ears;
the bodily relation is simply reversed, if I submit to his direction or advice. In all our cooperation with our neighbour something
happens, of which the engagement of one cog-wheel with another is
a tolerable diagram. Whereas in the engagement of our action with
God's there is no sort of parallel to any of this. We are concerned
with his purpose and action solely as an operation to which we
commit ourselves. It is no part of our business to work any determinate system of communication. We do not find where and by
what means to touch God nor where and by what means to undergo his
touch. We enter into his action simply by acting, whether the
action be a movement of thought or an employment of the hand. We
believe, and even claim to find, that his action sustains or inspires ours; but the divine assistance is experienced simply in its
effect. To be assisted by a mountaineer I must put my weight on
a rope; to receive the divine assistance I have only to think or
act my trust in God.

I know that I am retailing the very platitude of spiritual
religion. Perhaps the consequence I propose to draw has not been
so generally remarked. It is that the causal joint (so to speak)
between infinite and finite action plays and in the nature of the
case can play no part in our concern with God and his will. We
can do nothing about it, nor does it bear on anything that we can
do. And so, on empirical ground, the question about it is a question which does not arise and may be condemned as no question at
all. Without finding the causal joint between my action-system
and my neighbours', still more evidently, between my action-system
and inanimate environmental systems, I cannot relate my action to
theirs or theirs to mine. The causal joint (could there be said
to be one) between God's action and ours is of no concern in the
activity of religion; the very idea of it arises simply as a

by-product of the analogical imagination, as we explained above.
Surely it is nothing new that imagination should fall over its own
feet, or symbolism tangle into knots.

Turn from symbolism to action, and the problem vanishes.
We can, in the only possible way, experience the active relation of
a created energy to the Creator's action by embracing the divine
will. Everyone who prays knows that the object of the exercise
is a thought or an aspiration or a caring which is no more ours
than it is that of God in us. The philosopher who sets out to
examine the religious fact, and who brushes away such an account of
prayer as mere *Schwaermerei* or pious rant,[1] may as well close the
enquiry at once. He has said his last word; the whole thing's
nonsense. Let him devote his attention to a more serious topic.

The position which we have outlined, if it is accepted, carries some significant corollaries. First, the vanishing of the
problem of freewill and divine predestination in the achievement
of salvation. We know that the action of a man can be the action
of God in him; our religious existence is an experimenting with
this relation. Both the divine and the human actions remain real
and therefore free in the union between them; not knowing the
modality of the divine action we cannot pose the problem of their
mutual relation. All a spiritual guide need do is append anathema
to any proposition which denies the personal reality of either the
human action or the divine, or which, admitting both, inverts the
hierarchy and makes the divine action consequent upon the human
rather than *vice versa*.

A second corollary is that Grace ceases to be a special problem or even a special concept. It is superfluous to postulate a
supernaturalising extra imparted to the creature, and unnecessary
to take refuge by way of reaction in the shallow description of
Grace as mere influence. Grace is an action of the Creator in
the creature. He acts in the creature everywhere; when he acts in
the rational creature he is pleased to act in that creature's
mental and voluntary life, bringing them into his own. For of such
a conformity or union with the divine, mind and will can be made
capable. Physical or animal energies cannot.

NOTE

[1]Many philosophers would see themselves excused from examining
any such account by the supposed demonstration that a reference of
human duty to divine will is either vacuous or immoral. For an
examination of this argument see Mr. B. G. Mitchell's forthcoming
book, *Religion and Morals*.

ANIMA MUNDI

We have made a comparison between causal systems, and especially two, one formalist, the other activist; the Aristotelian,
and that which on our part we wish to commend. Aristotle placed
being before becoming, and so came back to a first being who simply
and absolutely was. We place determinators before determinates,
and so come back to a determinator who is nothing but what he determines to be--a free Spirit. But whatever considerations we
have been able to advance in favour of our system we have so far
cast little if any light on the nature of the causal relation--the
joint, as it were--between the action of the First Determinator,
and the finite activities determined by him.

When we were discussing the interpretation of existence which
is of practical concern to religion, we were happy to point out
that the joint just referred to does not come into question. For
man's business is to set himself in the line of the divine intention, not to manage a contact with supernatural force or transcendent process. We believe that, being conformed to the will of God,
we are used by him in the way such conformity expresses. The
divine operation is God's secret; the effect is displayed in what
we are enabled to do. It may be a tolerable language to describe
our action as a cooperation with God; but such cooperation is nothing like cooperation with our fellow-beings, when our work and
their work dovetail together in specifiable ways. On occasion, we
may accept the action of other finite agents as the work of God, and
set ourselves to dovetail with it; but it is evident that instances
of the sort cast no light on our problem. The mystery is, how
the action of any finite agents, whether severally or jointly, is
subject to the causality of God.

An austere empiricism might decide that what does not enter
into the pattern of our active concern is nothing to us; and that
having no experimental evidence on which to settle the question,
we cannot meaningfully raise it. But an empiricism so abrupt as
this is surely self-stultifying. For the activity we can exercise
in relation to God is so far comparable with the relations we culti-
vate towards our neighbour, that it supposes belief in him as in
a person whose will so acts that we can embrace it. And a belief
without which practice is impossible, cannot be called wholly

unpractical. We live the belief, and in so doing, we cannot leave
it utterly undefined. The idea of the relation of our activity to
God's causality cannot play its part in our imaginations while remaining to us just 'some relatedness, we know not what'. It is at
least so far definitely conceived by us as to exclude certain accounts of it; for example, it cannot be the simple relation of part
to whole; for if our will or action is a mere part of God's, we can
have no adjustment to make of ours to his.

However else the relation may be viewed, it is taken to be a
moral relation; that is, it is assimilated to relation with our
neighbour, whatever qualifications may be appended. One might say,
Relation to another active self, only not 'out there' but (as has
recently been claimed) 'in the ground of our being'. Or should we
say 'In the springing-point of our act'? The phrase may strike us
as less opaque, but it is no less composed of gross physical metaphor. It represents our activity as a jet of water spreading from
the fine aperture through which a pressure below, invisible to us,
forces it; or as a shoot thrown out from the parent stem by a life
invisible beneath the cover of the bark. Such metaphors serve only
to place the Creator's act in sheer priority to ours; a priority
which is of no less concern to a theology of nature than it is to
a theology of grace.

Should not a philosopher try to do better? Perhaps analogical
terms cannot be avoided; it should nevertheless be possible to
discard gross metaphor. We may not have a primary concern for the
perfect clarification of notions admittedly metaphysical, which do
not give immediate shape to our action. Yet the secondary concern
we have is not negligible, if our religious existence is in some
sense a living of our belief in a causality passing over from Infinite into finite act.

'Ought not you to go further?' says our critic. 'Can you, as
a theologian, admit that your concern here is secondary in any degree? You are not, I take it, prepared to have the religious life
simply reduced to the moral; you see it as a life of obedience to
an actual God. But it appears to me that you hope to draw a line
between your conception of God (for that, if anything is, must be
of primary importance to a theologian) and your conception of his
efficacy in determining his creatures. And I cannot see how such
a line can be drawn. You cannot pretend to know God except as
Creator--creator of finite entities, or of further perfections or
achievements in such entities. And Creation is a sort of efficacy;
your Creator is one who exercises it, as the baker is one who bakes.

The verb defines the noun, the action reveals the agent. A baker
does not become a baker by being the *cause* of bread, (say) on the
supposition that he grows it on trees in the form of breadfruit.
That would not be baking, it would be fruitfarming.

'You tell me that you work very happily in your religion with
the idea of a Person whose will is determinative and to be embraced.
I want to know whether this is poetry, commenting, I dare say fruit-
fully, on the moral destiny of man; or serious doctrine, enshrining
in analogical language a core of metaphysical belief. You reply
that if theology is a mythology, it is mythology about a God taken
to be non-mythical; it is not a God-mythology about mundane realities. If asked to justify your statement, you reply that the divine
action is taken as the cause of mundane activities, never as the
exercise of them. Very well; let *cause* be the lifeblood of your
faith. But what do you mean by cause in this connexion? Cause,
we have agreed, is a mere generic term for an act, circumstance or
event which in any way serves to explain what occurs. How, then,
can you be convinced of the operation of a cause, unless you can
specify the way it operates?

'Consider the following dialogue: Why did you get in the way
of the traffic?--A girl caused me to step off the pavement.--How
did she do that? Did she push you? Did she so walk that you
stepped aside to give her room? Did she ask you to do it? Did her
charms, glimpsed on the other side of the street, draw you across
the roadway? Or strike you all of a heap, so that you lost control
of your feet?--No, it was none of these things--What was it, then?--
I can't say; but I am sure it was a girl made me do it.

'What are we to make of such an answer? It could only hope
to pass as the record of an imperfect memory. He made a mental note
at the time that it was a girl who caused it; how, he can no longer
recall. But evidently our claim that God is the universal First
Cause cannot represent imperfect memory of this sort, unless it be
on the strength of Plato's myth--that the soul was clearer-sighted
in a previous existence, and able to observe what she now confusedly
remembers.

'Indeed my parable was too favourable to the agnostic believer
in divine causality. For the girl on the pavement is a girl, however it may have been about her diverting you into the roadway. But
a creator is not a creator irrespective of his creating. To make
the parallel strict, we should need to rewrite the conversation on
a level of utter futility: What diverted your steps into the roadway?--I was diverted by a divertent.--Meaning by a divertent,

what?--An agency which diverted.--Diverted in what way?--Not in any
way rather than in any other.'

   Ah, but now you have let yourself be carried away by the
pleasures of satire. You have forgotten the conditions of the question before us. Had we not agreed that the practice of religion
and the logic of theistic reflection are at one in seeing the Primary Determinant as personal will? This being so, the specifica-
tion of the causal relation is not as crucial an issue as you al-
lege. Your parable will need to be reconstructed. You take it to
be a person who made you step off the pavement, and you take that
person to have meant you to do what he made you do. There is only
one point which remains undecided--how his meaning you to act came
to bear in causing you to act. And, in the human case, that is an
issue we often leave unexplored. If, for example, we were told
that one of Queen Elizabeth the First's courtiers broke off an intended marriage because such was the royal will, we might not
trouble to enquire how the sovereign displeasure was brought home
to him.

   'I dare say; but then there are several easily imaginable ways
in which the Queen could make her wishes felt; if you are uncertain,
it is because you do not know which of several perfectly adequate
suppositions to adopt. In the theological case, it is all we can
do to think of one which tolerably fits. Still, I do not see that
we need despair. I was arguing against pious agnosticism, by reducing it *ad absurdum*. I am still entitled to argue in favour of
positive belief. Let us take the question up on the terms you have
just laid down. The hypothesis shall be that a personal activity
of mind or will, all-embracing in scope, determines the many particular acts of the world's constituents; and the question shall
be, What model do we possess for such a scheme? Surely there is no
need for us to look far afield. Does not every act of rational volition do what we suppose the divine will to do? We know nothing
of any will or mind existing or acting otherwise than by the employment of a bodily instrument. And to use a bodily instrument
means bringing into play a great number of bodily constituents,
which so act by their own proper motion as to further the voluntary
purpose. Will you not wish to say, then, that as my mind is the
mind of my body, so God's will is the soul of the world?'

   Thank you for so positive a suggestion. We shall need to look
at it with some care. But there is one point in the relation you
propose for comparison which offers immediate consolation; and
that is its unintelligibility. We believe the body to be a

physiological system organising a vast number of minute parts. We
have no insight whatever into the way in which our act of will
directs their multiple activities. Yet we have a practical belief
that it does so. Thus it is plain that an ignorance of the mode
by which will fulfils itself in its instruments is no bar to a conviction that it does so fulfil itself. Where I am the universal
operator in my microcosm, I have no awareness of the relation by
which I determine the cellular operators; where I am a cellular
operator in the macrocosm, I have no awareness of the relation by
which the universal operator determines me.

But I do not think you invoked the analogy to justify a prag-
matic agnosticism; you meant on the contrary, to define the nature
of the creature-creator relation as nearly as possible. If your
positive contention holds good, it will carry an important consequence for metaphysics; it will mean that the proper form for theism
to take is a Philosophy of Total Organism. If that is the thesis
we have to consider, we ought to scrutinise somewhat closely the
parallel on which it is built. Is it as persuasive on a second
view as it seems at first sight? There are certainly radical differences between the matters you have so confidently compared.

On either side there is thought and will (mine, God's) and
a plurality of constituents (the cells etc. of my body, the things
constitutive of the universe). On either side the thought is taken
to rule the constituent parts. So far, perhaps, so good. But we
have just observed that thoughtful purpose in ourselves rules the
multitude of its bodily constituents by ignoring them. The actions
I heedfully perform are bodily indeed, but the thought which animates them takes my body to be one thing and my act to be a total
effect. I am concerned with what I, the animal person, do, not
with the constituent activities of those minute parts in and through
which my animal person has its being. If, then, the parallel is
to be drawn at all strictly, with God's will the mind of the Universe as I am the mind of my body, then the action which concerns
the divine will must be the action of the whole, not the actions
of the multitudinous constituent parts in which the whole subsists.
We shall be back again by another route to a modified Aristotelian-
ism; God's thought will govern the grand movement of the universe,
a movement which employs the constituent movements, but is uncon-
cerned with them except as *conditiones sine quibus non* for its
majestic gyrations.

'Not Aristotle again! Whichever way we turn, we are confronted by that tedious ghost. Would it not be better if we resolved to ignore him, and to pursue the question on its merits? I

am not much impressed, I must say, by the point you have just
brought forward. "If," you say, "the parallel is to be drawn at
all strictly." But surely it cannot be drawn so strictly as to
saddle the deity with every limitation of our finitude. Human intention shows its finite scope by going no further into the detail
of its own action than a grasp of the macroscopic effect requires.
It must be our hypothesis that the Universal Mind is infinite; it
goes to the bottom of detail, it wills the total action through and
through.'

I am happy to agree with you. All I want is to see the necessary qualifications made, and you have introduced one that is certainly vital. There are more yet to come, however. You suggest
that we might speak of God's will as though it were purpose ani-
mating a body so comprehensively as to penetrate the minutest detail
of being or of action which goes to the make-up of it; the 'body'
in this case being the universe. Very well. But to talk like
this is still to take one's start from the great totality and work
down into the detail; and that again is to take it for granted that
there really is a totality--a totality, I mean, which adds up to
some sort of vital unity. Were there no dominant system of vital
functions in my body for my mind to be the mind of, my mind would
lose its physical setting and I should not know what could be meant
by calling it the mind of this body. My body is an organism; to
all evidence, the universe is no such thing.

The difficulty I am raising is familiar in connexion with the
traditional 'Argument from Design'. It is a shockingly rash and
careless presentation of the case which claims that the universe is
a designed whole. Only it seems easier to save that Argument than
it is to save your thesis. The Argument may still have some force
if it abates its pretensions, and points simply to elements of
design (if any such there be) not plausibly traceable to the action
of natural forces unaided. Your claim that the universe is an organic whole, such as to supply God's will with a 'body', is, as an
allegation, more staggeringly false even than the claim that it is
a total design. What is worse, your claim does not allow of modification or abatement, it is all or nothing. Elements of organisa-
tion here or there among the galaxies will not help to save it in
any form.

'This is not fair. The Argument from Design is an argument.
I never dreamt of arguing from the superorganic structure of the
sum of things to a Mind of the Universe. On the contrary, I accepted by way of hypothesis your own basis of reasoning, your

conventional inference to a First Cause, a Primal Determinant, a
free and sovereign Will. I merely ventured to help you over the
puzzle, how to conceive the joint (as it were) between the action
of the universal Will, and the actions of finite agents whether
voluntary or merely natural. And I said that we could scarcely
do otherwise than follow the model our own being provides--a relation between a rational organic agency and the cellular agencies
it organises. Now you appear to be saying that I have no right to
apply the model unless the sovereign mind's concern for the whole
takes precedence over his concern for the actions of the constituent
parts; and that this can scarcely be so unless the universe appears
to be a whole in a more than trivial sense; to be, indeed, the
organism of all organisms.

'If that is your contention, then I reject it. Did not we
agree in attributing to our finitude the incarnation of our own
mind or will in a single level of organising pattern? Once we have
admitted an infinite Mind, embracing all detail and penetrating
every level, why should we make it a matter of principle that it
should be any more yoked to the action of the whole, than to that
of the part? We have no interest in falsifying the balance of the
universe; let it be whatever it appears to be--no organism, if you
like, but a loose society, of which the organised activity is
centred in the parts rather than in the whole. The distribution
of the divine volition may correspond to the distribution of cosmic action, whatever that may be.'

You will scarcely expect me to quarrel with you, when you so
obligingly move in the direction I want you to take. What I wonder
is, once we have gone so far, how much substance there remains in
the analogy you originally proposed. But before we can decide that
issue, we have still further to go on the road we have been
travelling.

You declare your readiness to admit the apparent balance between whole and part in the universe, and to accept the verdict of
scientific observation. But suppose the verdict of scientific observation to be, that there neither is nor can be any such thing as
a universal whole. Then what becomes of your balance? You cannot
hold a balance between the real and the fictitious, still less between the intelligible and the nonsensical.

And the universe is not a whole. The cosmic paradoxes of
space and time should have convinced us. No one denies that the
human mind can place whatever it knows or comprehends of cosmic
fact in a single generalised diagram; but the real order of things

is diagrammatisable, not diagrammatic; the diagrammatic unity is in
the mind, not in the world. It is nothing but the great Newtonian
fiction of a space-time continuum viewed from no point in space and
from no moment in time. It was shown up for what it was almost as
soon as Newton had defined it; Leibniz wrote it off as the *phenomenon bene fundatum*. Realities do not coexist by absolute position
in a Newtonian continuum; they coexist by constituting a field of
conditions for any single piece of organised agency. The universe
is indeed organised, or drawn together into unity; but it is so
organised or drawn together a million million times over at all the
single points where a field of forces finds a focus; and that is
wherever any single active existence is present. All of these
focal points have a certain extension--they are patterns of activity. Our own sentient animal existence is a highly-developed
example. But to all evidence, there is no world-pattern pulling
the universe together; it is pulled together by each of the infinite overlapping multitude of focal patterns, the patterns of actual
and active existences.

If that is so--and to the best of our knowledge it is so--what
can this analogy of yours do except mislead? Thought and purpose
in a man animate or direct a pattern of action which organises and,
as it were, builds upon a multitude of cellular activities. There
is no such organising pattern on the cosmic scale, so how can the
universal will bear upon us and our fellow-creatures in any way
significantly analogous? If the God of Nature pulls the universe
together, he must be presumed to do it through his creative employment of the energies which do pull the universe together. And
these, as we have seen, are nothing but the individual 'creatures'
in their focal capacity.

'It is not easy to counter what you say, so long as we are
tailoring our theology to fit our natural philosophy. But one
learns prudence, even in philosophising; and experience of the game
should have taught us that just when theology has been trimmed down
to a perfect fit with natural fact, the theology vanishes. It is
not surprising; for the theistic postulation, even when it is made
in answer to questions posed by the world of nature, demands belief
in a reality which is itself non-natural, the divine. In any
settlement of boundary-issues between God and nature, there must be
give-and-take; the divine has its own logic and must be allowed its
own rights. It is as vital that God should remain God, as that
nature should remain nature.

'If, then, God is to be God, it may be necessary to postulate schemes of divine action in or upon nature, which are not visible in the pattern of natural events as they are naturally interpreted by us. The notion of a world-form organising the million million constituents, may be such a necessary postulate. Who indeed can doubt that it is so? Who that is ready to entertain the idea of God at all can be content to limit his action in the way you appear to suggest? Is God simply to support each of nature's constituents in being itself? Shall he do nothing to unify the whole otherwise than it is unified by the action of each constituent in drawing the field of environing forces into its focus? Then the action of God simply reduces to the action of nature; and the claim that the action of natural forces is divinely willed reduces to the statement that they act. Every theist of any kind wants, surely, to say that natural activities or processes are placed by divine wisdom in some general scheme, a scheme transcending any built-in self-orientation of their own, and proper to the scope of a divine agent.'

I agree, of course, with the substance of what you say. The divine must have its rights or there will be no theology. Divine thought must comprehend the whole. Divine intention must extend more widely than the immediate functioning of each agency among the many constitutive of nature. None of this is in dispute. The question is, how all of it can be asserted in a form which best allows nature to be natural or, if you like, adds to nature working extensions least out of keeping with what we know of her. The action of a cosmic superorganism is a very violent hypothesis, which fits none of our scientific or other natural knowledge; and we have no need to suppose anything of the kind, since a less extravagant supposition is open to us.

If we want light on the divine mind's covering the world, we turn inevitably to our own mind's covering of it. As we were observing, we cannot get the cosmos into our heads except in the artificial diagram of a neutral continuum. On a smaller scale, however, we can proceed more realistically. If we are merely considering the coexistence of a limited number of our sentient fellow-creatures, we can adopt the standpoint of each in turn and, while we do so, see the others as constituting his field or environment. That, if you like, is an artificial exercise. But when we are in discourse or in personal relation with our fellows, we see simultaneously from their centre and from our own by the mere fact of taking their meaning; for their meaning is what *they* intend, it is not a theorem of our own thought.

Now agreeable as it often is simply to appreciate and sym-
pathetically to enjoy the active existence of our fellow-beings,
the aim of mutual understanding is commonly more practical. Our
object is harmonisation, co-operation, common enrichment of life;
in a word, society. Social aims are entertained in some measure by
the most selfish; and they unquestionably extend beyond the natural
objectives of individuals singly regarded. On the other hand, the
social frame is not a superorganism; to take it as such has been
the tragic error of philosophical thought, a mistake not merely
academic, but carrying political implications nothing short of
disastrous.

What we in fact think of the divine will in its application to
ourselves is that its extension is a social extension. We take it
that the divine purpose is to achieve our individual good through
social action and mutual concern. And when we look behind our
existence and see the divine will as having placed or created us,
we take that will to be animated by a social providence. If God
meant to make an individual person, he cannot have intended him
without intending the society he would form with others; for apart
from that he could not have been himself.

To give value to the providence of God there is no need to
make the universe out to be *a* society, let alone the society of
societies, normative of all others. It is enough to say that God,
knowing each of his creatures from within its action, and viewing
its world from the standpoint of its being, cares for such mutual
harmonisations of natural agents as are necessary to the existence
or the development of the creatures he creates. Here is a theme
on which one might endlessly enlarge, and I have indeed expatiated
on it elsewhere; especially in comment on the patience (as it were)
of the creative Wisdom in achieving his combined effects without
forcing the limited and often brutal principles of activity native
to the several agents he employs; a patience which shows itself in
the toleration of much that we call waste, chaos and disaster.

The theme belongs to another occasion. We are considering
the proper and improper applications of the analogy embodied in
the formula, 'God, or the divine thought, is the mind of the
world.' And after so much urged against improper applications, it
is time that something was said about the proper way to take it.
God is the mind of the world--Yes, indeed, and that is how he differs from my mind which can never be more than the mind of me.
True, I attempt to enter into the subjectivity of a limited number
among my fellow-beings, but my power to do so is very imperfect;

and even then I cannot become their mind, so as to cause or operate
their proper action; it is theirs, not mine. But God is the Mind
of the World, that is, he is not tied to any base of operation that
is exclusively his; he enters fully into the subjectivity of all
the world's constituents. What is more, he does not enter into
them simply after the event, with a sympathy perfect, perhaps, but
still impotent; he enters into them by prior causality, willing
them the existence and the activity they exercise; and so he is indeed *the Mind* of the world.

So much for a brief statement of the force attaching to the
analogy. It will be seen that it takes as its foundation the
heights our mental activities aspire to reach, not the limitations
they endure. It virtually amounts to a statement of transcendence
and of first causality. To be the mind not merely of you or of
me but of all creatures, God must be a free Spirit, whose action
is prior to the actions of them all. Such being the value of the
analogy, it is clear that it casts no light whatever on the mysterious causal joint between prime agency (the Creator's) and second agency (the creature's); a relation which it simply presupposes.
God's being the mind of the world does nothing towards identifying
his action with that of an organic whole, to which the actions of
the cellular constituents are geared.

'Well, but surely the divine mind may be allowed to confer
unity on the universe by embracing it in his own single and in-
finitely multiform activity.'

Yes, of course; the statement is true in so far as it is
tautological. By concerning himself with a plurality he unites it
in the unity of his concern. The unity is the unity of the divine
initiative. Only, in making even so innocent a statement as this,
we need to be on our guard against the false suggestions of the
human model. When a man confers a sort of unity on a miscellaneous
collection of persons, animals and objects by giving them a place
in his multifarious activities or interests, he does impose upon
them a scheme of order which is his own, and alien to them. For
the possible patterns of human interest or activity, though indefinitely numerous, remain specifically human. However varied,
they are variations on set themes. Whereas it would surely be
irrational to suppose in God a determinate nature, like that of a
finite species, prescribing an order in his concern with things
particular to himself and foreign to the things. Surely his concern for his creatures is for them to be themselves, or more than
themselves; not for them to act as pawns in some specifically

supernatural game which any divine hand is bound to play. A man's
concern for his fellow-beings, however generous, must be a strait-
jacket compared with the openness of God's concern for the world.

13. THE CORPOREAL WORLD AND THE EFFICACY
OF SECOND CAUSES

Etienne Gilson

An examination of the universe as a whole certainly must begin
with the study of pure intelligences. But the next step in the
process is not so obvious. Indeed two different procedures are
possible. They correspond to the two principles by which the ar-
rangement of this universe is directed. One procedure is to follow
the hierarchy of created beings, taken in their diminishing order
of perfection, and so pass from the study of the angels to the
study of man. The other procedure is to abandon the above point
of view and to regard the order of ends. This attitude is suggested by the account of creation in Genesis. Man, who so far as
the order of perfection is concerned, ranks immediately after the
angels, does not appear in the Scriptural account until the completion of creation of which he is the true end. It is for man
that the incorruptible heavenly bodies have been created. It is
for him too that God divides the waters with the firmament, and
calls the dry land to appear from under the waters and peoples it
with animals and the green herb. Consequently, it is quite legitimate to place the study of corporeal things right after that of
the purely spiritual. In this way it is possible to conclude with
the examination of man who is the bond of union between the world
of intelligences and the world of bodies.[1]

The field of natural philosophy is the one where St. Thomas
has made fewest innovations; that is, at least, if we restrict it
to physics and biology, properly so-called. Here the Christian
doctor adds nothing to Aristotle, or so little that it is hardly
worth mentioning. We will not find in him the curiosity of a
Robert Grosseteste for the fertile speculations of mathematical
physics. No doubt the very spirit of his Aristotelian philosophy
was opposed to this; although it was not opposed to his following
the studies of his master, Albert the Great, in the field of zool-
ogy and in the natural sciences. Yet, here again we see him
escape. The questions of the *Summa Theologiae* given to the

commentary on the work of the six days provide him with many an
occasion to exercise his natural ingenuity in one or other of these
two directions. But St. Thomas has no heart for the task and saves
his ingenuity for other subjects. The essential thing in his
eyes is to preserve the very letter of Scripture intact. He is
well aware, however, that the Book of Genesis was not a treatise
on cosmography for the use of scholars. It was a statement of the
truth intended for the simple people whom Moses was addressing.
Thus it is sometimes possible to interpret it in a variety of
ways.[2] So it is that when we speak of the six days of creation,
we can understand by it either six successive days, as do Ambrose,
Basil, Chrysostom and Gregory, and as is suggested by the letter
of the text, which, however, is not addressed to scholars. Or we
can, with Augustine, take it to refer to the simultaneous creation
of all beings, with days symbolizing the various orders of beings.
This second interpretation is at first sight less literal, but is,
rationally speaking, more satisfying. It is the one that St.
Thomas adopts, although he does not exclude the other which, as
he says, can also be held.[3]

In whatever way or ways he judges it possible to reconcile the
visible universe as he sees it with the account of Genesis, St.
Thomas accepts essentially the universe of Aristotle. It consists
of a series of seven concentric, planetary spheres. These spheres
are contained within an eighth sphere, that of the fixed stars;
and they themselves contain the Earth which is their center.[4] The
matter of each of the celestial spheres is strictly incorruptible,
because for a thing to corrupt it must change. But for it to change
it has to be capable of becoming something other than it is. It
must, as we say, be capable of being *in potency*. Now the matter of
the heavenly spheres is in some way saturated by its form, and is
no longer in potency to any kind of being whatsoever. It is all
it can be; and can no longer change except in place. To each
sphere is assigned a motive Intelligence which maintains and directs
its circular movement. But it is not, properly speaking, either
its form or its soul. Beneath the lowest sphere, that of the Moon,
the four elements, fire, air, water, earth, are ranged. By rights
each of these ought to be completely gathered together in its
natural place. When it is in its natural place it is in a state of
rest and equilibrium. Actually, however, the elements are more or
less mixed up. It is their tendency to return to their natural
place which produces the various movements by which they are agi-
tated. Fire moves upwards; earth downwards; air and water settle

between the two in the intermediary places where they belong. This
whole cosmology falls within frameworks drawn from other sources.
Where St. Thomas is at home and able to perform with ease the task
that comes more naturally to him is in the metaphysical investigation of the principles of natural philosophy. Here once again the
Christian philosopher proves his originality. Here it is a question of the relation that binds being and the efficacy of second
causes to God. Here he feels himself directly interested in its
exact determination.

In studying the notion of creation, we came to the conclusion
that only God is a Creator, since creation is an act proper to
Him[5] and since nothing exists which was not created by Him. Perhaps it is not out of place to recall this general conclusion when
we are about to launch into the study of bodies. The more so since
the error that the nature of bodies was itself something bad and
that they were consequently the works of some evil principle other
than God had become very widespread.[6] This was a doubly pernicious
error. First, because all existing things have at least one constitutive element in common--their *esse*. There must be some principle from which they have this element and which causes them to
be, whatever may be their manner of being, whether invisible and
spiritual or visible and corporeal. Since God is the cause of
being, his causality extends necessarily to bodies as well as to
spirits. Secondly, there is a reason based on the end of things,
which is capable of convincing us that God has no other end than
Himself. But things have an end other than themselves--God. This
is an absolute truth, which holds for every order of reality whatsoever, and for bodies no less than spirits. But there is something
that must be added to it. A being cannot exist for God unless it
also exists for itself and for its own good. Thus in this huge
organism called the universe each part has first its own act and
its own end, as the eye is for seeing. In addition, each of the
less noble parts exists with a view to the more noble, as creatures
lower than man are in the universe with a view to man. Further,
all these creatures, taken one by one, are only in the universe
with a view to the collective perfection of the universe. Finally,
the collective perfection of creatures, taken all together, is only
here in the universe as an imitation and representation of the
glory of God Himself.[7] This radical metaphysical optimism does
not exclude anything deserving, in any sense whatsoever, the name
of being. It does not exclude the world of bodies any more than
anything else. Matter exists with a view to form; lower forms with

a view to higher, and higher forms with a view to God. Whatever
is, therefore, is good.[8] Consequently, whatever is, has God for
its cause in spite of the objection raised.

In analyzing this conclusion, we see a first consequence issue
out of it: God is the first and immediate cause of bodies, that
is to say, not of their form taken by itself, nor their matter by
itself, but the substantial unity of their matter and form. Here
is how we are to understand this.

What experience gives us to grasp immediately are bodies subject to perpetual change and movement. It is this concrete data
which analysis must break up into its constitutive elements. In
the first place, the very fact that beings become something other
than they were supposes the basic distinction of two points of view
toward being: what being is; what it can still become. This is
the distinction between *act* and *potency*, to which we have been
constantly referring. That which is capable of being a certain
thing, but is not that thing, is that thing in potency. That which
that thing already is is so in act.[9] This notion of possibility or
passive potency does not express sheer nothingness, absolute lack
of actuality. It signifies, rather, the aptitude toward a certain
eventual actuality which is realizable even though not yet realized.
The block of marble is in potency to the form of the statue; a
liquid mass is not. It is not that the outline of the statue is
more present in the marble than in the liquid. It is not in the
marble, but can be drawn out of it. The marble is *in potency* to it
as long as no sculptor makes it a statue in act.

Of all the kinds of potentiality, the first to present itself
is the potency to substantial being. What is "that which can become a substance?" This pure "possibility of being a substance"
is called *prime matter*. Taken by itself and separately, it cannot
be conceived, for the simple reason that it possesses no being of
its own. *Nullum esse habet*, Averroes says of it. That it is
nothing in itself does not prove that it is incapable of existing.
Prime matter exists in the substance from the very moment that the
substance itself exists, and by virtue of the act which makes it
exist. This act which constitutes the substance is the *form*. From
and by the form, substance receives whatever is positive in its
being, since, as we have said, it is in and by the form that its
act-of-being penetrates it. This also remains true of matter:
forma dat esse materiae.[10] Prime matter is the very possibility
of substance. It is to the form of the substance that matter owes
whatever actual being it has.

Form, accordingly, is an act. The form of the substance is
the act which constitutes the substance as such. Hence this is
called the *substantial form*. Once substance is constituted by the
union of form with matter it is in potency to further determining
factors. Substance, regarded as in potency to such factors is
called a *subject*. The further determining factors are themselves
called its *accidents*.[11] The relation of matter to form is the in-
verse of that of subject to accidents. Matter has no being but
what it has from the form, while accidents have no being but what
they hold from the subject. Moreover, this whole ontological
structure is, in each substance, but the unfolding of an individual
act-of-being created and continually kept in existence by God's
power. In and by its form, the creative *Esse* penetrates substance
to its very matter, and the subject to its very accidents.

These elements permit us to understand the complex act of becoming. Form explains what a substance is, because it is the act
and the reality of its being. Form will not explain, by itself,
how a being can acquire something which it is not or lose something
which it is. In either case there is the actualizing of a potency
or possibility. This actualization of any kind of possibility is
called movement or change. For there to be movement, there must
first be a being which moves. There must be a being and, consequently, an act. On the other hand, if this act were perfect and
complete, the being which it constitutes would have no possibility
of changing. For there to be change, therefore, there must be an
act which is incomplete and which admits of a margin of potency for
actualizing. Thus we say that movement is the act of what is in
potency, insofar as it is merely in potency. A good example of
change is to be found in the act of learning a science not already
known. In order to learn a science there must be an understanding,
and an understanding which already knows something. Insofar as
this understanding exists, and insofar as it knows, it is in act.
But this understanding must also be capable of learning if it is
to be in potency. Finally, this understanding must not already
possess the science in question. This is a privation. The very
change which we call learning is, accordingly, the progressive
actualization of an already existing act. And because it has act
it actualizes, step by step, its possibilities. Because to learn
is to transform step by step an aptitude to know into acquired
knowledge, to learn is a kind of changing.[12]

Thus conceived in its most general sense, movement is a passage from potency to act under the impulse of an act which is

already realized. Or again, it is the introduction of a form into
matter suitable to receive it. These terms and expressions must
not be allowed to make us forget the concrete reality they express:
an imperfect act that is being completed; or more simply, a being
on the way to realization. If this is the way it is, the body we
have been speaking of cannot be reduced either to its matter or
to its form. For a pure form, capable of subsisting apart, as an
Intelligence, would not be suitable for a body. And as for pure
matter, since it is mere possibility of all becoming without actually being anything, it would truly be nothing and consequently
could not subsist. The correct expression for designating God's
production of bodies and of their substantial principles is to say
that God *created* bodies and *concreated* their form and their matter;
that is, the one in the other indivisibly.[13]

We must realize that God governs by Providence beings constituted in this way. He is intimately present in their substance
and operations. But the intimacy of the assistance He gives them
leaves their efficacy absolutely intact. That the world is governed
in the first place is clear to unprejudiced eyes when they examine
the universal order of things. But we are forced to the same
position by the very idea of God which we obtained from the proofs
for His existence. For reason demands such a God as the first
principle of the universe. And since the principle of a being is
also its end, God must be the end of all things. Hence He relates
and directs them to Himself. And this amounts to governing them.
The final term in view of which the Creator administers the universe would seem, therefore, to be transcendent and exterior to
things. Once again, what is true of the principle is equally so
of the end.

The aspect richest in metaphysical consequences which God's
government of things presents to the reflecting mind is the notion
of their conservation. St. Thomas takes us to the heart of his
metaphysics of bodies by a steady progress of thought. He first
develops rigorously all the rigid implications of this notion of
divine conservation. Then, when he has, so to speak, left to things
nothing in their own right, he shows that the divine concursus
which seems to take away their powers and their being, in reality
actually confers these things upon them.

Every effect is dependent upon its cause. It depends upon
its cause in the very measure in which it is produced by it. The
word "cause" here designates something very different from that
"constant relationship between phenomena" to which empiricism had

reduced it. For St. Thomas, an efficient cause is an active force;
that is, it is a being which produces being.[14] Now if we look
into this closely, we find that acting or causing is still being.
It is only the unfolding or procession of being from its cause in
the form of an effect. There is no occasion for introducing any
new notion in order to pass from being to causality. If we regard
the act-of-being as an act, we shall see in this first act, by
which each thing is what it is, the root of this second act by
which being, which is first posited in itself, is also posited outside of itself, in its effects. Hence it is that just as God's
causality extends to the act-of-being of all beings, it extends to
all their operations.

To begin with, the divine efficacy extends totally to the being
of creatures. Let us consider the case of the artisan who produces
a work, or of the architect who constructs a building. This work
or this building is indebted to its author for its exterior form
and for the outward shape of its distinguishing parts. But it is
indebted to him for nothing else. The materials out of which the
work is fashioned already existed in nature. The artisan did not
have to produce them; he had only to make use of them. The definite nature of the causal relationship is very well expressed by
the manner in which the two terms (the artisan and his work) depend upon each other. Once it has been made, the work subsists
independently of the artisan. Since it is not indebted to him for
its being, it has no need of him in order to preserve its being.

It is precisely the same with natural beings. Each generates
other beings by virtue of a form which it has itself received and
of which it is not the cause. But it generates them in such a way
that it produces their form but not the act-of-being by which their
effects subsist. Thus we see that the infant continues to live
after the death of its father in the same way as a house remains
standing long after its builder has disappeared. In both cases
we have to do with causes which make a thing *become* what it is but
which do not cause it to exist.[15]

It is quite different with the relationship between things
and God. First, because God is not only the cause of the form
which clothes things, but of the very *esse* in virtue of which they
exist, so that for them to cease for a moment to depend upon their
cause would be to cease to exist at all. Secondly, this relationship between things and God is different because, somehow or other,
it would be contradictory that God should make creatures capable
of doing without Him.[16] It is of the essence of a creature that

it have its existence from another, whereas God has His existence
from Himself and subsists independently. For a creature to be able
to subsist even for an instant without God's assistance, it would
have to be existing by itself during this instant. That is, it
would be God.[17] Thus the first effect of the Providence of God
over things is the immediate and permanent influence by which He
assures their conservation. This influence is, in some way, but
the continuance of the creative act. Any interruption of this continued creation by which God maintains things in being would send
them instantly back into nothingness.[18]

Now let us go further and follow closely God's influence within things and we shall see that it extends from their existence to
their causality. Since nothing exists save in virtue of God's
being, neither can anything act save by virtue of the divine efficacy. Accordingly, if any being causes the existence of another
being, it only does so because God confers on it the power. This
truth is immediately evident if we but remember that *esse* is an
effect proper to God alone. Creation is His proper action and to
produce being is, properly speaking, to create.[19]

We must go still further, however, and say that what is true
of the causal efficacy of beings is equally so of their operations.
God is the cause of and the reason for the operation of all beings.
Why so? Because, in a way, to act is always to produce. What
produces nothing does nothing. Now we have just pointed out that
every real production of being, insignificant as it may be, belongs
properly to God alone. Therefore, every operation presupposes God
as its cause. Let us add to this that no being acts save in virtue
of the faculties at its disposal. It applies to the effects of
these faculties the natural forces which it is able to utilize.
Neither these forces nor these faculties come, in the first instance, from the being itself, but from God who is its author in
that He is the universal cause. So much is this so that, in the
last analysis, it is God who is the principal cause of all actions
performed by His creatures.[20] In His hands, creatures are like a
tool in the hands of the workman.

Because He is the supreme Act-of-Being, God is everywhere
present and acting by His efficacy. He is intimately present in the
very *esse* whose operation proceeds from creatures. He supports
them. He animates them from within. He leads them into their
operation. He applies them to their acts in such a way that they
neither are nor do anything except by Him, just as they would not
exist without Him. This is the teaching of the Holy Scripture:

"Do not I fill heaven and earth sayeth the Lord."[21] Or, again:
"If I ascend into heaven, thou art there; if I descend into hell,
thou art present." It must also be the necessary conclusion to
which we are led by the notion of a God who is the universal cause
of all being. Thus envisaged, the entire world is but a unique
instrument in the hands of its creator.

At this very point, where St. Thomas seems to be dissolving
beings in the divine omnipotence and submerging their activity in
His efficacy, he turns brusquely against those irreconcilable
enemies of his who would strip natural things of their own operations. This is the most unexpected change of direction for the
unsuspecting reader of the *Summa Contra Gentiles*.[22] Nowhere is
this characteristic trait of St. Thomas's technique--never to
weaken one truth in order the more firmly to establish another--
more perceptibly illustrated. Although we do not actually have to
take back a single word of what we have just said, we do have to
establish now quite a new proposition. Thomistic philosophy, in
which the creature is nothing and does nothing without God, is
set off against any teaching which would refuse to confer upon
second causes the full share of being and efficacy to which they
are entitled.

The varieties and shades of error misrepresenting the proper
activity of second causes are innumerable. It is not a question
here of adopting or rejecting any particular solution but rather of
taking a position for or against an entire philosophy. Behind each
of the doctrines he is refuting, St. Thomas detects the hidden
presence of Platonism. If he rejects them it is because he feels
that the philosopher's task is to interpret the real world of Aristotle, not the world of appearances described by Plato. And if he
attaches himself firmly to Aristotle's real world it is in order to
verify simple good sense, beyond which it is impossible to go.
Causes and effects regularly generate one another in the sensible
world. A warm body always warms a body that is brought near it.
It never chills it. A man never begets anything but a man. Clearly,
the nature of the effect produced is inseparably bound to the nature
of the cause that produces it. It is this constant relationship
between natural effects and their second causes which prevents our
supposing that there is a pure and simple substitution of God's
power for theirs. For if God's action were not diversified according to the different beings in which it operates, the effects which
it produces would not be diversified in the way that the things
themselves are, and anything might produce anything.[23] The

existence of the laws of nature prevents our supposing that God
has created beings deprived of causality.

A more remarkable thing, perhaps, is that those who deny all
efficacy to second causes in order to reserve the privilege of
causality to God Himself do no less injury to God than to things.
The excellence of the work shows forth the glory of the workman,
and how poor indeed would be a world entirely bare of efficacy!
In the first place, it would be an absurd world. In giving the
principal, no one denies the collateral. What sense would there
be in creating heavy bodies incapable of moving downwards? If
God, in imparting being to things, gave them some likeness to Himself, He ought also to have given them more of this likeness in
imparting to them the activity which issues from being, by attributing to them actions of their own. Moreover, a universe of inert
beings would point to a less perfect first cause than a universe
of active beings capable of communicating their perfections to one
another, when they act upon one another, just as God communicated
to them something of His own in creating them, bound and ordered
by the reciprocal actions which they perform. The urge by which
certain philosophers are driven to withdraw everything from nature
in order to glorify the Creator is inspired by a good intention,
but a blind one. Actually, *detrahere actiones proprias rebus est
divinae bonitati derogare:* to deprive things of actions of their
own is to belittle God's goodness.[24]

The problem in the final analysis comes to this. We must
hold firmly to two apparently contradictory truths. God does
whatever creatures do; and yet creatures themselves do whatever
they do. It is a question of understanding how one and the same
effect can proceed simultaneously from two different causes: God
and the natural agent which produces it. At first sight this is
incomprehensible. Most philosophers seem to have cringed before
it. They could not see how one action could proceed from two
causes. If a natural body is doing it, then God cannot be doing
it. Nay more! If God is performing the action, then it is much
less intelligible that a natural body can be performing it at the
same time, because God's causality reaches to the very depths of
being and no longer leaves anything to be produced by its effects.
Indeed, the dilemma appears unavoidable, unless we are to resign
ourselves to placing contradiction within the very heart of
things.[25]

Actually the opposition which metaphysics here encounters is
not so irreducible as it seems. Perhaps, indeed, it is only

superficial. It is contradictory to say that God and bodies are
causes of natural effects at the same time and under the same relationship. They are such at the same time but not under the same
relation. An example will enable us to see how this is so.

When an artisan produces something, he must of necessity employ
tools and instruments of one kind or another. His choice of instruments is justified by their form. He himself does nothing
more than move them in order to put them to work and make them
produce their effects. When an axe cuts a piece of wood, the axe
is certainly the cause of the effect produced. However, we can say
with reason that the workman who wields the axe also causes it.
We cannot divide the effect produced into two parts, one coming
from the axe, the other from the workman. The axe produces the
whole effect and so does the workman. The real difference is that
the two of them do not produce it in the same manner. The axe
only cuts the wood by virtue of the efficacy which the workman imparts to it. He is the first and principal cause, while the axe
is the second and instrumental cause of the effect produced.

We must imagine some analogous relationship between God, the
first cause, and natural bodies which we see acting before our
eyes. We say *analogous relationship* because God's influence upon
the second cause penetrates far more deeply into it than does the
influence of the workman into his tool. When God imparts existence
to things, He confers upon them at the same time their form, their
movement and their efficacy. Nevertheless, it is to them that this
efficacy belongs from the moment they receive it. Hence it is they
who perform their operations. The lowest being acts and produces
its effect, even though it does so by virtue of all the causes
superior to the action it is subjected to and whose efficacy is
transmitted to it by degrees. At the head of this series is God,
the total and immediate cause of all the effects produced and of
all the activity released therein. At the foot comes the natural
body, the immediate cause of the proper action which it performs,
even though it only performs it by virtue of the efficacy conferred
upon it by God.

When we examine in this way the operations and movements continually performed in the universe, we notice that no part of this
double causality can be considered superfluous. God's operation
is clearly necessary to produce natural effects, since second
causes owe all their efficacy to the first cause, God. But it is
not superfluous that God, who can produce all natural effects
Himself, should accomplish them by the mediation of certain other

causes. These intermediaries which He has willed, are not necessary to Him in that He is unable to do without them. Rather it is
for themselves that He willed them. The existence of second causes
points to no lack in His power but to the immensity of His goodness.[26] The universe, as represented by St. Thomas, is not a mass
of inert bodies passively moved by a force which passes through
them, but a collection of active beings each enjoying the efficacy
delegated to it by God along with actual being. At the first
beginnings of a world like this, we have to place not so much a
force being exercised as an infinite goodness being communicated.
Love is the unfathomable source of all causality.

   This is also, perhaps, the best point from which to view the
general economy of the Thomistic philosophy of nature. From here,
too, arise the various criticisms which such a philosophy directs
against all other existing systems. Looked at from without, such
a doctrine appears to its adversaries rather like a defense of the
rights of creatures against those of God. This accusation is the
more dangerous in that St. Thomas is ostensibly inspired by Aristotle. In this, at least, he appears to be yielding to the influence of pagan naturalism. Those who take their own interpretation to the extreme have never forgiven him for introducing *natures*
and *efficacious causes* between natural effects and God.[27]

   Looked at from within, St. Thomas's metaphysics seems, on the
contrary, to extol a God whose principal attribute is not power,
but goodness. Certainly productive fecundity and efficacy are
divine things. If God did not communicate them outside of Himself
to the multitude of beings which He has created, none of them would
be able to provide itself with the least particle of them; and it
is in His power that all efficacy originally shares. Or better,
divine power is so perfect and eminent in itself that we can readily
imagine how a religious soul will be very slow to attribute to
itself the slightest share of it.

   But we saw, when we studied the nature of the creative act,
that the infinite expansiveness of the Good is at its first beginnings. Consequently, the conception of a universe willed by a
Good which communicates itself cannot be that of a universe willed
by a Power which reserves its efficacy to itself. Whatever this
power would have the right to retain, the Goodness will wish to
give away. And the higher the gift, the higher will be the brand
of love with which it will be able to satisfy itself. The profound
metaphysical intuition which welds together these two key pieces
of the system is that a universe like Aristotle's demands as its

cause a God like the God of Denis the Areopagite. Our highest
glory is to be the coadjutors of God through the causality we wield:
Dei sumus adjutores.[28] Or, as Denis says elsewhere, what is most
divine is to be God's co-operator: *omnium divinius est Dei cooper-
atorem fieri.*[29] Therefore it is into the original effusion, which
renders this co-operation possible, that the efficacy of second
causes returns as to its source. No other kind of universe would
be equally worthy of infinite goodness.

    A consequence of this doctrine is to make its meaning true
to what is called the "naturalism" or the "physicism" of St. Thomas.
If no philosophy was so constantly busy safeguarding the rights of
creatures, it is because it saw in this the one means of safeguarding the rights of God. Far from encroaching upon the Creator's
privileges, the perfections attributed to second causes can only
increase His glory, since He is their first cause and since this
is a new occasion for glorifying Him. It is because there is
causality in nature that we can go back step by step to the first
cause, God. In a universe stripped of second causes the most obvious proofs of the existence of God would be impossible, and His
highest metaphysical attributes would remain hidden from us. In-
versely, this whole swarm of beings, natures, causes and operations
which the universe presents us with, can no longer be regarded as
existing or acting for itself. If God has conferred efficacy upon
them as the highest mark of their divine origin, then it is their
constant effort to assimilate themselves with God which makes them
work and moves them toward their operations. Beneath each natural
form there lies hidden a desire to imitate by means of action the
creative fecundity and pure actuality of God. This desire is quite
unconscious in the domain of bodies, which we are examining for the
moment. But it is that same straining toward God which, with intelligence and will, will blossom forth into human morality. Thus,
if a physics of bodies exists, it is because there exists first a
mystical theology of the divine life. The natural laws of motion,
and its communication from being to being, imitate the primitive
creative effusion from God. The efficacy of second causes is but
the counterpart of His fecundity.[30]

    As soon as we realize the significance of this principle, all
shadow of antinomy between God's perfection and that of created
being disappears. On the contrary, a universe which is only willed
by God as resembling Him will never be too beautiful nor too powerful. It will never realize itself too completely. It will never
tend too vehemently toward its own perfection in order to reproduce,

as it should, the image of its divine model. "Anything which tends
toward its own perfection, tends toward the divine model."[31] This
is a principle of inexhaustible fruitfulness in Thomistic philosophy
because it governs both human morality and the metaphysics of nature.
Let us be perfect as our heavenly Father is perfect.

Looked at in this way, St. Thomas's real reason for criticizing
earlier systems of metaphysics is easily grasped. He sees all
systems, save Aristotle's from which he drew his inspiration,[32]
falling into two classes according to two ways of denying to second
causes the efficacy which is theirs by right.

First, there is Platonism and its derivatives--the systems
of Avicenna, Ibn Gabirol, etc. According to this doctrine, anything new appearing in the world of bodies comes from outside.
Hence it is a question here of a basic extrinsicism, whether the
exterior cause of forms or operations of the sensible world reside
in the efficacy of the Ideas as with Plato, in that of a separated
Intelligence as with Avicenna, in that of the divine Will with
Gabirol. In every case, the problem is amenable to the same solution, whether it is a question of explaining the physical operations
of bodies, the cognitive operation of the reason or the moral
operations of the will. In the three cases the entire efficacy
resides in an extrinsic agent which imparts from without the sensible form to the body, or the intelligible form to the intellect,
or virtue to the will.

Secondly, there is what may be called Anaxagorism, with all
the modifications under which it may disguise itself. Here we have
an intrinsicism no less basic than the extrinsicism which we have
just been discussing, and its result is about the same. In this
second case, the various effects we have been speaking of come,
not from outside, but are already performed and realized virtually
from within. There are seminal reasons included in matter and
developed under the excitation of an exterior agent. There are in-
nate ideas included in the soul, and which blossom forth of themselves under the gentle shock of sensation. There are natural virtues, residing in a crude way in the will, and which perfect themselves spontaneously as life provides them with an occasion for
doing so. In the first case the second cause did nothing at all
because it was receiving everything from outside. Here in the
second case, it does very little more since the effects which it
seems to produce are already virtually realized either in itself
or in others. Its action is limited to removing the obstacles
standing in the way of its development.[33]

These errors are closely related, in spite of their apparent contradiction, and hence certain philosophers do not hesitate to combine them. For such as these, knowledge comes to the soul from outside by way of divine illumination, while sensible forms develop in matter from within, thanks to seminal reasons enclosed therein. Actually we have here but two different ways of derogating from the order of the universe whose very structure is fashioned from the order and the connection between causes. All causes are indebted to the infinite goodness of the first cause both for the fact that they are and that they are causes. This we are now about to verify in the particularly important case of the human composite.

NOTES

[1] *S T*, I, 65, 1, Proem.

[2] *S T*, I, 66, 1, ad 2: "Aerem autem, et ignem non nominat, quia non est ita manifestum rudibus, quibus Moyses loquebatur, hujusmodi esse corpora, sicut manifestum est de terra et aqua." Cf. in the same sense: "Quia Moyses loquebatur rudi populo, qui nihil, nisi corporalia poterat capere . . ." *Ibid.*, 67, 4. "Moyses rudi populo loquebatur, quorum imbecillitati condescendens, illa solum eis proposuit quae manifest sensui apparent . . ." *Ibid.*, 63, 3, 2. "Moyses autem rudi populo condescendens . . ." *Ibid.*, 70, 1, ad 3; and also, 70, 2. The guiding principles of the Thomistic exegesis are as follows: "Primo, quidem, ut veritas Scripturae inconcusse tenatur. Secundo, cum scriptura divina multipliciter exponi possit, quod nulli expositioni aliquis ita praecise inhaereat, ut si certa ratione constiterit hoc esse falsum, quod aliquis sensum Scripturae esse credebat, id nihilominus asserere praesumat, ne Scriptura ex hoc ab infidelibus derideatur, et ne eis via creadendi praecludatur." *S T*, I, 68, 1. St. Thomas is here in full agreement with St. Augustine, and expressly claims to have taken this double principle from him: 1. to maintain steadfastly the literal truth of Scripture; 2. not to be so exclusively attached to one of the possible interpretations as to cling to it even when its opposite has been scientifically demonstrated. See Father Synave, O. P., "Le Canon scripturaire de saint Thomas d'Aquin," *Revue Biblique*, 1924, pp. 522-533; also by the same author: "La Doctrine de saint Thomas d'Aquin sur le sens littéral des Écritures," *Revue Biblique*, 1926, pp. 40-65.

[3] *In II Sent.*, 12, 1, 2, Solutio.

[4] Above the sphere of the fixed stars, the invisible world begins. Naturally, its structure is more Aristotelian: the heaven of waters, or the Crystalline sphere; and the heaven of light, or the Empyrean. *S T*, I, 68, 4.

[5] See above, p. 122.

[6] St. Thomas is constantly preoccupied with the Manichaean doctrine which he wishes to refute. This is owing to the development of the doctrine in the Albigensian heresy, a heresy which the Order of St. Dominic fought from the very moment of its birth.

[7]*S T*, I, 65, 2. Cf. my *The Spirit of Mediaeval Philosophy*, ch. 6: "Christian Optimism," pp. 108-127.

[8]See above, p. 156.

[9]Quoniam quoddam potest esse, licet non sit, quoddam vero jam est: illud quod potest esse et non est, dicitur esse potentia; illud autem quod jam est, dicitur esse actu." "De principiis naturae" in *Opuscula*, I, 8 (ed. Mandonnet).

[10]*Ibid*. This absence of form in matter is called *privation*. Thus marble is being in potency, or matter. Its absence of artistic form, is a privation. Its shape as statue is a form.

[11]Matter is not a *subjectum*, for it only exists through the determination it receives. Of itself, it is not there in order to receive it. On the contrary, because the *subject* is a substance, it does not owe its being to accidents. Rather, it lends them its being. See above, Part I, ch. 5. Cf. *S T*, I, 66, 1. Note that matter, being in potency, cannot exist apart. However, it is not potentially good but absolutely good, because it is ordained to form. This of itself constitutes it as a good. Thus there is a relationship under which good is more extensive than being. See *C G*, III, 20.

[12]For a purely technical analysis of becoming, see *In III Physic*, I, 2: Leonine ed., II, 104-105.

[13]St. Thomas accepts Aristotle's classification of the four kinds of causes, material, formal, efficient, final (*De Principibus naturae*, in *Opuscula*, I, 11). In fact, matter and form are only causes in that they are constitutive elements of being. Matter cannot actualize itself, nor can form impose itself upon matter. Marble does not make a statue of itself. Form does not sculpture itself. For actualization of matter by form, there must be an active principle: "Oportet ergo praeter materiam et formam aliquid principium esse, quod agat; et hoc dicitur causa efficiens, vel movens, vel agens, vel unde est principium motus" (*Ibid*.) Whether Aristotle ever truly got beyond the level of motor cause to efficient causes still requires examination. If not (and see A. Bremond, *Le dilemme aristotélicien*, p. 11 and pp. 50-52), then St. Thomas's notion of the efficient cause must grow out of his analysis of *esse*. In this case, St. Thomas's philosophy of nature must be as far beyond Aristotle's as his natural theology is.

[14]"Hoc vero nomen Causa, importat influxum quemdam ad esse causati." *In V Metaph*., I, Cathala ed., n. 751, p. 251. This is why the operation of a being (second act) is only an extension of the act which this being is: "Actus autem est duplex: primus et secundus. Actus quidem primum est forma, et integritas rei. Actus autem secundus est operatio." *S T*, I, 48, 5. The expression is not perfect because it does not push out beyond the form to the act-of-existing. In this sense, the classical adage "operatio sequitur esse" is better. Note that we actually know the second act first. A being operates, therefore it acts, it performs an act. It is this that we see. Tracing our way back from there by means of thought to the active energy which causes its act or operation, we locate its origin in the first act-of-being. This act-of-being reaches being by its form and confers *esse* upon it. Thus this first act is posited by a judgment proceeding from its observable effect, operation. See *In IX Metaph*., lectio 8; ed. Cathala, n. 1861, p. 539.--J. Owens, C.SS. R. "The Causal Proposition--Principle or Conclusion?" *The Modern Schoolman*, XXXII (1955), 159-171, 257-270, 323-339.

[15]To this corresponds the technical distinction between the
causa fiendi and the *causa essendi:* when man engenders a man independent of himself, he is his *causa fiendi;* when the sun engenders
light and the light ceases just as soon as the sun disappears, it
is its *causa essendi.*

[16]*C G,* II, 25.

[17]*S T,* I, 104, 1.

[18]"Nec aliter res (Deus) in esse conservat, nisi inquantum eis
continue influit esse; sicut ergo antequam res essent, potuit eis
non communicare esse, et sic eas non facere; ita postquam jam
factae sunt, potest eis non influere esse, et sic esse desinerent,
quod est eas in nihilum redigere." *S T,* I, 104, 3.

[19]*C G,* III, 66.

[20]"Causa autem actionis magis est id cujus virtute agitur,
quam etiam illud quod agit, sicut principale agens magis agit
quam instrumentum. Deus igitur principalius est causa cujuslibet
actionis quam etiam secundae causae agentes." *C G,* III, 67.

[21]Jeremias, 23, 24. For the text following, see Psalm 138,
8. Cf. *C G,* III, 68. *S T,* I, 8, 1.

[22]Here is the order of the chapters in the course of which
this rectification takes place: cap. 65, "Quod Deus conservat res
in esse"; cap. 66, "Quod nihil dat esse nisi inquantum agit in
virtute divina"; cap. 67, "Quod Deus est causa operandi omnibus
operantibus"; cap. 68, "Quod Deus est ubique et in omnibus rebus";
cap. 69, "Quod opinione eorum qui rebus naturalibus proprias sub-
strahunt actiones."

[23]"Si enim nulla inferior causa, et maxime corporalis, aliquid
operatur, sed Deus operatur in omnibus solus, Deus autem non variatur
per hoc, quod operatur in rebus diversis, non sequetur diversus
effectus ex diversitate rerum in quibus Deus operatur. Hoc autem
ad sensum apparet falsum; non enim ex appositione calidi sequitur
infrigidatio, sed calefactio tantum, neque ex semine hominis
sequitur generatio nisi hominis; non ergo causalitas effectuum
inferiorum est ita attribuenda divinae virtuti, quod substrahatur
causalitas inferiorum agentium." *C G,* III, 69.

[24]On the Arabian and Latin adversaries whom St. Thomas opposes
here, see Etienne Gilson, "Pourquoi sant Thomas a critiqué saint
Augustin," *Arch. d'hist. doctr. et litt. du moyen âge,* I (1926-
1927), 5-127. Maurice de Wulf has severly criticized the plan
of this article in "L'Augustinisme 'avicennisant,'" *Revue néo-
scolastique de philosophie,* 1931, p. 15. His reproach falls really
on the plan of the *Contra Gentiles,* III, 69, on which the article
is but a commentary.

[25]*C G,* III, 70.

[26]"Patet etiam quod, si res naturalis producat proprium
effectum, non est superfluum quod Deus illum producat. Quia res
naturalis non producit ipsum, nisi in virtute divina. Neque est
superfluum, si Deus per seipsum potest omnes effectus naturales
producere, quod per quasdam alias causas producantur. Non enim hoc
est ex insufficientia divinae virtutis, sed ex immensitate bonitatis
ipsius per quam suam similitudinem rebus communicare voluit, non
solum quantum ad hoc quod essent, sed etiam quantum ad hoc quod
aliorum causae essent." *C G,* III, 70.

[27]From this point of view, the philosophy of Malebranche is the absolute antithesis of Thomism. In Malebranche God alone is cause and reserves efficacy exclusively to Himself. Moreover, the preface to *Recherche de la vérité* opens with a protest against the Aristotelian, and therefore pagan, inspiration of Thomist scholasticism. Cf. the two rich and suggestive volumes of Henri Gouhier, *La Vocation de Malebranche*, Paris, Vrin, 1926, and *La Philosophie de Malebranche et son expérience religieuse*, Paris, Vrin, 1926.

[28]I Cor., 3, 9.

[29]*De coel. hierarchi.*, c. 3. Texts cited in *C G*, III, 21.

[30]Cf. *The Spirit of Mediaeval Philosophy*, ch. 7, "Glory of God," pp. 128-47.

[31]*C G*, III, 21, at Praeterea, tunc maxime perfectum.

[32]We are here speaking of Aristotle as St. Thomas looked at him, or wish to do so. If, as we have suggested, St. Thomas went far beyond the Aristotelian notion of motive cause to a truly efficient cause, it was Aristotle's Platonism he was effectively leaving behind.

[33]"Utraque autem istarum opinionum est absque ratione. Prima enim opinio excludit causas propinquas, dum effectus omnes in inferioribus provenientes, solis causis attribuit: in quo derogatur ordini universi, qui ordine et connexione causarum contexitur, dum prima causa ex exminentia bonitatis suae rebus aliis confert non solum quod sint, sed etiam quod causae sint. Secunda opinio in idem quasi inconveniens redit: cum enim removens prohibens non sit nisi novens per accidens . . . , si inferiora agentia nihil aliud faciunt quam producere de occulto in manifestum, removendo impedimenta quibus formae et habitus virtutum et scientiarum occultabantur, sequitur quod omnia inferiora agentia non agant nisi per accidens." *Quo. disp. de Veritate*, XI, 1.

14. SUMMARY ANALYSIS

We have considered a number of views of the activity of God
in the world. Our task now is to analyze these various approaches,
to determine how many distinct positions are represented, to explore their relations, to inquire whether they are addressing the
same question, and to see what further light can be shed on the
issue at hand.

Let us review briefly the approaches represented in the
selections. Wright's view of God's activity in the world is basically an analogy of personal action, but the relation of the divine
action to finite causes is not explored. Both Gilkey and Dilley
distinguish a liberal view which sees God as acting in and through
finite causes and a conservative approach in which God performs
outright miracles, and they inquire whether there is a middle way
as implied by the biblical theologians. Bultmann's position is
that God's action in the world is hidden in finite causes and is
visible only to the eye of faith, while the finite causal nexus
itself is completely intelligible to modern science. Furthermore,
God's action on persons is understood on the analogy of human
personal relations. Ogden proposes three analogies for the relation of God to the world: the person-body relation, the action of
the self by which it constitutes itself, and the mind-brain relation. Cobb and Griffin following Whitehead see the divine action
in the form of the offering of an initial aim to each event such
that God influences each event by being experienced. Kaufman
claims to use the analogy of personal action but in fact repeats
the liberal view that God acts in and through the natural and
historical processes without disrupting them. Kirkpatrick develops
the analogy of personal action. Wiles proposes the view that God's
purposive action in the world is uniform and not special or particular. Farrer presents the analogies of personal action and mind-
body and also the theory of double agency. Gilson elaborates the
traditional Thomist position on primary and secondary causes.

There seem to be five distinct positions offered in these
selections:

1. Personal Action. This approach is based on the analogy
of human personal action in the world as elaborated by the philosophy of action. It is explicated fully by Kirkpatrick and is

referred to by Kaufman. It is essentially an analogy without a
theory. It offers an interpretation of God's intervention in the
world through the interruption of the finite causal nexus, but it
does not explain God's relation to ordinary events. In effect it
is the same as the conservative view referred to by Gilkey and
Dilley.

2. Primary Cause. This is the traditional approach to God's
activity in the world in which God as primary cause acts in and
through all secondary causes in nature and history. It is the view
represented by Thomism, Protestant orthodoxy, and in this volume
by Farrer and Gilson. When God's activity apart from secondary
causes in miracles is excluded, this approach becomes identical
with that of the liberal theology, Bultmann, and Kaufman. In its
traditional form this view is a complex theory with the occasional
use of the artisan-instrument analogy. In its liberal form it is
neither a theory nor an analogy but simply an affirmation.

3. Process. This is the position of the process theologians
Ogden, Cobb, and Griffin. It holds that God acts in all events
by influence or persuasion. By being prehended or experienced God
offers an initial aim to each emerging event, which aim may be
accepted in varying degrees. It is thus a complex theory based
on the philosophy of Whitehead and Hartshorne. The analogies offered are those of self-body, mind-brain, and self-constitution.
These analogies, however, have quite distinct implications for the
nature of divine activity in the world, as we shall see later.

4. Uniform Action. In this approach God's action in the
world is understood as uniform and universal, and the appearance
of particular divine activity is given by the variety of human
response. This view is represented only by Wiles, who offers
neither a theory nor analogy. It was noted in the Introduction
that the analogies offered by Pike for this position are impersonal
in nature. The concept of uniform purposive activity is somewhat
obscure, and it is not clear whether God is understood to act in
natural processes. This approach is similar to that of the liberal
theology, but the latter seems to involve a variety of particular
activity in and through finite activity. It is similar to some
versions of the primary cause view which emphasize the divine
creation, preservation, and empowering of all finite causes.

5. Two Perspectives and Languages. In this view science
and faith in God's providential activity are understood to be two
different ways of looking at the natural historical process. They
are expressed in two different languages, that of scientific

description and that of faith assertions about the purpose and
activity of God. This approach is touched on in Kirkpatrick's
essay and expressed in Bultmann's statement: "This is the paradox
of faith, that faith 'nevertheless' understands as God's action
here and now an event which is completely intelligible in the
natural or historical connection of events." (p. 64)
Since this view is not fully elaborated in any of the selections
in this volume, we shall explore it briefly here.

John J. Compton, professor of philosophy at Vanderbilt
University, explicates this approach in connection with the personal action view. He states that a movement of one's arm can be
understood and analyzed in terms of neurology and physiology and
also in terms of personal intention as in the philosophy of action.
"My arm motion is an action *at the same time*, if not in the same
respect, in which it is a succession of causally linked events.
Between these two perspectives there is no conflict whatsoever."
Likewise the natural-historical process can be seen from the
scientific perspective or from the perspective of faith in God's
providential activity. "Each story has a complete cast of charac-
ters, without the need for interaction with the other story, but
quite compatible with it. What happens is that the evolution of
things is *seen* or *read*, in religious life--as my arm's movement
is read in individual life--as a part of an action, as an expression of divine purpose, in addition to its being viewed as a
naturalistic process."[1]

This is essentially a perspectival or linguistic approach to
the relation of science and faith which does not offer a theory of
the actual relation of divine and finite activity. Compton offers
an analogy, but the point of the analogy is that there is no relation, no interaction between the two perspectives. They are two
unrelated "language games."

The main difficulty in this view is that both religious
language about the activity of God in the world and scientific
language of the world process are usually held to be cognitive and
to refer to the same actual world.[2] (See Barbour, *Issues*, chs.
6-iii, 9-i.) Thus it becomes necessary to understand the relation
between the two kinds of assertions and to explain how they can be
true of the same world process. The two perspectives and languages
approach ignores these issues and thus avoids the fundamental
question at hand.

Several points should be noted about these five views of
God's activity in the world. First, some are analogies, some

are theories, some involve both, and some neither. Let us understand a theory in this connection to be a detailed metaphysical
analysis of the relation of divine and creaturely activity, and
an analogy to be the interpretation of this relation through comparison with some better known relation. In this sense theories
are usually elaborations of analogies or of clusters of analogies
in models. The personal action approach is essentially an analogy.
Although the philosophy of action has elaborated a complex theory,
it is a theory of human action, and its use as an analogy for divine
action is only beginning to be explicated. The primary cause and
process views are primarily theories. Both have offered analogies,
but they have not been uniform or predominant. Process theologians
have suggested the mind-brain, self-body, self-constitution, and
experiential influence analogies. The proponents of the primary
cause theory are obviously using a general analogy of finite causality, but the artisan-instrument analogy for the concept of primary
cause is not very illuminating. As we have noted the uniform
action approach offers neither an analogy nor a theory, and the
two perspectives view offers an analogy but no theory. It would
seem that a successful interpretation of divine activity in the
world would involve both a fundamental analogy or model and a fully
elaborated metaphysical theory. The process view seems to have
come closest to this goal at the present.

Now the question arises as to whether these five approaches
are complementary or mutually exclusive. It is clear that as
theories or implicit theories they are mutually exclusive. For
example, while the first three views affirm particular divine action, the uniform action position denies it. Also whereas the personal action and primary cause positions involve determinative
divine action, the process view asserts influential or persuasive
action. However, at least some of the points being affirmed in the
various analogies may be complementary. For example, the personal
action, artisan-instrument, and mind-body analogies seem to be coherent, since the latter two are aspects of the first. We shall
return to this point later.

Another question about these various views of divine activity
in the world is whether or not they are addressing the same question. Let us assume that they are treating the general question,
How does God act in the world? Of the eighteen different meanings
of "how" in the Oxford English Dictionary six are relevant to this
question.

1. By what means? E.g., God acts in the world through
secondary causes.

2.   In what way or manner? E.g., God acts in the world uni-
formly, purposively, persuasively.

3.   To what effect? E.g., God acts in the world to heal
diseases and to inspire good actions.

4.   With what meaning or for what reason or purpose? E.g.,
God acts in the world to achieve the divine purposes of justice and
peace.

5.   To what extent or degree? E.g., God acts in the world
everywhere and always.

6.   On analogy with what? E.g., God acts in the world as the
mind acts on the brain.

Now which question is each of the five main approaches addressing? The personal action view is addressing question 6. The
primary cause view is treating primarily questions 1 and 5. The
process approach is addressing all of the questions. The uniform
action view is addressing questions 2 and 5. The two perspectives
position addresses questions 5 and 6. Thus the various views we
are considering are interpreting the question formally rather than
materially. As might be expected they are addressing primarily the
questions of the means, manner, and extent of the divine activity
rather than its content or purpose. It is clear that the various
approaches can be compared only in so far as they are treating the
same question. Much of the debate between the various views is
vitiated by failure to observe this.

Is there also ambiguity about the term "act"? Do the five
main views of divine action have the same understanding of "act"?
There is a variety of types of action or activity: physical,
chemical, electro-magnetic, organic, mental, personal or spiritual,
and social or collective. Thus "activity" can be called a metaphysical term which is required in all languages or areas of
discourse.[3]

The personal action view has treated this question most fully
through its employment of the philosophy of action and its focus
on human intentional action. In the primary cause approach analogies of human action are sometimes offered, but in the idea of a
primary cause acting through secondary causes the concept of act
is obscure. In the process view various analogies of mental and
personal action are proposed, as we have seen. When the divine
action is held to be uniform, the meaning of "act" is left quite
obscure or is interpreted by means of physical analogies. So we
can see that the various views of divine action in the world have
rather different understandings of the concept of action, and any

proposal in which this concept is left unclarified will be to that
extent less useful.

It is apparent, however, that the most pervasive analogy for
the divine action in the world is human action. This is clearly
the case in the Bible and throughout the tradition. God's actions
in the world are understood to be the manifestations of the divine
purpose and intention on analogy with human actions. The most
common analogy of the divine transcendence has been the transcendence of the mind or self over the body and the world. But the
different views we have explored have focused on different aspects
of this analogy. The personal action approach emphasizes the
totality of human action from intention to change in the world.
The process position concentrates on the mind-brain and self-body
aspects of human action. The primary cause view focuses on the
body-world aspect in its artisan-instrument analogy.

It is important to note that an emphasis on different aspects
of the general analogy of human action leads to quite different
results in regard to divine activity in the world. A focus on the
totality of human action results in a view of divine activity involving miraculous interventions and interruptions in the finite
causal nexus, as in the personal action view. An emphasis on the
body-world aspect of human action would seem to lead in the same
direction, although the artisan-instrument relation is proposed as
an analogy of the primary-secondary cause relation. If the focus
is on the mind-body aspect of human action, the results are not
at all clear since the mind-body relation involves such a wide
range of different activities from immediate action on certain
brain cells through the complex chain of causes involving nerves,
muscles, and bones, to various unconsciously controlled bodily
actions such as heartbeat and digestion. Finally, attention is
often focused on the mind-brain relation and specifically on those
brain cells which are immediately affected by the mind, since this
is taken to be an example of the action of spirit on matter. In
this case we probably have a view of divine activity which is determinative and even interruptive in relation to finite causes much
as the totality of human action is found to be. But this is not
at all clear since the mind-brain relation is so obscure. The
philosopher Jerome Shaffer states:

> The mind-body problem remains a source of acute discom-
> fort for philosophers. . . . It may well be that the
> relation between mind and body is an ultimate, unique, and
> unanalyzable one. If so, philosophical wisdom would

consist in giving up the attempt to understand the relation in terms of other, more familiar ones and accepting
it as the anomaly it is.[4]

If Shaffer is correct, the mind-body relation and more specifically
the mind-brain relation may be an important analogy for the mysterious nature of the relation of divine and finite activity, but
it certainly is not very illuminating as to its actual character.

    In the light of these clarifications we can inquire as to the
central questions which need to be addressed in a fully satisfactory
analogy and theory of the activity of God in the world. The following seem to be fundamental: Does God act in all events or only
in some? Is God the sole cause of any events or a partial cause
of all or some events? What is the relation of divine and finite
activity? Is it identity, independence, complementarity, interdependence, inclusion, exclusion, or causality? Any proposal concerning the nature of the activity of God in the world can be assessed by the degree to which these questions are clearly addressed
and resolved. Let us investigate how the five positions outlined
above deal with these questions.

    According to the personal action view it seems that God acts
only in some events and is the sole cause of these events. The
relation of divine and finite activity seems to be one of independence, that is, there is no significant relation between them. In
the primary cause approach God acts in all events and is the sole
cause of some, namely, miracles. The relation of divine and finite
activity is vague in this view. It can be characterized as complementarity, inclusion, or causality, since they act together and
God as primary cause encompasses the secondary causes and is said
to cause them. In the process approach God acts in all events, is
the partial cause of all events, and the sole cause of none. The
relation of divine and finite activity can probably best be characterized as interdependence, since God is understood to be one
among many efficient causes but the preeminent one which influences
all the others as well as being influenced by them.

    In the uniform action view it seems that God is active in
relation to all events and a partial cause of some, but it is not
clear whether or not God can be a cause in natural events. The
relation of divine and finite activity would seem to be causality,
since God's activity elicits human action. Finally in the two perspectives approach God is understood to be potentially active in
all events; that is, every event can be seen to be an act of God.
Presumably God could also be interpreted to be the sole cause of an

event. The idea of God being a partial cause would seem to be
meaningless from this point of view. The relation of divine and
finite activity is left unclear. There is no significant relation
between the two perspectives and languages, but how their referents
are related is unexplored. They could be interpreted to be complementary, that is, different aspects of one reality. In summary,
it seems that the process view treats these questions most clearly
and fully, whereas the uniform action and two perspectives approach
seem to be the least successful in addressing them.

Since many of the essays in this volume focus their treatment
of divine activity in the world on God's action in Christ, we should
explore whether or not christology provides us with a pattern for
ordering and illuminating the approaches to this question. God's
action in Christ is usually understood to be paradigmatic for the
divine action elsewhere in the world. If it is considered to be
unique or different in kind from the divine activity elsewhere, then
christology may not be very illuminating for our question. But
if God's action in Christ is different only in degree from the
divine action elsewhere, then it may shed considerable light on the
question.

If we consider the traditional patterns of christological
orthodoxy and heresy, an interesting correlation emerges. The
personal action view in which the divine action is understood to
be not through finite causes but beside and apart from them seems
to be an example of Apollinarianism in which the divine nature takes
the place of the human spirit in Christ. The primary cause approach in which God and creaturely causes are both fully operative
represents the Chalcedonian formula where Christ is understood to
be fully human and fully divine, without confusion, change, divi-
sion, or separation. The process view in which the relation of
divine and creaturely activity is described as one of influence
or persuasion, can be seen to represent Nestorianism where the relation between the divine and human in Christ is interpreted as
a moral union. Finally, the uniform action position, in which
there is a variety of human response to the uniform divine action,
can perhaps be interpreted to be an example of Adoptionism, where
Jesus' response to the divine presence results in his being declared the Christ.

It is not being suggested in these comparisons that the validity of the various views we are considering is to be determined by
the orthodoxy of their christological correlates. Rather these
comparisons simply illuminate the variety of possibilities for

interpreting the divine action in Christ and elsewhere which have
been explicated in the tradition and which are still prevalent
today.

Modern christology has tended to move away from the traditional categories of substance and nature toward dynamic and functional categories. One example of this tendency is the view based
on the "paradox of grace" as developed by D. M. Baillie.[5] Here
the experience of grace is taken as the clue to the action of God
in Christ. Baillie appeals to Paul's statement: "By the grace of
God I am what I am. . . . I worked harder than any of them though
it was not I, but the grace of God which is with me." (1 Cor 15:10)
This is interpreted to mean that the divine action of grace is not
in competition with the free human response such that the more
grace the less human freedom and activity and vice versa. Rather
it is understood to mean that the more the divine action of grace
is present, the more human freedom and action are enhanced. The
incarnation of God in Christ is interpreted to be this experience
of grace taken to the absolute degree.

This approach to christology is based on a particular human
experience and is apparently an elaboration of the analogy of
personal influence. It suggests that divine activity in the world
is identical or conjoint with at least some human activity. Its
limitation is that its implications for non-human finite activity
are not elaborated. It is similar to the process view in that both
use the analogy of personal influence. It is closest to the primary cause view since it asserts a double or conjoint agency of
divine and human action. Thus, although it is based on human
experience, it leaves the relation between divine and creaturely
activity quite mysterious, as in the case of the Chalcedonian
formula and the primary cause view.

Finally, how are we to choose among these five main positions
on the divine activity in the world and their elaborations in the
essays in this volume? This depends on our philosophical and
theological criteria. Most generally our judgment will have to be
based on the criteria of inner consistency, coherence with everything else we hold to be true, and adequacy to our experience.[6]
The most widely held theological criteria have always been coherence
with the Bible and the theological tradition as critically reinterpreted.[7] On the basis of these or other criteria the readers
will have to judge for themselves.

NOTES

1.   John J. Compton, "Science and God's Action in Nature,"
op. cit., pp. 37-39.   This view is criticized by Barbour in his
book *Issues in Science and Religion*, pp. 437-39.   For a similar
approach see Robert H. King, *The Meaning of God* (Philadelphia:
Fortress Press, 1973), pp. 76-79.

2.   See Barbour, *Issues*, chs. 6-iii, 9-i.

3.   See I. T. Ramsey, "Miracles: An Exercise in Logical Map-
work," in *The Miracles and the Resurrection* by Ramsey et al.
(London: S.P.C.K., 1964), pp. 16-17.

4.   "Mind-Body Problem," *The Encyclopedia of Philosophy*, 8
vols., ed. Paul Edwards (New York: Macmillan Publishing Co.,
1967) 5:345a.   In another book, however, Shaffer comes out tentatively for epiphenomenalism.   See *Philosophy of Mind* (Englewood
Cliffs, N. J.: Prentice-Hall, 1968), p. 76.

5.   See *God Was in Christ* (New York: Charles Scribner's
Sons, 1948), ch. 5.

6.   For a straightforward discussion of these criteria see
Kent Bendall and Frederick Ferré, *Exploring the Logic of Faith*
(New York: Association Press, 1962), sect. 10; and Frederick Ferré,
Basic Modern Philosophy of Religion (New York: Charles Scribner's
Sons, 1967), ch. 13.

7.   For a recent discussion of the relation of philosophical
and theological criteria, see David Tracy, *Blessed Rage for Order*
(New York: Seabury Press, 1975), esp. ch. 3.